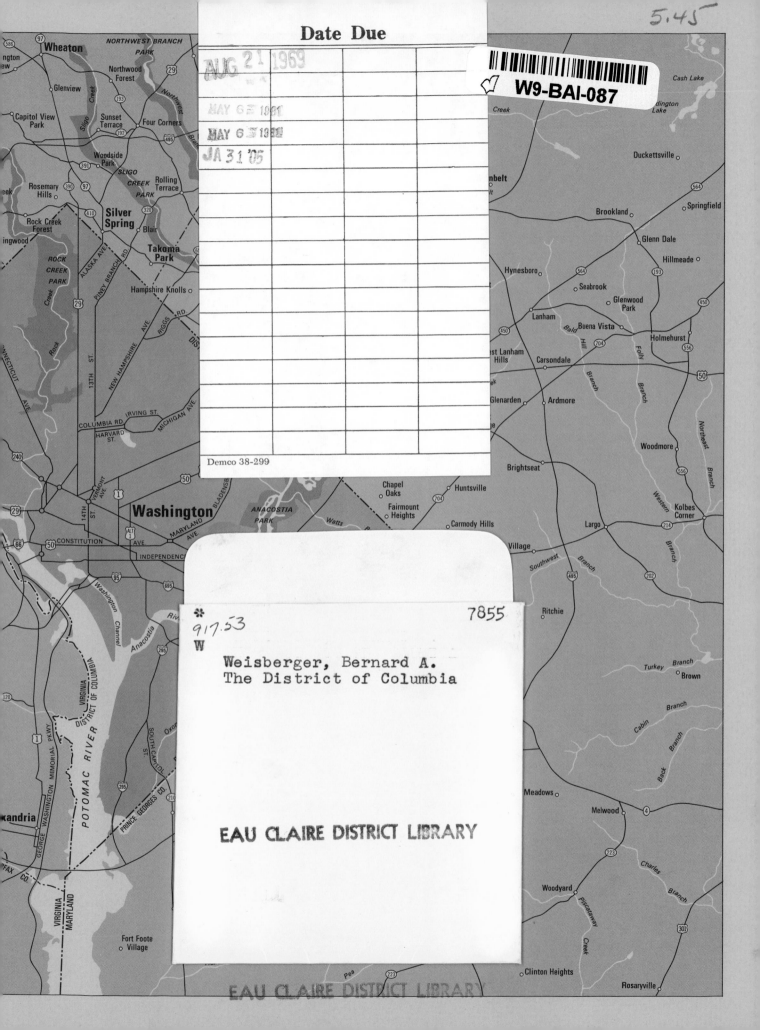

5.45

The District
of Columbia

The District of Columbia

The Seat of Government

By Bernard A. Weisberger
and the Editors of
TIME-LIFE BOOKS

TIME-LIFE BOOKS, New York

The Author: Bernard A. Weisberger, a native of Hudson, New York, is a noted historian, teacher and writer on American history. Formerly Professor of History at the University of Rochester—a post he left to devote more time to writing— he is now Adjunct Professor of American History at New York University. In addition to writing essays and articles in professional journals, Dr. Weisberger is the author of a number of books, including *Reports of the Union, They Gathered at the River, The American Newspaperman* and two volumes of the LIFE History of the United States. His most recent book is *The New Industrial Society.*

The Consulting Editor: Oscar Handlin, Charles Warren Professor of American History at Harvard University and director of the university's Charles Warren Center for Studies in American History, is one of America's foremost social historians. His work on U.S. immigrants, *The Uprooted,* won the Pulitzer Prize in 1952.

District of Columbia Consultant: Andrew Hacker, Professor of Government at Cornell University, is the author of numerous books and articles on the American political scene.

The Cover: In the twilight of a summer evening, the U.S. Marine Band gives a concert on the steps of the Capitol beneath the softly lit dome.

TIME-LIFE BOOKS

Editor
Maitland A. Edey

Executive Editor
Jerry Korn

Text Director   **Art Director**
Martin Mann   Sheldon Cotler

Chief of Research
Beatrice T. Dobie

Picture Editor
Robert G. Mason

Assistant Text Directors:
Harold C. Field, Ogden Tanner

Assistant Art Director:
Arnold C. Holeywell

Assistant Chief of Research:
Martha Turner

Publisher
Rhett Austell

Associate Publisher: Walter C. Rohrer
Assistant Publisher: Carter Smith
General Manager: Joseph C. Hazen Jr.
Business Manager: John D. McSweeney
Production Manager: Louis Bronzo

Sales Director: Joan D. Manley
Promotion Director: Beatrice K. Tolleris
Managing Director, International:
John A. Millington

TIME-LIFE Library of America

Series Editor: Oliver E. Allen

Editorial Staff for *The District of Columbia:*

Assistant Editor: James A. Maxwell
Picture Editor: Sheila Osmundsen
Designer: John Newcomb
Assistant Designer: Jean Lindsay
Staff Writers: Lee Greene,
Frank Kendig, William Longgood,
Victor Waldrop, Peter Wood
Chief Researcher: Clara E. Nicolai
Text Research: Sondra Albert, Ruth Silva, Val Chu
Picture Research: Toby Solovioff, Elizabeth Evans,
Myra Mangan, Ellen Youngblood, Marcia Gillespie,
Rhea Finkelstein, Louise Samuels, Doris Coffin,
Margo Dryden

Editorial Production

Color Director: Robert L. Young
Assistant: James J. Cox
Copy Staff: Marian Gordon Goldman, Patricia Miller,
Florence Keith
Picture Department: Dolores A. Littles,
Marquita Jones
Traffic: Arthur A. Goldberger
Art Assistants: Jean Held, Virginia Wells

The text of this book was written by Bernard A. Weisberger, the picture essays by the editorial staff. Valuable aid was provided by the following individuals and departments of Time Inc.: LIFE staff photographers Fritz Goro, Francis Miller, Charles Phillips and Arthur Rickerby; Editorial Production, Robert W. Boyd Jr.; Editorial Reference, Peter Draz; Picture Collection, Doris O'Neil; Photographic Laboratory, George Karas; TIME-LIFE News Service, Richard M. Clurman; Washington Correspondents Edwin W. Goodpaster, Neil MacNeil, Hays Gorey, John F. Stacks and Martha Bucknell.

Contents

Introduction

In this perceptive portrait of the District of Columbia, Bernard Weisberger describes Washington as "perhaps the most electric 70 square miles of urban America." Unlike the author, I am not a historian and therefore am not bound by his professional restraint. To me, the nation's capital is unquestionably the most electric 70 square miles on earth. That is so because it is a community doubly in ferment. It is in ferment as an urban center reflecting all of the problems and ills of our modern crowded society—and adding a few extra ones all its own. And it is in constant, boiling ferment as a developing, changing, expanding capital of a rich and powerful country that strives to live up to its role as the lodestone of democracy throughout the world.

I have been especially fortunate to have seen both Washingtons at close hand. Washington was my hometown all the time I was growing up. My family's circumstances were relatively comfortable —my father was an attorney for the Veterans Administration—and although we were Negro we lived in a pleasant neighborhood in Northwest Washington that at the time was partially integrated. The houses were red brick, identical three-story buildings attached in a row to each other, like innumerable other "row" structures all over Washington. Unlike many disadvantaged Negroes who even then were living in slums, our family was secure and happy. But in some ways the middle-class Negro world of Washington in the 1920s and 1930s was an unreal one. The city was actually just an overgrown Southern town, and the attitudes of most of the white people were what you might expect. Our neighborhood was quiet and friendly, and everyone knew just about everyone else, but it just happened that most of the Negroes' world tended to be segregated. We had our own

churches, stores and clubs and so we lived quite a separate existence. As a teenager I was lucky enough to be able to go to the Paul Laurence Dunbar High School, an exceptionally fine institution whose faculty members were the best anyone could hope for; most of its graduates went on to college— I had no trouble getting into Howard University. But of course Dunbar High, like all the other schools that most Negroes went to, was segregated. So the world I grew up in, while highly beneficial in some respects, did have a number of limitations that some of us might have found disturbing, at least in retrospect.

By the time I returned to Washington as a newly elected Senator in 1967, after living and working for two decades in Massachusetts, the city had changed greatly, and with it my old neighborhood. Today the neighborhood is totally segregated—it is now all Negro—and the surroundings are not quite as comfortable as they once were. When rioting broke out in the city in 1968, I felt a special twinge of despair because the violence and disorder were taking place not far from the old neighborhood I had known and loved. And although I could not condone the violent activity that was rending the community, I could well understand the kinds of feelings and circumstances that had caused it.

The task of alleviating these conditions will necessarily fall to the other Washington—the city which is the focus of political power and influence for the entire country and which, as Mr. Weisberger points out, has grown so much in size and complexity over the past several decades. This other Washington has been in ferment, too, and again I have had a ringside seat. The city I grew up in and in which my father worked was in many respects quite parochial. Washington of the 1920s and 1930s was beginning to take on some of the burdens it carries today, but these concerns did not seem so weighty. In those days there were still trolley cars in the streets, and the general atmosphere was more leisurely and slow-paced. Now the city is encircled with freeways like every other metropolis, high-rise buildings are shooting up everywhere, and there is not much leisure left. Just as the world of the blacks had changed when I came back to the city, so had "official" Washington, the world of the bureaucrats, the politicians and the civil servants. Everything was much busier and more crowded—and the problems of today's world crowded in on everyone.

For many years it has been the habit of certain political figures, many of them admittedly in my own party, to decry bigness in government. The federal government, they say, is destroying the American character and bringing disaster to the American economic system. I recall that Herbert Hoover said the New Deal was "the most stupendous invasion of the whole spirit of Liberty that the nation has witnessed since the days of Colonial America." The same sentiments, somewhat modified, are still heard nowadays. But the legacy of negativism obscures the very real needs of contemporary life that urgently demand attention. As this book demonstrates so vividly, Washington has taken on more and more cares and duties simply because they are cares and duties that must be attended to. The tendency to regard "massive" federal government as an adversary is a wasteful error. Of course there are inconveniences, annoyances and even dangers inherent in the existence and operation of a strong central government. But it is a mistake to believe that government, even strong central government, is the natural adversary of the American people. Our real adversaries are

not governmental programs but the "massive" conditions of 20th Century American life that have given birth to "massive" government. Our true adversaries are the circumstances that lead with dismaying regularity to our national ills: the cluttering and despoiling of our land and our air, the deterioration of our cities and our countryside, the continuing threat of war, the accumulation of racial and religious resentments and all the pent-up aspirations caused by what we think of as progress —progress in a land shrinking in distances and exploding in population. These are the challenges that transcend racial, religious and ethnic barriers. They are the problems that fill the dockets of the Congress and cause lights to burn late in the administrative offices of the government of the United States. There is no avoiding them. And it is exciting to feel that here they are being attacked with zeal and courage.

Since coming to the Congress I have been particularly impressed by two things. One is the sheer difficulty of getting things done; tremendous patience and persistence are needed to get bills passed and signed into law. The other is the sense of opportunity that one feels everywhere in Washington—the opportunity to accomplish something for America, especially for the ailing cities like the capital itself. Both of these characteristics are conveyed admirably by Mr. Weisberger. He has spelled out the atmosphere of crisis and ferment and expectancy that excites everyone in this driving, pulsing town. He has also given us a feeling of the complexity of the government and the dedication of its personnel. These are things the American people should know about, and they will find what they are looking for in this volume.

—EDWARD W. BROOKE
U.S. Senator from Massachusetts

1

The Seat of Empire

The District of Columbia, i.e., the city of Washington, occupies a small area at the convergence of two branches of an Atlantic-bound river whose economic heyday was passed not long after the beginning of the 19th Century. No exotic or enriching cargoes are swung ashore at Washington's docksides; no strings of boxcars line up in its rail terminal with the gathered wealth of continents; no factories hum themselves alive each morning; no billion-dollar corporate mergers are likely to be arranged in its carpeted lawyers' offices. It bears no remote resemblance to San Francisco or Chicago or Detroit or New York.

Yet to a greater extent than any of these cities, Washington is vital—perhaps the most electric 70 square miles of urban America. For in this magnetic and maddening, fulfilling and frustrating city, the commodity whose presence dominates life is not oil or grain or machinery, but power. In the buildings of the United States government at Washington's heart take place the daily transactions in power that, to a great extent, determine

President John F. Kennedy delivers his inaugural address at the Capitol in January 1961. Underlying the festive air of any Presidential inauguration is the awesome fact that on this one man falls the power of the world's most influential political post.

the structure, pattern and tempo of events in San Francisco, Chicago, Detroit or New York. True, the ultimate source of that authority lies outside Washington, with the voters of the United States, and the agents of authority are always mindful that what has been conferred by the American people may eventually (though not easily) be taken away.

But for the working day it is Washington that dispenses the conferred power of the electorate in measurable quantities to particular ends. Though Washington is not the country's business headquarters, it pumps economic life into thousands of communities through an intricate capillary system of installations, field offices and subagencies. Though it has been both the sport and the stock in trade of some Congressmen and editors to lament the growth of the federal bureaucracy, the 20th Century has inexorably inflated the number of the national government's employees. There were nearly three million federal workers in March of 1968, or one employed person out of 25 in the country as a whole. Only about 10 per cent of them work in Washington. The rest receive their share of the $1.8 billion monthly payroll elsewhere, often in faraway countries.

They work for offices and departments so numerous that it takes the *United States Government*

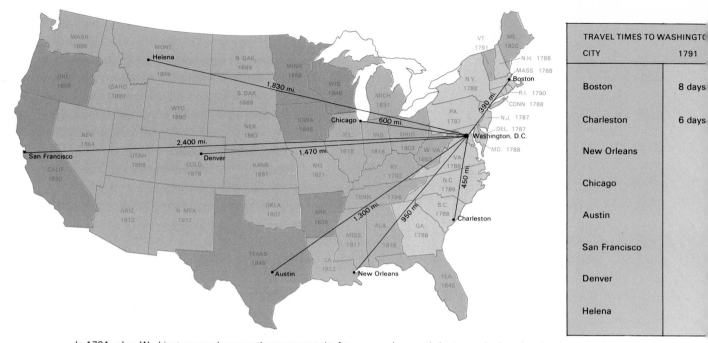

TRAVEL TIMES TO WASHINGTO	
CITY	1791
Boston	8 days
Charleston	6 days
New Orleans	
Chicago	
Austin	
San Francisco	
Denver	
Helena	

In 1791, when Washington was chosen as the permanent site for the nation's capital, the city lay in the middle of the 13 states strung along the East Coast. Boston was 390 straight-line miles away *(see map),* an eight-day trip by stagecoach *(see chart).* Charleston was farther—450 miles—but ships made the run in six days. By 1830, new states to the west were coming into the Union (map and chart are color-keyed to show periods when new states entered) and Washington's location became less centered. The 600-mile overland journey from Chicago took 18 days. Meanwhile, better roads and faster ships reduced the travel times back East. By 1860 Washington was almost the breadth of a continent away from some of the newer states—a 34-day voyage around the tip of

Organization Manual more than 800 pages to list and describe them. The federal presence is everywhere —in the more than 33,000 post offices, the 440-odd federal hospitals, the Coast Guard lighthouses and the customs offices of the Treasury Department, the depots, forts, yards and bases of the armed services (which employ more than a million civilians), the launching pads for space vehicles, the 34 federal penal and correctional institutions of the Justice Department, the thousands of installations of the Department of the Interior scattered over the national domain and doing everything from stocking lakes with fish to assisting oil prospectors. In addition there are the official accretions of the nation's 20th Century efforts to make good the promise of American life for everyone. The successive waves of that effort have borne different public-relations labels—New Freedom, New Deal, Fair Deal, New Frontier, Great Society—but each, in receding, has left additional programs and agencies deposited either in existing or new Cabinet departments or independent or quasi-independent agencies. The long list stretches from the Department of Labor in 1913 to the Office of Economic Opportunity in 1964.

Thus the city sits at the center of lines of force that radiate to every corner of the nation, every quarter of the globe and even into outer space. The pulses of energy that it daily generates direct men and women to specific action in a slum in Toledo, a county engineer's office in Butte, a classroom in Anchorage, a laboratory in Cambridge, a hospital in an African village and, perhaps one day soon, an insectlike, gleaming exploration module on the moon. This mighty reach is Washington's primary, functional distinction among the cities of America.

Its second distinction is, in a sense, demographic. It is the capital of the United States, belonging to all the states and to none. As originally laid out in 1791, the 100-square-mile District of Columbia was approximately at the center of the young United States, halfway between Vermont and Georgia. Of necessity it was carved from Maryland and Virginia (the latter eventually reclaimed its portion); but though it was Southern in location, the District was even then national in conception. Today, as a second century of American expansion moves toward its end, Washington is still, in a sense, at the country's center. Its more than 300,000 civil servants form the living aspect of the federal establishment. Drawn from every state in the Union, most of the capital dwellers live in a curious suspension between points of reference. They are always transients, psychologically if not actually,

key dates in the growth of the U.S.)			
330	1860	1915	TODAY
4 days	1 day	11 hrs.	1¼ hrs.
3 days	1½ days	15 hrs.	1¼ hrs.
4 days	5½ days	1½ days	2½ hrs.
8 days	2 days	20 hrs.	1 hr.
	14 days	2½ days	3 hrs.
	34 days	4¼ days	5½ hrs.
		2¼ days	3½ hrs.
		2¾ days	9¼ hrs.

South America from San Francisco. Trains were drastically cutting travel time in many of the cities farther east. By 1915 nationwide railroads brought all cities within a few days of Washington, and today's jets have reduced that time to hours. Seeming discrepancies in time—11 hours by train from Boston in 1915, 9¼ hours from Helena today—are due to lack of direct connections.

expecting the change in Administration, the assignment outside Washington or the reduction in staff that will remove them from the capital. Yet they are no longer participant members of their home communities. Because of this estrangement from local affairs, their relationship to the nation as a whole and its purposes has a unique intensity. Their parochial loyalty is to the United States as it is made manifest in the agencies and departments for which they work. Whether they are Cabinet officers or file clerks, they belong to their country in a way that leaves abundant room for intense anger, maddening frustration or even bitter disillusionment with it, but none for indifference.

Paradoxical Washington is therefore a place bearing the stamp of no one state or region, yet influenced by the constant importation of the styles of all of them. As Americans, most of its inhabitants are simultaneously untypical and quintessential. This was less true three quarters of a century ago, when the federal bureaucracy was minuscule, legislative sessions were briefer, and the capital's life rested more securely in the hands of rooted families that gave it a social flavor of Virginia and southeastern Maryland. But that has changed since Washington was burdened with the responsibilities of the 20th Century and with the

management of a large part of the world's destiny. Washington is now irresistibly modern, increasingly cosmopolitan and at the convergence of every contemporary current. Neither a cultural nor an economic headquarters, nor a birthplace of trends, it is nonetheless where much of the action occurs. For those who want to know the score, whether they are scholars, publishers, journalists, tycoons or foreign heads of state, it is the place to watch.

In its evolving role, Washington has become something special and separate on the American scene. It is endowed with a metropolitan personality of its own—a bit republican, a touch imperial, sauced with the frontier and laced with suggestions of every aspiration, noble and comical and greedy, that has stirred the American people.

Washington is, for one thing, handsome as are few American cities. When Pierre L'Enfant drew up its original plan in 1791, he envisioned a grid of streets opened up by wide boulevards sweeping through them on the diagonal. Where these boulevards intersected there would be spacious parks. Heroic statuary, pure, harmonious public buildings, a nobility stemming from space, nature, and virtuous intentions rather than mass and ornamental detail—this was the theme. Time has been kind to L'Enfant's original vision. The broad avenues are still there, yielding their visual pleasure ungrudgingly to the sightseer. The best known of them are Pennsylvania, along which flow the parades to honor new Presidents, national heroes and visitors of distinction; Connecticut, the avenue of fashionable stores, apartments, hotels and restaurants; and Massachusetts, along whose upper (i.e., northwestern) reaches are old and stately mansions, many of which now house embassies. Where the avenues and streets join, often in circles around which confused drivers centrifugally whirl, there are indeed parks and statues of Presidents, explorers, inventors and especially Civil War generals— Scott, Logan, McClellan, Thomas, Sherman, Sheridan—who grasp their sword hilts and stare from under weathered, green-bronze hat brims at the capital of the Union they saved.

The major public buildings and monuments, too, are built and placed for looks. The Capitol dominates, as it should, the view from many parts of downtown Washington. Sweeping west from the Capitol is the wide, green expanse of the Mall, which the eye follows to the great exclamation point of the Washington Monument. To the west of the monument is the long Reflecting Pool that lies before the Lincoln Memorial; to the north, across a broad ellipse of green, is the White House;

11

to the south, beyond the Tidal Basin ringed with cherry trees, is the round, colonnaded marble of the Jefferson Memorial. The working buildings are integrated into the scene. Those of the so-called Federal Triangle, just west and north of the Capitol—the Post Office, the Internal Revenue, the Interstate Commerce Commission, Justice, Federal Trade Commission, Federal Bureau of Investigation, Commerce, Labor and National Archives buildings—have a fortresslike solidity that looks placidly on tempests of change. Such outlandish structures as the sandstone gingerbread towers of the original Smithsonian Institution on the Mall, the blatantly overdecorated "Second Empire" Executive Office Building across from the White House and the monolith of the Pentagon across the Potomac in Virginia somehow seem to be forgiven their ugliness in this purposeful, historical setting.

Washington's awareness that it had beauty to preserve grew on it slowly. The grand design had to be completed by post-L'Enfant generations. It took 36 years, beginning in 1848, to raise the Washington Monument. The streets did not receive their first real attention until the Administration of Grant, when Washington temporarily got a territorial form of government and a political boss, Alexander R. Shepherd, who provided pavements, sewers, lights and a debt of some $20 million before Congress, in alarm, snatched back control of the District. Not until 1901 was a Park Commission created; not until 1910 was there a Commission of Fine Arts; and many of the best-known monuments and buildings date from the 20th Century. Current crusades to glamorize the capital city may, in fact, threaten to provide too much of a good thing and turn Washington into a quickly outdated super world's fair. But there is no doubt that, for the time being, the city's official architecture is calculated to please and impress, and does.

Not all of Washington's handsomeness is confined to public exhibits, moreover. Some of the best residential addresses in the city are to be found in Georgetown, whose narrow streets and beautifully restored old houses are guarded by its residents, proud inhabitants of what is an almost unspoiled 18th Century Potomac River town. (Alexandria, farther south and in Virginia, is equally 18th Century but less convenient of access and so has never become Georgetown's equal as a status community.) And along with its own colonial town, Washington has its own wilderness preserve. This is Rock Creek Park, some 1,800 acres of preserved woodland in northwest Washington, with jumbled

and towering rock masses, deep gorges, a profusion of wild flowers, ferns and trees, numerous songbirds, flying squirrels, deer, opossums, raccoons, weasels, muskrats, foxes and other animal life not usually found 15 minutes from city traffic jams. In this park Theodore Roosevelt used to lead perspiring knots of diplomats and newspapermen on point-to-point dashes, scrambling through the underbrush, sliding down rocks and leaping into the creek itself with zesty abandon. Nature lovers who hike its 15 miles of trails or ride its 18 miles of bridle paths still find it irresistible, as do the youngsters who come to its National Zoological Park in vacationing droves.

The city has its unattractive features, too. There are appalling slums to the north and east of the Capitol itself; in the Virginia suburbs especially, there are rows of boxlike apartment buildings and individual family houses checkered with garish shopping plazas. Washington's downtown business district, especially to the east of the White House, is hardly attractive, and in many places there are ugly encrustations of bad taste and exploitive haste in building, the resulting structures often succumbing to abandonment, decay and the onset of honkytonk. Nevertheless, Washington overall would be hard to equal as a visually satisfying theater for the drama of decision making. Even its most jaded longtime residents admit that.

The human tide that churns through intersections at any Washington noon hour is made up of a number of population elements. A Washingtonian crowd, in cross section, will show a division among short-term transients, permanent residents and what might be called transients for the long haul. The proportion is in favor of the first group, and this is a fact of considerable significance for the social and cultural life of the capital.

The short-term transients, birds of passage whose stay is a day or a week or two, are themselves divided among the tourists and those who have come to knock upon one of the doors in the labyrinthine corridors of government. The tourists are always in evidence, though there are huge migrations on special occasions like inaugurations, during school vacations, at Christmastime, and in the Easter season, when the annual blooming of the cherry trees is an extra attraction. Tourism is, as everywhere, combined with conventions, and of the 16.8 million visitors to Washington in one year in the late 1960s, about 512,000 were delegates to business, fraternal, professional and scholarly gatherings, many of them bringing their wives and

Arrangement © 1947 by Carl Fischer, Inc., New York.

With a lively march in six-eight time, the Washington-born "March King," John Philip Sousa, turned the name of his city's noted newspaper, *The Washington Post*, into a national household word. The history of his immortal "The Washington Post March" began in June 1889, when the paper's owners sponsored a writing contest. They asked Sousa to compose a special piece in honor of the award presentation. The resulting march soon became one of Sousa's most popular pieces—it sold more than a million copies in five years—although under the terms of his publishing contract he received only $35.

children to take in the sights. In every color, size and style of dress, chattering on in every variety of regional accent and foreign language, cameras swinging around their necks, guidebooks in hand, eyes slightly glazed and heads swiveling relentlessly, they pass in line before the arches, columns, domes, display cases and murals, then plunge out into the unfamiliar streets to regroup in families or classes for the next visual assault on the nation's heritage.

Among the other short-time visitors are the seekers after funds, authorizations and contracts. While the tourists come in goodly numbers in buses, trains and private automobiles, it is the petitioners who fill most of the planes that touch down at National Airport—40 an hour in peak traffic periods. These petitioners come because the center of power of the vast governmental structure is on the north bank of the Potomac River; this is where one must come to trace a problem to its source or to appeal to some final arbiter.

The problems and appeals are numerous and constant, for there is hardly a farm, county seat, schoolroom, airfield, hospital, home for the aged, housing development, power plant or waterworks in the country that does not, in some way, bear a relationship to a federal agency or that does not

share, one way or another, in the more than $125 billion annually that the government now spends in this broad area. In addition, private business now has more dealings than ever before with the government in its dual role as regulator of industry and the nation's biggest customer.

It is for these reasons that the man hailing a taxi at National Airport is likely to be a mayor, a park commissioner, a state chief highway engineer, a school superintendent, a labor mediator, the chairman of a farmers' cooperative committee, a housing coordinator or a welfare supervisor. And the passenger who sat next to him on the plane was likely to have been a businessman, coming to sell the government anything from a fleet of jet aircraft to a part of the million dollars' worth of pencils and paper clips that are bought annually, or to present arguments for a merger that has brought frowns in the Antitrust Division of the Justice Department. Public men or private men, they are making their pilgrimage to the powerhouse, hoping to see the Congressman or official who can get things done—or the man with access to the Congressman or official who can get things done.

The capital's permanent residents include the affluent dwellers near the apex of the social pyramid and the unsung multitudes who perform such routine servicing chores of a metropolis as laundering and bus driving. Washington's continuous social elite (as opposed to the high society that varies with the fortunes of Republicans and Democrats) is especially rich in distinguished widows, of whom the most distinguished is probably Alice Roosevelt Longworth, daughter of the first Roosevelt to reach the White House. There are Washingtonians in the right clubs who still live on the inherited fruits of carefully invested fortunes and those who have made fortunes of their own in merchandising, transportation and real estate. A prominent feature of Washington's social structure is its incredible number of lawyers. There were 13,000 of them in the late 1960s (8,000 of these in government service), or one for every 200 persons in the metropolitan area. The capital is, in fact, a lawyers' paradise. They are the guides through the sunless jungle of interlocking, overlapping and entangling regulations, and their share of the game brought back by the hunting parties they lead is enough to make them very much at ease in Zion. Some of the most successful are former Cabinet members, Congressmen and chairmen of the regulatory agencies. They have used the skills and contacts they acquired in public service to remain profitably in Washington after their tours of duty.

Other regulars of Washington life are the directors of the lobbies. The word itself still has a slightly suspicious ring to it. It summons up remembrance of Gilded Age crudity—mustachioed men in flowered vests proffering champagne and crisp Treasury notes to Congressmen in plush private dining rooms. But in fact lobbying has become modernized and has adapted itself to a variety of causes, profane and sacred. If the American Iron and Steel Institute and the American Bankers Association have Washington offices, often in elegant new buildings on 16th Street, Connecticut or Massachusetts Avenues, so do the AFL-CIO, the American Association of Retired Persons, the National Association of Letter Carriers, the National Federation of Business and Professional Women's Clubs, the National Association for the Advancement of Colored People, and so on for 13 columns under the heading "National" in the District telephone book. Universities, religious bodies, philanthropic organizations, and professional and scientific societies must also look to their own interests —perhaps even more assiduously than the trade associations that are more likely to speak a Congressman's language in the first place. The man who manages a successful Washington headquarters is valuable and usually well paid, and he has

no actual counterpart in any other American city.

Among the poor permanent residents of Washington, a disturbing percentage, as is the case throughout urban America, is black. It is in fact one of the distinctions of the District of Columbia that it has a Negro majority—approximately 60 per cent of some 810,000 District residents as of 1968. It must be borne in mind that the Washington metropolitan area as a whole shows a different picture. Counting in the surrounding suburban Maryland and Virginia counties, into which few Negroes penetrate, the population is slightly more than 2.6 million. Nevertheless, the Negro majority in the District itself is a deeply significant fact. It is one of the reasons why Congress has been traditionally reluctant to grant home rule to Washingtonians. With the exception of reservation-based Indians, they are America's only colonials on the North American continent with no representative government. Moreover, the prevalence of blacks in the District has vastly complicated the inherently agonizing problem of effective school integration.

Negro Washington is not entirely a fortress of deprivation. It boasts of one of the oldest Negro social registers in the country and the best U.S. Negro university, Howard, with all the cultural fringe benefits attached. It has a Negro middle class of civil servants, which has grown steadily for several decades and which rises from a base in the janitorial services of government buildings to a lofty peak in Supreme Court Justice Thurgood Marshall. (In September of 1967 it even acquired a Negro commissioner, Walter Washington, appointed by President Lyndon Johnson under a new reorganization plan. But Washington, though billed as a Negro "mayor," was given neither a voting constituency nor any significant power.)

Despite the evidences of solid Negro advance everywhere in the offices of the government, there is no avoiding the fact that in black Washington, as in the black cities that exist in the nation's other urban centers, unemployment, crime, decay and despair are festering, along with their illusory antidotes of alcoholism and drug addiction. And black Washington cannot be painted out of any realistic portrait of the capital city.

Lastly, there are the long-term transients, those who come and go on rotating assignments. They can be as prosaic as the sweatered students at Washington's five universities of standing or the enlisted men serving lengthy hitches in the capital area. Or they can be as romantic-looking as the foreign diplomats and their staffs.

Chained to an uprooted tree, an angry group of women protest a plan in 1938 to remove the Japanese cherry trees around the Tidal Basin to make way for the Jefferson Memorial. The fracas was largely the result of an emotional campaign against the project conducted in the columns of two Washington newspapers, the *Times* and the *Herald*, by their publisher, Eleanor "Cissy" Patterson. (The papers later merged and became the Washington *Times-Herald*.) The female activists—not including Mrs. Patterson—led a march on the White House and organized a "chain-in" at the construction site, demanding that President Roosevelt "save the cherry trees." Roosevelt's reply was simply that Mrs. Patterson was flimflamming the public to boost her papers' circulation. Eventually the furor died down, and when the memorial was completed in 1942, only 83 of the area's 1,700 cherry trees had been removed—and there were plans to add 1,000 more.

Like any capital, Washington gets a touch of the exotic from the presence of its foreign colony. Embassy Row is a reminder that the entire world does business here. Behind the gates of 2520 Massachusetts Avenue, Japanese clerk-typists drink pale green tea. Tulips bloom in the garden of the Embassy of the Netherlands. On Queen Elizabeth's birthday, the more-than-500-man staff of the British Embassy participates in a reception featuring strawberries and Devonshire cream. Elephants impassively gaze with stone eyes in front of India's embassy. The chancery where the business of Iran's embassy is conducted is decorated with blue-and-white ceramics. In a curbside swirl of rush-hour pedestrians, African robes vie for attention with miniskirts. (More than nationalistic pride is involved in the costuming; it is one sure way that a black man from abroad can reduce the risk of embarrassing racial incidents.)

Among the most prestigious temporary residents of Washington are the several hundred men (and an occasional woman) who occupy the top policy-making posts in the Executive department. The roster begins with the family that lives in the White House, at 1600 Pennsylvania Avenue. It goes on to number the Vice President, the members of the Cabinet, the Justices of the Supreme Court, the uniformed Joint Chiefs of Staff, and the heads of the great and powerful agencies—the Federal Reserve Board, the Interstate Commerce Commission, the United States Information Agency, the Central Intelligence Agency, the Bureau of the Budget, the Atomic Energy Commission. These men, at the highest level, are the ones who are usually driven to work in chauffered limousines, who are never more than a moment away from a telephone connection to the White House, and who willingly pay for their well-cut clothes, good homes and social standing with work hours that a steel puddler would have found excessive 50 years ago. The times are long past when they were accessible to anyone who walked through the department doors or when they refreshed themselves with strolls and horseback rides down the main avenues. Their time and privacy are jealously guarded as official secrets. When they do speak to the public, it is likely to be through television speeches or statements to the press corps. That corps itself is a feature of Washington life, numbering about two thousand accredited correspondents for newspapers, magazines and electronic networks and representing the presses of nearly 30 countries.

The 100 Senators and 435 Representatives are also among the capital's illustrious long-term transients, though some of the luckier ones get re-elected often enough to assure a virtually permanent Washington address along with their committee chairmanships. No seniority, of course, is as impressive as that of the Justices of the United States Supreme Court, who hold office for life, but there are Congressmen with longer records of consecutive service than many Justices.

Below these participants in splendor are the more than 300,000 workaday civil servants of Washington. They are not officially transients, and the civil service system itself was created to guarantee that merit would not be swept away with each turn in the political tide. Yet in the higher reaches of many agencies, assignment outside Washington is routine and expected. Moreover, it is a curious fact that thousands of federal employees who come to Washington look upon it as a waystop. They may be stenographers who come "temporarily" from Terre Haute or Fargo to taste a little of the capital's glamor and to see if they can triumph over an unfavorable ratio of 100 females to fewer than 90 males. Or they may be at the top of the ratings, GS-18s in the civil service code, making more than $30,000 annually. In that case they are likely to be such scarce specimens as solid-state physicists, experts in rare Asian languages or economic analysts with doctorates in mathematics, and they are given to making plans for departure to a professorship or a job with private industry. These dreams take on fresh intensity when Congress threatens to deny pay raises or is agitated by an economy drive that threatens sweeping cuts in personnel.

But despite such fantasies of departure, thousands of the government workers, employed by a hundred or more departments and agencies and rated by 2,000 job skills listed in the personnel manual, remain throughout their lives. Even those who do not stay on are bound together in a fellowship. As part of the Washington scene, they are indefinably special. There is an attraction that makes even teaching school or directing traffic in the nation's capital something more intensely felt than it could be elsewhere. It is the lure of feeling at the center of things. In prosaic fact, the Washingtonian may not really be closer to the inside than the New Yorker or the San Franciscan. The news he gets from his local papers and television stations is being flashed to the entire country in the precise form in which it reaches him. But the news does take place, for the Washingtonian, in *his* town, even if it is only his adopted town pro tem. What is more, he may, if he is lucky, actually see the chairman of the Senate Foreign Relations Committee or the Vice President's wife emerge from a taxi in front of a hotel. As a civil servant, he will occasionally be given time off and urged to help welcome a visiting prime minister or conquering general in ceremonial parade. And his (or her) girl friend or neighbor's cousin or tailor's daughter actually does the First Lady's hair or served breakfast to Walter Reuther and Senator Mansfield yesterday or types correspondence for the Secretary of Defense.

This feeling of participation in the great currents of history is balm to the Washingtonian's ego, and never more so than when the capital dweller puts himself on display for out-of-towners. The higher the Washingtonian's rank, the more exhilarating is the sensation. Perhaps one reason that many former top officials remain in the city is not merely the prospect of cashing in on their experience and knowledgeability, but the awareness that they cannot really go home again—that law practice in Ohio or Tennessee can never again be the same.

Perhaps this assumption by some Washingtonians of an importance not really earned mirrors a facet of the city's character. Washington, too, lives to some extent on borrowed identity. Much of its handsomeness comes from monuments to heroes who earned their laurels somewhere else: on battlefields or in offices and laboratories far away. It is true that great transactions of statesmanship have taken place in the capital, and many a provincial lawyer has become a great man only because of what he has achieved in Washington. But generally the events to which political leaders have responded transpired elsewhere. They belong, just as the heroes belong, to the nation. But Washington has appropriated the national past to itself with every memorial and historic document.

And it must, for in a sense Washington has no real past of its own. What happened to the town in war and peace happened because it was the seat of government. It had no independent economic or strategic value. It has always been, as someone has said, a city within a capital, never a capital within a city.

Yet this very functionalism—this way of defining itself by its single great task of governing—has clothed Washington with greatness as the capital has passed from the headquarters of a minor republic to the nerve center of an empire. In addition, Washington has chosen as well to be the mirror of the nation's past, present and future—therefore, a mirror in which the figures are never still.

From the south balcony of the White House, Army Herald Trumpeters play a fanfare to welcome a visiting head of state. A recent tradition in Washington, the Trumpeters were formed to greet Queen Elizabeth of Great Britain in 1957.

Ruffles and flourishes

The pageantry, customs and traditions that have grown up with the business of government in Washington are a curious combination of the ancient and the relatively modern, the aristocratic and the plebeian. A visiting head of state is sometimes greeted with ceremonies befitting a medieval king, but a new ambassador to the United States may equally well be met at the White House by an informally dressed President. The House of Representatives cherishes a symbol that dates back to republican Rome, but a more important symbol to an individual lawmaker is his special license plate. A Senator may feel one with history when he dines at the White House and eats from dishes used by President Lincoln. But more cherished in his day-to-day life is the traditional bean soup served in the Senate dining rooms. To a foreigner, the mixture of pomp and informality is often baffling, but if he stays long enough, he recognizes that both reflect facets of the nation's character.

Welcome for a Prime Minister

Carrying state flags, an honor guard chosen from all arms of the military service awaits Thanom Kittikachorn, Prime Minister of Thailand, on the South Lawn of the White House. The Prime Minister has been flown to Washington from Andrews Air Force Base in a Marine helicopter landing beyond the South Lawn; protocol demands that a visiting chief of state or head of government be furnished with official transportation from the point where he first touches U.S. soil. (Visiting heads of state from the Far East often land in Hawaii and must then be flown by military jet to Washington.) After the helicopter lands, the Prime Minister will be taken by limousine to the South Lawn in front of the honor guard. There he will be greeted by the President, and the howitzers in the background will fire a 19-gun salute.

Fireworks for a visiting dignitary

Following a state dinner and a parade given for the Prime Minister of Thailand, fireworks light up the sky above the White House. President and Mrs. Johnson and their 140 guests viewed the display from the Truman Balcony above the South Lawn, where the brilliant light of the fireworks etched the Washington Monument and the Jefferson Memorial against the dark sky. Since 1874, when President Ulysses S. Grant was host to King Kalakaua of the Sandwich Islands (now Hawaii), the first reigning monarch to be greeted by a U.S. President, the White House has been providing special entertainment for visiting dignitaries. Usually the diversion is planned to suit the individual taste of the guest. For a visit of officials of the Italian government, for example, opera stars performed at the White House.

Historic china for a banquet

One of the most popular attractions for visitors to the White House is the China Room, where tableware of the Presidents is on public display. Started in 1889 by Mrs. Benjamin Harrison, the collection includes examples of china used by every President since George Washington. Many pieces from this collection are used even today. The place setting below, for example, used at a state dinner given by President Lyndon B. Johnson for the President of Tunisia, includes glassware chosen by Mrs. John F. Kennedy, a service plate purchased during the Truman Administration, and original pieces or faithful copies of the French vermeil flatware purchased by President James Monroe.

Among the china still being used at the White House are the plates at right. The

Lincoln China (1) bears a band of purple and has the motto *"E Pluribus Unum"* inscribed on the clouds surrounding the eagle. President Grant selected a design (2) of native American flowers and the U.S. coat of arms. To bring the flavor of American life to the White House table, Rutherford B. Hayes commissioned a pattern (3) using U.S. flora and fauna for his service of more than 1,000 pieces. Mrs. Benjamin Harrison, herself a skillful china painter, designed for her dishes (4) a corn-tassels-and-ears border with a band of stars encircling the coat of arms. The service of Theodore Roosevelt (5) bears a border of radiating gold lines and the U.S. coat of arms, while the Wilson China (6), the first American-made dinnerware to become an official White House service, introduced the Presidential seal to the Chief Executive's table. President Franklin D. Roosevelt included a detail from his own family's coat of arms—the Roosevelt roses and feathers—in his china (7), and Harry Truman selected a service of yellow-green-bordered ware (8). President Dwight D. Eisenhower ordered plates rimmed in pure coin gold (9), and the Lyndon B. Johnson China (10) utilizes various state flowers in its design.

6

7

8

9

10

Gown for an inaugural

When Sarah Childress Polk attended the ball on March 4, 1845, celebrating the inauguration of her husband, James K. Polk, the nation's 11th President, she wore the lace-trimmed silk dress pictured below. It is one of a collection in the First Ladies Hall of the Smithsonian Institution in Washington, an exhibit that includes a dress worn by every President's wife or official hostess since Martha Washington. The collection was started in 1912, when Mrs. William Howard Taft, then the First Lady, presented her inaugural gown to the museum. Two socially prominent Washington women, Mrs. Julian James and Mrs. Rose Gouverneur Hoes, filled out the collection by gathering dresses worn by previous First Ladies. Each President's wife since Mrs. Taft has donated one of her own dresses to the exhibit to keep it up to date.

Honors for a diplomat

Nicaraguan Ambassador Guillermo Sevilla-Sacasa, clad in formal diplomatic attire, is the dean of the diplomatic corps, having the longest service in Washington. He has represented his country in the United States since 1943. Like all ambassadors, Sevilla-Sacasa enjoys certain privileges in accordance with international law and custom. He is immune to arrest and exempt from local taxes, and his communications with his own country may not be tampered with or severed. And in Washington he is given other privileges. An accredited ambassador is outranked only by the President, the Vice President, the Speaker of the House of Representatives, the Chief Justice of the United States, former Presidents and the Secretary of State. At a formal state reception, for example, an ambassador is always presented before any American Senator.

Many new ambassadors are struck by the lack of ceremony they find in the U.S. In some nations a new ambassador would not consider meeting the chief of state dressed in anything but full formal attire, and in some countries, such as Great Britain, he could expect to be driven to this meeting in a state coach drawn by matched horses and attended by liveried footmen in flowing scarlet cloaks. In Washington a new ambassador may be greeted by a President who is wearing a simple business suit.

Formal garb for a day in court

Ready to argue a case, Solicitor General Erwin N. Griswold poses on the steps of the Supreme Court in the morning coat and striped trousers that custom decrees he wear when appearing before the nation's highest tribunal. Appointed by the President and confirmed in his office by the Senate, the Solicitor General is the third-ranking officer in the Department of Justice and may at the request of the Attorney General represent the federal government in any U.S. or state court. Although the tradition of wearing formal morning dress before the Supreme Court—thought to be an adaptation of a European custom that calls for the advocate, as well as the judge, to appear in court in robes—is upheld by all government lawyers and a few old-school private attorneys, technically Griswold could appear before the Court in a sport coat.

Regiment to guard a capital

The color guard of the United States Third Infantry, known as The Old Guard, appears at a Washington function in traditional uniforms, exact replicas of those worn by enlisted men of the unit when it was formed in 1784. Predating the Constitution, The Old Guard has fought valiantly in virtually every war the nation has waged, and from its ranks have come a host of celebrated soldiers and statesmen, among them President Zachary Taylor. In recognition of its high standards and brilliant record, The Old Guard was assigned in 1946 to protect the nation's capital. Some of its other duties are ceremonial: serving as personal escort to the U.S. Presidents, participating in arrival and departure ceremonies for dignitaries, and standing round-the-clock watch over the Tomb of the Unknown Soldier.

"... known but to God

"Here rests in honored glory an American Soldier known but to God" reads the inscription on the Tomb of the Unknown Soldier in Arlington National Cemetery, just across the Potomac from Washington. In the sarcophagus, under the 50-ton block of marble that caps the tomb, lies the body of an unidentified soldier who fought and died in World War I. Flanking the tomb are the graves of two other unknown soldiers who were interred beneath the gray granite plaza on Memorial Day in 1958 to commemorate the unidentified American dead of World War II and the Korean conflict. Only the dates of the two wars mark the graves.

To ensure that the three unknown soldiers are never left alone, a sentinel selected from The Old Guard keeps a day-and-night vigil, pacing the narrow mat in front of the graves 42 times each hour. He takes 27 steps of 30 inches each during every pass, keeping his bayoneted rifle on the shoulder away from the tomb. He is not permitted to smile, to talk to visitors or even to pick up his hat if it is blown away by the wind. During the day, he is replaced every hour on the hour; the night tour is two hours. Each day thousands of visitors watch the guard-changing ceremony *(right)*.

A genial functionary for the House

William M. "Fishbait" Miller is the Doorkeeper of the House of Representatives. He ushers in the President and other dignitaries when they visit the House in joint session with the Senate and provides the official introduction. Before the President enters the chamber Miller strides down the center aisle, stops at the third row and announces in his Mississippi drawl, "Mistuh Speakuh, the President of the United States." But Miller is more than a herald. Heading a staff of more than 300 employees, he is in charge of the House pages, the House publication and distribution service, five barbershops and all the public rooms in the House. Miller was raised on the Mississippi Gulf Coast and was scrawny and small as a boy—a shrimp. "And down there," he says, explaining his nickname, "shrimp is used for fish bait."

Youthful pages for Congress

Taking a rare break from their duties, the pages of the Senate and House of Representatives pose for a photograph on the steps of the Capitol. The first page, a nine-year-old boy, was appointed by Daniel Webster and Henry Clay during the Administration of President Andrew Jackson. Today they must be older, between 14 and 18 years of age. They run all kinds of errands and provide minor services for the members of Congress, but they also attend school—the Capitol Page School is located on the top floor of the Library of Congress—starting their classes at 6:30 each morning so that they are free by 10 to man their positions in the Senate or House. They are given a rare introduction to the workings of Washington politics and yet, curiously, relatively few pages make their adult careers in that field.

Flags for the voters

Lost to history is the name of the savvy Congressman who first courted constituents by giving local organizations American flags that had flown over the Capitol. In recent years, however, the custom has become enormously popular. In 1937 only six such "courtesy" flags were sent out; three decades later the flag below, obtained by Senator Mike Mansfield for the Ladies Auxiliary of Post 2252, Veterans of Foreign Wars, Glacier Park, Montana, was one of 18,000 being provided annually. The flags are sent out by Congressmen but supplied to them by the Architect of the Capitol, who purchases thousands of flags each year and flies each one briefly before delivering it. At one time all such flags were flown on the two main flagpoles, but the demand has become so great that nine additional poles for courtesy flags have been erected on the Capitol's roof.

An ancient symbol to keep order

The Sergeant-at-Arms of the House of Representatives, Zeake W. Johnson Jr., holds the House Mace, the symbol of his office. Originally a weapon of war—a mace was used by cavalrymen in Europe as late as the 16th Century—its function as a symbol of authority probably dates back as far as the Roman Republic. The House Mace consists of 13 ebony rods, bound together with strips of silver. On top is a globe of solid silver. Since the establishment of the House of Representatives in 1789, the Mace has been used only a few times to restore order. In 1885, for example, Representative John D. White of Kentucky, after erupting with a stream of abusive language, was directed to sit down by the Speaker. White ignored the order. At the Speaker's command the Sergeant-at-Arms confronted White with the Mace, and the Congressman meekly took his seat.

Status for a Senator

In Washington low-numbered license plates are as much a status symbol as "good" addresses or invitations to the White House—one newspaper publishes a list of the first 1,250 D.C. numbers for dedicated tag watchers to keep in their glove compartments as a handy reference. Some Senators, such as Senator Margaret Chase Smith of Maine, whose license plate is shown below, acquired these plates easily from their home states. But for Washington plates, the battle is more fiercely fought. The demand for low numbers far exceeds the supply, and every ploy from gentle persuasion to bribery has been used to obtain one. Besides conferring status, the low license numbers have a practical advantage: relatively few cars bearing these plates are stolen. But they also bring a risk: recently thieves have taken to stealing the low-numbered plates for themselves.

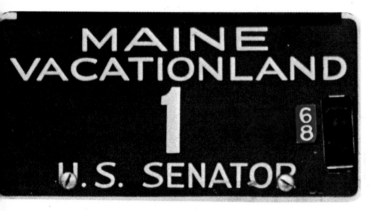

Famous Senate Restaurant Bean Soup

1½ lbs. dried Michigan pea beans

4 large yellow onions, chopped

2 tbs. butter

1 lb. smoked ham hocks

Tie in cheesecloth: 6 sprigs parsley, 1 clove garlic, ¾ tsp. dried thyme, 1 bay leaf, 1 chopped carrot, ½ lemon

Salt and pepper

Place beans in bowl; add cold water to a depth of 4 inches above beans and soak overnight. Drain and run hot water over beans until slightly whitened. Lightly brown onions in butter. Put beans in pot with 3 quarts cold water. Add onions, ham hocks, and flavorings tied in cheesecloth. Bring to boil, reduce heat and simmer, stirring occasionally, for about 3 hours, or until beans are tender and quantity is reduced by half. Set ham hocks aside to cool. Discard flavorings. Purée 2 cups of beans with a little of the liquid and return to pot, adding 2 cups of water. Finely dice meat from skinned ham hocks and return to soup. Season to taste with salt and freshly ground pepper. Bring to a boil and serve. (For 8.)

A hearty dish for a Senator

Every day on the menu of every restaurant in the Capitol Building can be found Senate Bean Soup; the recipe for this popular dish is given above. There is no record of the origin of this practice, but according to one story it originated not in the Senate but in the House, with a Representative who insisted that bean soup be served daily. Today, however, the soup is especially popular in the private dining quarters in the Capitol's Senate wing, two adjoining rooms, one for Democrats and one for Republicans. The Senators' fondness for the soup does not make them gourmets. The maître d'hôtel says, "If they don't choose Senate Bean Soup, they invariably ask for a hamburger."

A beacon for lawmakers

High above Washington, the 50-foot-tall lantern atop the Capitol dome announces to Washington that the lawmakers are meeting at night. Although the dome is floodlighted every night, the 12-columned lantern is lit only when one or both houses of Congress are in session after sunset. There is no law requiring that the lantern be lit for night sessions, nor is there any record of the origin of this practice, but it is thought that it began in the middle of the 19th Century when many members of Congress lived in hotels and boardinghouses near the Capitol. A blazing lantern meant official business was being carried on, and summoned the Congressmen. Another practice established by tradition rather than law—the flying of flags both day and night over the respective houses of Congress—indicates when the House and Senate are in session.

Marines: musicians and sentries

Usually pictured in the midst of bloody combat, the Marine Corps performs milder duties in Washington. One of its responsibilities is music for the President. The United States Marine Band *(upper right)*, known as "The President's Own," has played at every Presidential inauguration since Thomas Jefferson took office in 1801, as well as at other state functions. Out of its ranks have come some of the nation's finest musicians, among them John Philip Sousa, leader of the band from 1880 to 1892 and composer of the official Marine Corps march "Semper Fidelis."

The Marines also guard diplomatic establishments, such as U.S. embassies throughout the world, and in Washington, Blair House *(lower right)*, the President's official guesthouse on Pennsylvania Avenue. Converted from a private residence after World War II, when the influx of foreign dignitaries began to tax the crowded White House, Blair House had already played a part in U.S. history. It was here that President Lincoln wrote the first draft of the Emancipation Proclamation. President Truman and his family lived in Blair House from 1949 to 1952, while the interior of the White House was being rebuilt. After an attempt on the life of the President in 1950, the 32-room mansion was equipped with bulletproof windows and doors that open only from the inside. Since then such notable heads of state as Emperor Haile Selassie of Ethiopia, President William Tubman of Liberia, Prime Minister Jawaharlal Nehru of India and former Soviet Premier Nikita Khrushchev have slept in the mansion's large, antique-filled rooms.

The Marines who guard Blair House are part of the Guard Company of the Marine Barracks in Washington, the oldest Marine Corps post in the nation. All members of the Guard Company are volunteers; they are screened to meet strict standards of appearance and physical fitness, and most of them have seen combat duty.

30

2

Biography of a Small Town

There have always been two, and possibly three, Washingtons. First, there is the true "Federal City," the collection of buildings sheathing the bones, nerves and muscles of the national government. It occupies only a small portion of the District of Columbia's acreage, but it is the District's reason for being. From the days of the first drawings for the Capitol itself to the latest eruption of official magnificence in the new Congressional office buildings, this Federal City, Washington, has grown in spasms, depending on whether Congress was inclined to husband the money of the taxpayers or to build more stately mansions for their chosen agents to work in. Then there is the city of Washington itself, populated by humans who eat, sleep, marry, become ill, read newspapers, and require schools, sewers, pavements, street lights and other mundane necessities that are inconveniently expensive and low in their yield of purely esthetic pleasure. To these two Washingtons some chroniclers would add a third—a "secret city" of Negro residents, hardly ever considered an integral ele-

ment in the capital's life, yet an inescapable presence in its past and future development. The interwoven threads of relationship among official Washington and human Washington, and among white and black, form the texture of the District's history.

The pattern began to take form from the start. The very establishment of the capital on the Potomac was less the fruit of logic, geography and the exertions of local boosters than of an early instance of Congressional logrolling. The Southern states, in 1790, favored the location of a "Federal District" on the Potomac River between Maryland and Virginia, but numerous Northerners preferred a site closer to the established financial and communications centers of New York and Philadelphia, both of which had played temporary host to the capital. It came about that Alexander Hamilton, Secretary of the Treasury and no friend to Virginia's anti-Federalist planters, needed a few votes for a prized financial measure, the assumption of the states' debts by the national government. A deal was arranged with several members of the Virginia delegation to provide the needed votes and in exchange Hamilton's friends in Congress helped to put over the Potomac site.

Greatly pleased with the decision, George Wash-

A handsome Georgetown house, its entrance lit by gas lamps, is typical of many found in the District's oldest residential area. Georgetown has been designated as a national landmark area to protect its homes, some of which date from the 18th Century.

ington himself chose an area on the stream that would allow the District to include Georgetown and Alexandria. He sent Andrew Ellicott (already highly regarded as a public surveyor for his work on the New York and Pennsylvania state boundaries) to fix the borders and named Major Pierre L'Enfant, whom he knew from Revolutionary War days, to draw up a plan for the city proper. The existing local community, such as it was, consisted primarily of about a score of substantial landholders; their reaction to the honor descending upon them was to plan on a substantial rise in land values near whatever locale would be chosen. Washington cannily requested L'Enfant to run surveys near both Georgetown and the minuscule settlement of Carrollsburg, south of the present Capitol Hill, in order to keep the speculators guessing. Then Washington appeared in person, assembled the owners of tracts in the area encompassed by the Potomac, the Anacostia River and a line drawn roughly southeast from a point on Rock Creek, and convinced them that instead of competing to sell the nation a relatively small area on which to construct the government buildings, they should "make a common cause of it" and provide space for a really ample Federal City. They agreed to the persuasive President's proposal and ceded the entire stretch he wanted, with the understanding that they would get back every other lot after the city was surveyed and land was set aside for streets and public buildings.

This transaction gave the new nation a chance to create spacious headquarters at once, and also left room for future growth. The entire District, as surveyed, included the towns of Alexandria and Georgetown, two tiny settlements (Hamburg and Carrollsburg) that soon disappeared as separate entities, and a portion of unincorporated Maryland soil of which only a part went into the newly established city of Washington. In effect, the government was given about half the land in the capital city free. The government would pay the proprietors for any of their lots taken for its buildings (but not for streets) at the rate of "twenty-five pounds [about $67] per acre." But the owners' real reward was to come from the sale of their value-enhanced remaining lots to the public. The government would also sell its own unused land at public auction to pay for the cost of its structures.

No one was happier than L'Enfant with the large extent of the government-acquired area. Trained in engineering and architecture in Paris, he had been an enthusiastic volunteer in the American War for Independence and eventually had made his home in the United States. In 1789 he had written to the President to ask for the privilege of "acquiring reputation" by drawing the plans of "a Federal City which is to become the Capital of this vast Empire." With an enthusiasm that was a truer testament to his adopted Americanism than any citizenship papers, L'Enfant proposed that the plan be "on such a scale as to leave room for that aggrandizement and embellishment which the increase of the wealth of the nation will permit it to pursue to any period however remote." He had gotten that coveted privilege, and now, in 1791, with an expanse of 3,000 to 5,000 acres to plan for, he was presumably in a position to convert his optimistic visions into reality.

He did not reckon, however, with the prosaic and sometimes ungrateful side of the national character. He set busily to work designing those features of Washington that still form its visual core—the diagonal avenues and gridded streets; the squares designed for statuary and fountains; the Capitol on its hill and the "Presidential palace" about a mile away, connected by the tree-lined breadth of Pennsylvania Avenue; the broad Mall linking the landscaped grounds at the foot of Capitol Hill with those south of the President's home. But while he was meditating, the three commissioners of the District, appointed by Washington to oversee the actual construction, were planning the unromantic business of selling lots. They demanded finished plans from L'Enfant to show to buyers. He put them off, ignored their authority, and gave commands for expensive clearing and other jobs far beyond the resources available. He even ordered the demolition of a house belonging to Daniel Carroll of Duddington, an influential landowner and nephew of one of the commissioners, because it stood in the way of one of his avenues. Inside of a year he was reluctantly dismissed by Washington and spent the rest of his life convinced that the capital's rulers had neither rewarded his efforts fairly nor appreciated the superiority of beauty to bookkeeping.

His plans were completed by Andrew Ellicott, assisted by a talented and often overlooked free Negro named Benjamin Banneker. The work of actual construction dragged seriously, as did the sale of lots. By the summer of 1800, when the government officially moved in, almost nothing was in readiness. Only one wing of the Capitol was up; the single federal office building near the President's residence was not fully usable; and the "Presidential palace" itself was anything but palatial. It had neither fence nor landscaped yard. Some of the

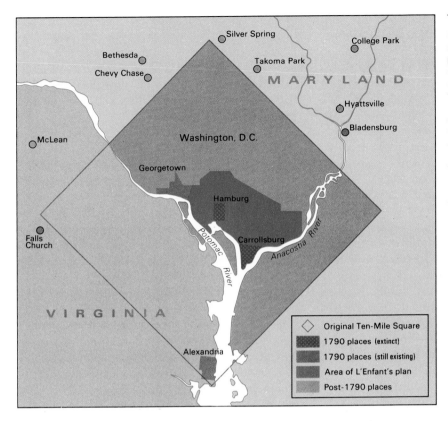

Map legend:
- ◇ Original Ten-Mile Square
- 1790 places (extinct)
- 1790 places (still existing)
- Area of L'Enfant's plan
- Post-1790 places

plaster in most of the rooms was still wet, carpenters' shacks huddled around its walls, and when Abigail Adams, wife of the second President, hung the family wash in the East Room, it probably added to the appearance of the place. Pennsylvania Avenue was a muddy gash cut through alder thickets. Many Congressmen turned up their noses and wondered how long it would take to write off a bad experiment in capital location and begin again. Oliver Wolcott, the Secretary of the Treasury, possibly noting the absence of any source of taxes, observed that "the people are poor, and as far as I can judge, they live like fishes, by eating each other," and a New Yorker with a wry sense of humor noted "we only need here houses, cellars, kitchens, scholarly men, amiable women, and a few other such trifles to possess a perfect city."

Nevertheless, a genuine community struggled into existence under the approving eye of two Virginia Presidents who followed John Adams into office, Thomas Jefferson and James Madison. Jefferson was nothing if not a scholarly man; the vivacious Dolley Madison, wife of his successor, was certainly an amiable woman; and nearby landowners soon put up some handsome houses, with cellars and kitchens, on the emerging streets. The lines of the Capitol and the Presidential residence (and of the first buildings to house the State, War, Treasury and Navy Departments and the Post Office), gradually completed, were as handsome as designers like William Thornton, Benjamin Latrobe, James Hoban and Charles Bulfinch could make them. They did give the city the beginnings of a rather imposing appearance, if an observer could ignore the desolate and untended spaces between them. In 1802 Washington proper was given a charter, providing for a mayor and a council chosen by property holders, as was deemed right and proper. The city developed a pleasant society of top federal officials and such local worthies as Samuel H. Smith, editor of the city's first newspaper, the *National Intelligencer*, and John Tayloe, planter and horse breeder, whose beautiful town residence, the Octagon House, survives to remind us of a young but gracious era. Visiting each others' homes to sip wine poured by liveried slaves, discussing European politics or the progress of the useful arts with the Secretaries of State and the Treasury, and ruminating on the city's attractive prospects of tapping the inland trade with western Maryland, Virginia and Pennsylvania (via the Potomac and its branches, plus a few needed canals), the members of this little elite saw no reason to feel apologetic about the rawness of their nation's capital. It would pass in time. The population of the District itself was a good index, having risen from almost nothing in 1790 to 16,000 whites, about 2,500 free Negroes and some 5,500 slaves in 1810.

While this sense of progress warmed and grew, the War of 1812 came and gave Washington the first, and most shattering, of its direct confrontations with armed conflict. In two hot August days of 1814 the British invaded and destroyed virtually the entire city. For the British, it was a minor operation. Their 4,500-man expedition, which landed on the shores of the Patuxent River, some 35 miles southeast of the capital, was a raiding party and not an occupying force. Government officials, doubtful of the power of the small and untrained militia to protect the city, began the evacuation of their records to various places in the surrounding country. General Robert Ross's Redcoats and Admiral Sir George Cockburn's marines scattered the American defenders on the afternoon of the 24th, entered the District, and that evening set fire to the Capitol, the President's residence and other buildings. (Later, during rebuilding, the scorched walls of the President's official home were painted in fresh white, leading to the legend that the White House then and there got its name.) A heavy rain prevented the complete destruction of the buildings. The next day, however, the British set fire to the offices of the Cabinet departments, the arsenal, the building housing the *Intelligencer* and some private homes. The Americans themselves burned the navy yard on the Anacostia to prevent the capture of ships and stores. A sudden windstorm of gale force caused further wreckage. When the British pulled out and moved on toward Baltimore, Washington was a ruin. The heroine and hero of the occasion were Dolley Madison, coolly directing the removal of the Gilbert Stuart portrait of George Washington from the White House, and Dr. William Thornton, Superintendent of Patents, who dissuaded a Redcoat officer from putting the torch to the structure that housed the Post Office and Patent Office. "Are you Englishmen or Goths and Vandals?" the learned doctor was said to have asked. He then lectured dramatically on the usefulness to all mankind of the models and drawings in his custody, and he convinced the British major that the proposed arson would earn the scorn of future centuries. Despite these heroics, the city was so badly wrecked that one woman resident remarked: "I do not suppose the Government will ever return to Washington."

Her estimate was needlessly glum. Congress, when it reassembled—crowded into the Post Office building, while other departments made the best arrangements they could in private homes—did consider the removal of the capital to a less vulnerable location. But it finally rejected what appeared to be the course of cowardice and voted substantial sums for rebuilding and enlarging the government's habitations.

Paradoxically, Washington's permanent hold on the capital's location was thus strengthened by the invasion. And although there were still occasional murmurs of a possible change, each year that the government remained in Washington moved it toward confirmation as the symbolic as well as the physical seat of government. When news of the Treaty of Ghent ending the War of 1812 reached the town in 1815, it celebrated freely and then entered on a 45-year period of uneven growth.

Washington now became the theater in which the growing young republic acted out its sometimes lively, sometimes tragic political productions. It was in the old Supreme Court chamber in the basement of the Capitol that John Marshall handed down decisions that upheld the majesty of the Union and that Roger B. Taney delivered the opinion in the Dred Scott case of 1857 that helped to tear the Union apart. Upstairs in the Senate chamber, Daniel Webster, in a day when great orators were as famous as movie heroes, thundered his devotion to liberty and union one and inseparable; John Calhoun unsuccessfully fought to save the political power of the declining South; genial Henry Clay engineered (or at least took credit for) compromises that averted the threat of civil war in 1820, 1833 and 1850. A parade of Presidents marched through the White House, the most spectacular easily being Andrew Jackson. At his inauguration reception in 1829 there was tumult when a throng of his supporters crowded into the mansion, trampled furniture and rugs under muddy boots, smashed china and glassware, and nearly smothered the aging hero of New Orleans in their devotion.

It was once historically fashionable to describe Jackson's triumph of frontier boisterousness as the onset of a social revolution in which former officeholders were mowed down wholesale to make room for loyal Jacksonians and Washington society lost its ordered grace to the shock wave of democratic manners. The facts are less spectacular but still significant. Although Jackson's lieutenants did pride themselves that "rotation in office" best kept the machinery of government geared to the popular will, only about 10 to 20 per cent of existing federal jobholders were replaced in the whole eight years of the Jacksonian Administration. One guess is that about 900 were retired or dismissed in all that time. Jefferson had done a comparably thorough housecleaning of political appointees in 1801—but after that there had been no such big changes for nearly 30 years, which made the Jacksonian "revolution" seem more raging.

On the other hand, the structure of capital society did undergo a subtle change. The new Jacksonian officeholders were more apt to think of themselves as birds of passage, due to be "rotated" out of the capital as a natural thing. "A new differentiation developed," says historian Constance Green, "between people who thought of the federal city as home and those ephemeral inhabitants to whom only her federal function seemed important." Then, too, the spirit of Jacksonianism was unquestionably leveling and had social consequences that turned unexpectedly and dramatically political. Jackson's Secretary of War, John Eaton, married the widowed daughter of a tavern and boardinghouse keeper, Peggy O'Neale Timberlake. Washington's Southern-trained society belles refused to admit her to their parlors or to call on her. ("God help the woman who must live in Washington," wrote Peggy many years later.) The ostracizing ladies happened to include the wives of the Vice President and several Cabinet members. Peggy was gallantly defended by Jackson and his widower Secretary of State, Martin Van Buren. The fracas developed other reverberations and did not end until there was a Cabinet shake-up in which several members resigned.

While these titillating events claimed public attention, Washington faced deeper problems. Its leading citizens engaged in a frustrating attempt to provide the city with a solid economic base. The expansion of the federal governmental establishment sharpened the question of dividing municipal costs fairly between the Union and the capital's local citizenry. Finally, the gathering storm over slavery had deep repercussions on Washington's own racial patterns.

The Washingtonians seeking economic security were as susceptible as their brother Americans to the allurements of promoters. In an age when young America's ambitions were being translated by Congress into national roads and banks and protective tariffs for home industries, it was natural for the city fathers of Washington and Georgetown to be visionaries, too. They invested heavily in the Chesapeake and Ohio Canal, begun in 1828, in high hopes that it would bring the coal and grain of the Ohio Valley, western Maryland, Virginia

Washington in 1800

President John Adams' wife, Abigail Adams, who is shown at left in a portrait by the American painter Mather Brown, was the first First Lady to reside in what was to be called the White House. When Mrs. Adams moved to Washington in 1800 she found the new city to be little more than a muddy, ugly village built on a great swamp. Her new home was far from finished—the grounds were cluttered with workmen's shacks and no single room was complete—and she had to keep 13 fires burning to warm the damp house. In a letter *(below)* to her daughter, Mrs. Adams described her first days in Washington.

My Dear Child,
I arrived here on Sunday last, and without meeting with any accident worth noticing, except losing ourselves when we left Baltimore, and going eight or nine miles on the Frederick road, by which means we were obliged to go the other eight through woods, where we wandered two hours without finding a guide, or the path. Fortunately, a straggling black came up with us, and we engaged him as a guide, to extricate us out of our difficulty; but woods are all you see, from Baltimore until you reach the city, which is only so in name. Here and there is a small cot [cottage], without a glass window, interspersed amongst the forests, through which you travel miles without seeing any human being. In the city there are buildings enough, if they were compact and finished, to accommodate Congress and those attached to it; but as they are, and scattered as they are, I see no great comfort for them. The river, which runs up to Alexandria, is in full view of my window, and I see the vessels as they pass and repass. The House is upon a grand and superb scale, requiring about thirty servants to attend and keep the apartments in proper order, and perform the ordinary business of the house and stables; an establishment very well proportioned to the President's salary. The lighting in the apartments, from the kitchen to parlors and chambers, is a tax indeed; and the fires we are obliged to keep to secure us from daily agues is another very cheering comfort. To assist us in this great castle, and render less attendance necessary, bells are wholly wanting, not one single one being hung through the whole house, and promises are all you can obtain. . . . Briesler [major-domo to the Adams family] entered into a contract with a man to supply him with wood. A small part, a few cords only, has he been able to get. Most of that was expended to dry the walls of the house before we came in, and yesterday the man told him it was impossible for him to procure it to be cut and carted. He has had recourse to coals; but we cannot get grates made and set. We have, indeed, come into a new country.
You must keep all this to yourself, and, when asked how I like it, say that I wrote you the situation is beautiful, which is true. The house is made habitable, but there is not a single apartment finished, and all withinside, except the plastering, has been done since Briesler came. We have not the least fence, yard or other convenience, without, and the great unfinished audience-room I make a drying-room of, to hang up the clothes in. . . . Up stairs there is the oval room, which is designed for the drawing-room, and has the crimson furniture in it. It is a very handsome room now; but, when completed, it will be beautiful. If the twelve years, in which this place has been considered as the future seat of government, had been improved, as they would have been if in New England, very many of the present inconveniences would have been removed. It is a beautiful spot, capable of every improvement, and, the more I view it, the more I am delighted with it.
Affectionately your mother,
A. Adams.

The burning of Washington

The invasion that brought about the burning of Washington, depicted in the painting at left by a British artist, began on August 19, 1814, when 4,500 British regulars, commanded by General Robert Ross, landed 35 miles southeast of Washington. The only defending troops were the District's ill-equipped militia quartered at Bladensburg, a battery of naval guns, and about a hundred troops guarding what was later to be called the White House. This resistance was quickly overrun, and on August 24 the British burned all the government buildings except the structure that housed the Post Office and the Patent Office. The British left the city the next night. A few days after Washington was put to the torch, Mrs. Margaret Bayard Smith, a lady prominent in Washington society, wrote to her sister describing the condition of her city. Excerpts from her letter are printed below.

In the afternoon we rode to the city. We pass'd several dead horses. The poor capitol! nothing but its blacken'd walls remained! 4 or 5 houses in the neighbourhood were likewise in ruins. Some men had got within these houses and fired on the English as they were quietly marching

and Pennsylvania down to Washington for profitable transfer to ocean-bound shipping. A vital link in the system was to be the already existing Washington Canal, cutting through the city along the north edge of the Mall and leading down to the deepwater wharves of the Anacostia. Later there were plans for a railroad bridge across the Potomac to link up eventually with railroads ribboning into the cotton South, and hopes that the swiftly flowing Potomac just above Georgetown could provide water power for flour and textile mills.

But somehow the visions never survived any longer than most dreams survive breakfast. The Baltimore and Ohio Railroad, begun on the same day (July 4, 1828) as the C & O Canal, brought the western trade not to Washington but to Baltimore, on Chesapeake Bay. The capital's only rail hookup with the North until after the Civil War was through that Maryland city. Though Washingtonians hoped to be a trade link between North and South, direct rail connections with Virginia were still not completed by as late as the beginning of the Civil War, and Dixieland's cotton went north by sea. The banking, managerial and labor resources for successful factory operation never coalesced. Even before a nationwide depression afflicted the economy in 1837, Washington was

nearly $1.75 million in debt. Congress finally had to bail it out (or face the prospect of foreign holders of canal bonds seizing large portions of capital real estate put up as collateral), an experience that did not increase Congress' confidence in the District's powers of self-government. By the 1850s there was no longer any real expectation of Washington's becoming a commercial center.

A consequence of these frustrated ambitions was a notable scrimping on city services. Whatever tax revenues could be generated fell heavily on real estate owned by a small group of permanent residents; federal property was tax-exempt. The permanent residents were the cream of the District's white population, which amounted to about 27,500 in 1830, approximately 30,000 in 1840 and some 38,000 ten years later. The permanent residents wanted taxes kept low, and since they dominated the municipal governments created under Congressional charters of 1820 and 1848, they usually succeeded. Congress itself insisted on rigid limitations on the city's borrowing power. Moreover, certain urban programs, such as street beautification, fell into a no man's land between Congress and the city council, each thinking it was the other's proper burden.

With civic revenues scant and responsibilities divided, Washington remained far behind most other cities in acquiring professional firemen and policemen, street lights or sewers. The largely unused Washington Canal became a dumping ground for refuse, and the capital stank in the summer heat. Dignitaries rode or walked between imposing government buildings through a gooey underfooting of mud and manure. Overgrown vacant blocks made a Portuguese minister's earlier description of Washington as "the city of magnificent distances" still applicable and anything but complimentary. "My God!" lamented a French diplomat. "What have I done, to be condemned to reside in such a city!" Congressmen at least had an option. Refusing to expose their families to the cholera, fevers and "fluxes" that the primitive water and sanitation systems made commonplace, the legislators lived in boardinghouses during the relatively short Congressional sessions, then fled home.

The businessmen of Alexandria were so pessimistic about the District's future that they repeatedly urged their representatives in Congress to have Virginia's portion ceded back to the Old Dominion, and it was done in 1846. Ironically, that was the very time at which Congress was beginning to accelerate a program of federal construction, as if eager to erect more symbols of a permanent Union the nearer the country drifted to the fragmentation of civil war. In the 1830s, to meet the needs of science, commerce and sea power, Congress had revived the Coast Survey and had created both a Depot of Charts and Instruments and a Naval Observatory. Such steps led the government further and further into the role of a patron of research and also added to Washington drawing rooms the presence of a body of distinguished scientists, a number in naval uniform. (Washington's intellectual life was more richly endowed by the government's hired brains than by the faculties of its two colleges, Georgetown and Columbian—later George Washington—a pattern still in force.) In 1847 the Smithsonian Institution began to go up on the Mall, followed soon thereafter by greenhouses for the botanical specimens brought back by the government's exploring expeditions in various parts of the world. In the 1850s, new wings were begun on the Capitol, as well as work on a new and more impressive dome. Congress also commissioned a soldiers' home, an insane asylum and several pieces of commemorative statuary, while private funds were being collected to complete the Washington Monument. And so Washington as a Federal City flourished, while Washington as a town continued to operate on a

Two views of Washington

The city of Washington in the first half of the 19th Century, described below by two English visitors, presented vistas of huge, raw open spaces broken by large government buildings. The reactions of the two observers to the city differed sharply, however. Viewing scenes like the one shown below, Mrs. Frances Trollope, mother of novelist Anthony Trollope, was moved to rare praise in her book *Domestic Manners of the Americans*, published in 1832. But novelist Charles Dickens, who visited the city in 1842, had only scorn for "the headquarters of tobacco-tinctured saliva" in his *American Notes*.

Trollope: "I was delighted . . ."

Our first object the next morning was to get a sight of the capitol. . . . The mists of morning still hung around this magnificent building when first it broke upon our view, and . . . we were struck with admiration and surprise . . . to see so imposing a structure on that side of the Atlantic. . . . It stands so finely too, high and alone. . . .

I was delighted with the whole aspect of Washington; light, cheerful, and airy, it reminded me of our fashionable watering places. It has been laughed at by foreigners, and even by natives, because the original plan of the city was upon an enormous scale, and but a very small part of it has been as yet executed. But I confess I see nothing in the least degree ridiculous about it; the original design, which was as beautiful as it was extensive, has been in no way departed from, and all that has been done has been done well. From the base of the hill on which the capitol stands extends a street of most magnificent width, planted on each side with trees, and ornamented by many splendid shops. This street, which is called Pennsylvania Avenue, is above a mile in length, and at the end of it is the handsome mansion of the President; conveniently near to his residence are the various public offices, all handsome, simple, and commodious; ample areas are left round each, where grass and shrubs refresh the eye.

THE CAPITOL AS SEEN FROM THE PRESIDENT'S HOUSE IN 1830.

Dickens: ". . . the City of Magnificent Intentions"

Here is Washington, fresh in my mind and under my eye. Take the worst parts of . . . the straggling outskirts of Paris. . . . Burn the whole down; build it up again in wood and plaster; widen it a little; throw in part of St. John's Wood; put green blinds outside all the private houses, with a red curtain and white one in every window; plough up all the roads; plant a great deal of coarse turf in every place where it ought not to be; erect three handsome buildings in stone and marble, anywhere, but the more entirely out of everybody's way the better; call one the Post Office, one the Patent Office, and one the Treasury . . . and that's Washington. . . .

It is sometimes called the City of Magnificent Distances, but it might with greater propriety be termed the City of Magnificent Intentions; for it is only on taking a bird's-eye view of it from the top of the Capitol, that one can at all comprehend the vast designs of its projector. . . . Spacious avenues, that begin in nothing, and lead nowhere; streets, mile-long, that only want houses, roads and inhabitants; public buildings that need but a public to be complete; and ornaments of great thoroughfares, which only lack great thoroughfares to ornament—are its leading features. . . . To the admirers of cities, it is a . . . pleasant field for the imagination to rove in; a monument raised to a deceased project, with not even a legible inscription to record its departed greatness.

niggardly scale. To cite only one example, the school "system" in the mid-1850s provided only 37 teachers and 24 rooms for more than 2,000 pupils.

In spite of such deficiencies, there was a genteel ease to life in Washington drawing rooms. The good manners and clubbiness of this Southern town enchanted many visitors who could avert their eyes and noses from the city's defects. The charm was not apparent, however, to Washington's Negro community. The slave population of the District rose from about 3,200 in 1800 to some 4,700 in 1840 before the Virginia portion was returned to the mother state. It was 3,185 in 1860. Although most of these slaves were house servants, and accordingly were considered more fortunate than hard-working field hands, the existence of slavery at the nerve center of freedom's homeland still incensed many Americans. Antislavery sentiment was openly expressed and violently contradicted in the capital city, and while slavery's opponents had never had much chance of wiping out the peculiar institution in the District, the trade in slaves at least was banned in 1850.

The real victims of the situation, however, were the free Negroes of Washington. There were about 8,500 in the District in 1840, or nearly one in five of the population, and about 11,000 twenty years later, forming a slightly smaller proportion of the total. Most were freed slaves or their descendants, and while a good many were servants, barbers and peddlers, some, like the restaurant and hotel proprietor James Wormley, had accumulated considerable amounts of property. The men who controlled capital life, however, were Southerners and Southern sympathizers. They lived in the common fear of slave revolt, and the rising tide of abolitionism turned fear into near panic. Seeing in every free colored man a potential rebel leader, the city fathers burdened black residents with grossly humiliating restrictions. Negroes were required to post bonds for their good behavior, to be off the streets by 10 p.m. and to secure official permission for any public gathering. They had to swallow mistreatment by police and white roughnecks without much hope of redress in courts and were in perennial danger of being picked up as fugitive slaves and sold south, with the burden of proof to the contrary on them. They could not vote. Nevertheless, they managed to support several private schools (the city providing none for black children) as well as a number of churches.

In April of 1861 the country finally gathered in the first installment of the harvest that had been ripening since "twenty Negars" were landed in

Virginia in 1619. The coming of the Civil War was the major earth shock in Washington's history. It opened an 18-year period that spelled fantastic growth, social upheaval, reshuffles in government and finally the end of home rule for the city.

When Lincoln took the oath of office, Washington was a town of some 75,000 residents, whose folkways were conditioned by the fact that half of them were either born in, or only recently removed from, the languid tobacco-and-cotton culture of the South. Four years of fighting completely altered this picture. Torrents of armed men poured into the city—first the healthy and exuberant youngsters from the North who drilled and marched in preparation for battle against the Confederacy, and then the pale and feverish wagonloads of sick and wounded who came back to fill the many hospitals that sprang up in the city. As a gigantic base camp, Washington was full of military activity. Uniformed Army clerks crowded into commandeered private homes; teamsters in blue cursed wagon-pulling mules through the crowded streets; thousands of horses whinnied and stamped in open spaces taken over for corrals. The Washington Monument grounds were used for cattle pens and for slaughtering beef. (The disposal of the animals' offal raised the pollution in the city canal to unbelievable levels.) Saloons and whorehouses did a booming business, the jails overflowed, and the small city police force was strained to the limit to cope with brawls, thefts and other offenses.

In July of 1864 Washington actually was under attack by the troops of Confederate General Jubal A. Early. Lincoln himself went out to Fort Stevens, some four miles north of the White House, to see the action. There is a story that he climbed on a parapet for a better look while sharpshooters' bullets were flying and was ordered away with a sharp "Get down, you fool!" by Lieutenant Colonel Oliver Wendell Holmes Jr.

Along with the troops came civilian workers who needed housing, and contractors and officials whose demands for hotel and restaurant facilities added to a flush of building activity. The sounds of saw and hammer rang around the clock, as the population climbed to 140,000 while wages and prices played frenzied leapfrog. And most significantly, among the newcomers were literally thousands of black fugitives, voting their way out of slavery with their feet as the Federal armies rolled southward. The influx of refugees and the emancipation of the District's slaves in 1862 gave Washington a population that was predominantly composed of poor, free Negroes. They found jobs at the bottom of the wartime economy, and living space in shacks without water, ventilation, light or sewerage. Most of these structures were built in the interior open spaces of many blocks of Washington houses. These alley dwellings, almost invisible from the street, were the core of the capital's slums for decades afterward.

But if living conditions for most Negroes were dreadful, their status as citizens did improve on the whole. From 1862 until the mid-1870s, a Congress dominated by Radical Republicans enacted model codes for the District that embodied the idealism—and the partial unreality—of Reconstruction as a whole. Negroes were enfranchised in 1866 and did in fact elect a number of black men to the popularly chosen city council that governed Washington until 1871. Free (though segregated) schools were provided, and stiff laws forbade discrimination on racial grounds in hotels, restaurants, theaters and streetcars. The old Negro elite of the city found its status improved by the ending of the prewar "Black Codes," restricting the rights and movements of Negroes, and a reporter noted many of the city's colored businessmen attending churches "in plug hats and kid gloves," with the women "wearing dresses that would not disgrace a White House reception." There was a growing middle class composed of those Negroes employed by the government and in the ministry, the professions or the faculty of Howard University, established in 1867. Welcome as these laws and changes were, they did not hit at the basic problem of Negro poverty, lack of skills and general exclusion from opportunities to advance. For every Negro near the apex of the social pyramid, like Senator Blanche K. Bruce, from reconstructed Mississippi, or District Recorder of Deeds Frederick Douglass, there were scores in rags and dirt. Eventually the momentum of the drive for civil equality was lost, as it was in the country at large. In Washington the issue was complicated by its entanglement with the establishment of a territorial government, which was short-lived but rich in impact.

Congress could no longer tolerate the primitive condition of the nation's headquarters in 1871. At Grant's inauguration, coachmen charged up to $40 a day for their services, knowing that no woman would drag her best gown in the filth of Pennsylvania Avenue. Shortly afterward Washington was rejected as the site of the upcoming Centennial Exposition because of a widely shared opinion, expressed by wealthy Senator William Stewart of Nevada, that the capital was the ugliest city in the country. Unwilling to leave the job of urban main-

The poet and the President

In 1862, seven years after the publication of his first volume of poetry, *Leaves of Grass*, the American poet Walt Whitman *(above)* went to Washington in search of his brother George, who had been wounded on a battlefield in Virginia. Finally finding George on the road to recovery near Fredericksburg, Whitman returned to Washington, visiting the wounded in hospitals, working as a clerk in government offices and writing. He probably never met Abraham Lincoln, but he was often moved by the sight of the President riding through the streets. Some of Whitman's impressions of Lincoln, taken from his *Specimen Days*, are printed here.

August 12th [1863]—I see the President almost every day, as I happen to live where he passes to or from his lodgings out of town. He never sleeps at the White House during the hot season, but has quarters at a healthy location some three miles north of the city, the Soldiers' home, a United States military establishment. I saw him this morning about 8½ coming in to business, riding on Vermont Avenue, near L Street. He always has a company of twenty-five or thirty cavalry, with sabres drawn and held upright over their shoulders. They say this guard was against his personal wish, but he let his counselors have their way. The party makes no great show in uniform or horses. Mr. Lincoln on the saddle generally rides a good-sized, easy-going gray horse, is dressed in plain black, somewhat rusty and dusty, wears a black stiff hat, and looks about as ordinary in attire, &c., as the commonest man. A lieutenant, with yellow straps, rides at his left, and following behind, two by two, come the cavalry men, in their yellow-striped jackets. They are generally going at a slow trot, as that is the pace set them by the one they wait upon. The sabres and accoutrements clank, and the entirely unornamental cortège as it trots toward Lafayette square arouses no sensation, only some curious stranger stops and gazes. I see very plainly Abraham Lincoln's dark brown face, with the deep-cut lines, the eyes, always to me with a deep latent sadness in the expression. We have got so that we exchange bows, and very cordial ones. Sometimes the President goes and comes in an open barouche. The cavalry always accompany him, with drawn sabres. Often I notice as he goes out evenings—and sometimes in the morning, when he returns early—he turns off and halts at the large and handsome residence of the Secretary of War, on K street, and holds conference there. If in his barouche, I can see from my window he does not alight, but sits in his vehicle, and Mr. Stanton comes out to attend him. Sometimes one of his sons, a boy of ten or twelve, accompanies him, riding at his right on a pony. Earlier in the summer I

tenance to local management any longer, but also unwilling to take full control, Congress merged Georgetown, Washington and the remainder of the District into a Territory. It was to be ruled by a Presidentially appointed governor and an 11-man council and a popularly elected House of Delegates of 22 members. A board of public works, also named by the White House, was to take charge of improving Washington. It was to assess part of the costs among property owners adjacent to its projects, and it was also to have the right to borrow. There were limits on loans and taxes, however, removable only by a popular referendum.

One of the members of this board was a 37-year-old contractor named Alexander R. Shepherd, one of those forceful businessmen-gamblers of the Gilded Age whom President Grant so much admired. Shepherd became a one-man revolution. Dominating the other commissioners by force of will, he set out to make Washington a modern city by a vast program of street paving and grading, tree planting and sewer construction, begun simultaneously at many points. Within six months he had the city nearly $10 million in debt; it rose to $20 million before he was through. But armies of grateful employed laborers were happy to give him the votes he needed at referendum time to raise the debt lim-

it. Householders left for work in the morning and returned to find excavations full of sewer pipe where their front yards had been, with a bill of charges soon to appear. Proprietors of condemned structures rushed off to court to get injunctions and came panting back as workmen cleaned up after the demolition job. One railroad refused to eliminate a grade crossing and parked a locomotive squarely across the disputed intersection. Shepherd's crews appeared with lanterns at 1 a.m. on a Sunday, ripped up the tracks on either side and left the iron horse stranded until its owners backed down. "Boss" Shepherd, operating from his gilt and carpeted office in the new headquarters of the Board of Public Works, was as flamboyantly dictatorial as his New York contemporary, William Tweed—except that no graft stuck to Shepherd's fingers. Repeated investigations found him clean. When he was through, the city was groaning under a huge debt burden, but it was no longer a frontier village.

Shepherd's career was checked—though many of his projects were later finished by other hands—by the Depression of 1873. Even though elevated to governor of the Territory by Grant, he could not borrow fresh money. In 1874 Congress stepped in, finally ready to accept the fact that it could not let

42

occasionally saw the President and his wife, toward the latter part of the afternoon, out in a barouche, on a pleasure ride through the city. Mrs. Lincoln was dress'd in complete black, with a long crape veil. The equipage is of the plainest kind, only two horses, and they nothing extra. They pass'd me once very close, and I saw the President in the face fully, as they were moving slowly, and his look, though abstracted, happen'd to be directed steadily in my eye.

March 4 [1865]—The President very quietly rode down to the capitol in his own carriage, by himself, on a sharp trot, about noon, either because he wish'd to be on hand to sign bills, or to get rid of marching in line with the absurd procession, the muslin temple of liberty, and pasteboard monitor. I saw him on his return, at three o'clock, after the performance was over. He was in his plain two-horse barouche, and look'd very much worn and tired; the lines, indeed of vast responsibilities, intricate questions, and demands of life and death, cut deeper than ever upon his dark brown face; yet all the old goodness, tenderness, sadness, and

canny shrewdness, underneath the furrows. (I never see that man without feeling that he is one to become personally attach'd to, for his combination of purest, heartiest tenderness, and native western form of manliness.) By his side sat his little boy, of ten years. There were no soldiers, only a lot of civilians on horseback, with huge yellow scarfs over their shoulders, riding around the carriage. (At the inauguration four years ago, he rode down and back again surrounded by a dense mass of arm'd cavalrymen eight deep, with drawn sabres; and there were sharp-shooters station'd at every corner on the route.) I ought to make mention of the closing levee [the public reception in honor of the inauguration] of Saturday night last. Never before was such a compact jam in front of the White House—all the grounds fill'd and away out to the spacious sidewalks. I was there, as I took a notion to go—was in the rush inside with the crowd—surged along the passage-ways, the blue and other rooms, and through the great east room. Crowds of country people, some very funny. Fine music from the Marine band, off in a side place. I saw Mr. Lincoln, drest all in black, with white kid

gloves and a claw-hammer coat, receiving, as in duty bound, shaking hands, looking very disconsolate, and as if he would give anything to be somewhere else.

The "dark brown face, with the deep-cut lines," and the "deep latent sadness in the expression" that Whitman described in his *Specimen Days* can be seen in this photograph of Abraham Lincoln taken in Washington in 1863 by Alexander Gardner, not long before the President delivered his famous Gettysburg Address.

Washington be either backward or bankrupt. In a reorganization completed in 1878, it gave the District the government it would have until 1967. Three Presidentially named commissioners—one always to be a member of the Army Engineer Corps, to oversee physical development—were to divide most of the functions of District rule among them. The health department, the board of education and other administrative bodies were likewise appointed. Washingtonians would vote neither for their own rulers nor the country's. The pill was sweetened by a Congressional commitment to pick up half the annual operating budget, a promise more or less honored until the end of the 19th Century. Local ratepayers, remembering Shepherd, were not overly disgruntled. It was the less affluent Washingtonians, especially those who were black, who had little to compensate them for becoming colonials.

Washington entered now on a 40-year period long recalled by oldtimers as a kind of golden age. The city grew out toward its limits, with elaborate mansions on major avenues, like Connecticut and Massachusetts, housing embassies, local men of means and tycoons who chose to maintain a residence in the capital. In between, more modest dwellings sheltered armies of government clerks;

they could now plan to settle down permanently in Washington as a result of the expansion of civil service regulations after 1880. It was a real-estate man's town. During the Administration of Benjamin Harrison (1889-1893), an observer predicted that Washington, "with its low taxation, will be the Mecca of the capitalist for years to come," and so far as capitalism was confined to dealing in lots and houses, it was true. The government itself steadily expanded into new quarters that were built with an opulence far removed from the chaste neoclassicism of the original designs for the White House or the Capitol; among the most flamboyant structures were the State, War and Navy Building, completed in 1888, and the Library of Congress building of 1897.

Fortunately the mood did not bury Washington under baroque piles of masonry. Part of the thrust of beautification was the setting aside of land for Rock Creek Park in the 1890s. In 1901 a special Senate Park Commission (known as the McMillan Commission) of outstanding architects and artists was formed. In their report they provided an overall plan for the orderly and tasteful future expansion of the city's park system and the government's building program. Their basic ideas, supervised by the later-created Commission of Fine Arts and

A statue of Alexander Shepherd stands by Pennsylvania Avenue in Washington, a community he helped transform from a squalid eyesore into a relatively modern city. A political leader in the 1870s, "Boss" Shepherd spent millions for paved, well-lit streets, improved sewer and water systems, and tree-filled parks.

the National Park and Planning Commission, were keyed to the resurrection of L'Enfant's century-old design. These ideas dominated public construction in the capital until the 1930s and produced neoclassic forms in Union Station, the early Congressional office buildings and the huge departmental structures of the Federal Triangle. Whatever posterity might think of the designs, they expressed a national commitment to the idea of a show place Federal City conceived in majesty. A century after the 130-odd federal government employees had moved into the three unfinished buildings in a semiwild Washington, Congress was willing to make the arrangement permanent.

In the four decades before World War I, life in Washington was enriched by the quality of the men who headed the growing panoply of government bureaus, particularly in the social and natural sciences. Henry Adams, Boston-bred, quintessential Harvard intellectual and descendant of two Presidents, felt great distaste for the ruder aspects of triumphant democracy. Yet he preferred the society of Washington to that of any other city. He might well have; in few other places was it possible to meet a collection of intellects that included astronomers like Simon Newcomb, statisticians like Francis A. Walker and Carroll Wright, geol-

ogists like Clarence King and John Wesley Powell, public health experts like John S. Billings and Walter Reed, and many others who worked for the Census Bureau, the Geologic Survey, the Naval Observatory, the Smithsonian, the Library of Congress. The new agencies that appeared as the Theodore Roosevelt, Taft and Wilson Administrations extended the sphere of national concern for public welfare—the Forestry Service, the Food and Drug Administration, the Public Health Service, the Federal Trade Commission—brought in still more brainy men.

The scholars in public service who staffed these bureaus were usually not wealthy but were able to achieve a professorial style of living that centered around stimulating lunches in clubs, dinner parties in large but not ostentatious homes, and rides and picnics in Rock Creek Park. Some called Washington a "city of conversation," and it was. Much of the conversation was gossip, but, as one commentator remarked, the gossip of Washington was the business of the world. And even Presidents and Secretaries of State were still socially available. The magnitude of the government's operations grew steadily—even District budgets had grown to $10.5 million by 1910—but the chief manipulators were not yet walled behind guards and secretaries. Despite McKinley's assassination, Theodore Roosevelt still came out occasionally to shake hands with White House tourists.

For black Washington, however, the years of high-button shoes were not golden. The Negro employees in federal service—there were some 2,400 in 1891—were often kept in the more menial jobs despite demonstrated ability that should have earned them promotions. What was more, an ugly tide of Jim Crowism rolled up from the South. Supreme Court decisions had rendered the old Reconstruction equal-accommodation ordinances invalid, and more and more restaurants, theaters, hotels and shops in Washington excluded black citizens. Segregation even officially invaded the offices of the government itself in the Administration of Virginia-born Woodrow Wilson, who approved separate washroom facilities for Negro workers despite the protests of the recently organized National Association for the Advancement of Colored People. "Segregation is not humiliating but a benefit," the President said, "and ought to be so regarded by you gentlemen." As for the Negro underclass, it furnished most of the destitute, most of the charity patients and the highest proportion of infant funerals in the capital. Still living in huge numbers in the appalling alley dwellings within a

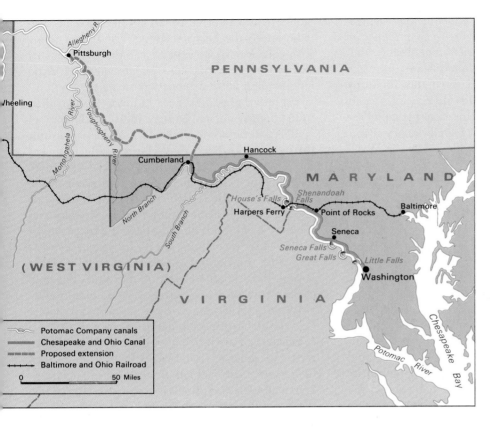

A link with the West

An old dream of making Washington the eastern outlet for western trade spurred two canal-building projects along the Potomac River during the late-18th and early-19th Centuries. The Potomac Company, which George Washington helped to organize in 1785, tried to open the Potomac River to traffic by building five bypass canals around dangerous falls and rapids. But the river's treacherous currents and frequent dry periods and floods defeated the undertaking. A more ambitious project, the Chesapeake and Ohio Canal, was begun in 1828. Intended to become a 360-mile route to Pittsburgh, the canal reached the halfway point at Cumberland, Maryland, in 1850, but was never completed. Trains of the Baltimore and Ohio Railroad, which reached Cumberland in 1842 and the Ohio River at Wheeling, West Virginia, in 1852, proved too much competition for the C & O's slow-moving barges. Used mostly to carry coal, the C & O Canal fell into disrepair and was finally abandoned in 1924. Purchased by the federal government in 1938, it is now maintained as a National Monument. About 22 miles of the canal between Georgetown and Seneca, Maryland, have been fully restored. No water is fed into the remaining 160-mile stretch although the towpath of this section is popular with hikers.

few minutes' walk of the Capitol (a favorite photographers' shot showed them with the dome looming in the background) were thousands of the Negroes who in 1910 made up nearly 30 per cent of the District population. Untouched by the centennial plans (which were concerned not with urban services but only with architectural symmetry), by the pulses of federal growth or by the expectations of the Progressive Era, Washington's Negroes might have been forgiven wry smiles on the April evening of 1917 when Woodrow Wilson stood before Congress and asked for a declaration of war to make the world safe for democracy.

That war spelled the end of Henry Adams' clubby Washington as surely as the firing on Sumter forever buried the sleepy little Southern town that he had visited as a recent college graduate in late 1860. It was not that the social texture binding old Washington families or long-resident civil servants was torn apart. It was, rather, that 1917 marked the first of successive thrusts of expansion that made the Washingtonian elite a progressively smaller element in the picture of capital life and that confronted it with urban problems that could not be ignored behind the drawn blinds of elegant parlor windows. Each new expansion of governmental power inexorably dictated an enlarged capital and

made the city a prey to creeping metropolitanism.

World War I saw the quartering of many government workers in once tranquil homes that were commandeered for the duration and the clustering of bureau headquarters in the raw "temporary" structures that proliferated like fungi on such spots as the Mall between the Capitol and the Washington Monument. The population grew from about 350,000 to an estimated 526,000 in a year. Dollar-a-year executives working for the War Industries Board or the War Shipping Board jostled into elevators with their secretaries freshly arrived from the countryside, all mutually flushed with patriotism and all repressing the irritation of crowding and shortages.

The irritation burst out after the armistice in somber forms, among them a five-day race riot in 1919 that killed an undetermined number of people and took 800 troops to put down. It was less than a year since the streets had been full of hearses carrying away 3,500 known victims of the 1918 influenza epidemic, which raged with most effect in crowded cities, exacting a special price for urban living. Washington was once more, as in the 1860s, drinking a full cup of sadness. Like the nation, the city had left a certain innocence behind it.

The darkest drops in that cup were drained 13

years later, however, in the depth of the Depression. For it was in 1932, in the very presence of American democracy's historical monuments, that men in the uniform of the United States marched against other men who had worn that uniform, some of them on the battlefields of France, 14 years earlier. Into the capital city that summer came the ragged ranks of the Bonus Expeditionary Force (B.E.F.), a collection of unemployed World War I veterans determined to stage what was an early kind of "sit-in" in the capital. They intended to stay until an economy-minded Congress voted to make immediate payment of a bonus scheduled to be paid in 1945. For weeks they squatted in shantyvilles built on mud flats along the Anacostia riverbank and (with official permission) in condemned government buildings along Pennsylvania Avenue. They were kept alive by donations of food and fuel arranged for by the District's understanding chief of police, a retired general named Pelham Glassford. But on July 28, after the Senate had adjourned without taking action on the bonus and the Hoover Administration had been panicked by persistent rumors of Communist penetration of the B.E.F., helmeted troops under the command of General Douglas MacArthur tear-gassed the veterans out of their makeshift camps and, wherever possible, burned their shanties down. (Though the B.E.F. lost the battle, it won the war, belatedly: in 1936 Congress authorized the payment of the bonus in nine-year bonds, convertible into cash.)

Then, in March of 1933, Franklin Roosevelt's New Deal roared into Washington, in a frame of mind that one of the new bureaucrats recalled as "filled with a vast enthusiasm, although we didn't know exactly for what. And we didn't know what we were going to do." What they did among other things was to give Washington both a building boom and a population boom. New buildings were put up for the host of new agencies and for the expansion of existing departments. Nearly 1,800 new apartment houses were built by private industry and some 2,300 row and separate houses went up. The tidal waves of official visitors washed as many as 40,000 people into Union Station daily in peak periods; they pumped as much as half a million dollars weekly into local cash registers. But the obverse of the coin was a capital suffering increasingly from congestion and desperately needing educational, medical and welfare services that Congress refused to provide. Though thousands of families still lacked electricity, plumbing and inside water taps in slum areas, one Congressman from Mississippi candidly explained to a public welfare

official why Congress would not increase its contribution to the District budget. "If I went along with your ideas," he said, ". . . I'd never keep my seat in Congress. My constituents wouldn't stand for spending all that money on niggers."

Explosive pressures were building in Washington's ghettos, but on Sunday morning, December 7, 1941, all domestic problems became irrelevant; the Japanese bombed Pearl Harbor and catapulted the United States into World War II. Once more Washington was plunged into a wartime expansion that tested facilities until they cracked, groaned and buckled. Swarms of government workers and soldiers, black and white, schemed like conspirators for apartments, queued up for seats on streetcars and trains, and created horrendous traffic jams at the bridges and circles. The great flat bulk of the Pentagon rising across the Potomac in Virginia was representative of the government's overflow of the District boundaries themselves.

When the war ended, in 1945, no one could foresee the decades of Cold War with the Communist bloc, the armed conflicts in such far-off places as Korea and Vietnam, or the vast federal programs that would dwarf anything dreamed of during the New Deal. But if the scale of government activities could not be guessed at, there was at least general recognition that a massive federal government was an enduring fact of life in the United States. The nation's new global responsibilities alone made that inevitable. Since the growth trend for metropolitan Washington was apparently irreversible—by 1960 the population edged toward the two-million mark—the city's attempts to cope with its old problems would be greatly complicated and aggravated by increasing numbers of people. Like city dwellers all over the nation, Washingtonians launched drives for school improvements, civil rights and urban renewal, plus one unique to the District—home rule.

Meanwhile, the Federal City and the white community, flowing out toward available land and dispersed locations in Maryland and Virginia, and the black community, largely confined to the old boundaries, were generating new tensions in their contacts. Would downtown Washington become an isolated camp surrounded by freeways, its older government buildings standing amid decay like jewels in mud, as they had once stood amid another kind of rawness? Or would the spirit embodied in what 19th Century rhetoric would unabashedly have called the "temples of democracy" reach out to uplift all of Washington? That was the question in the last decades of the 20th Century.

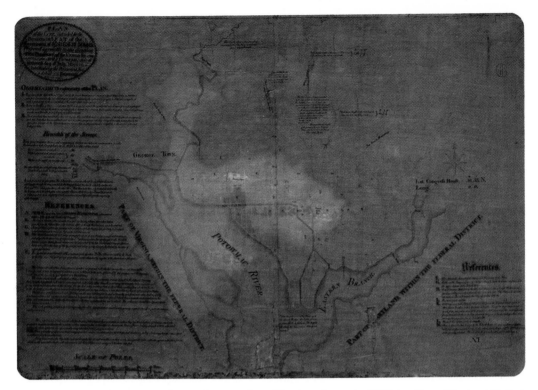

The origins of Washington, D.C., can be traced to this plan, drawn in 1791 by Pierre Charles L'Enfant.

Creating the National Center

PART 1: DREAMS REALIZED AND LOST

The original plan for Washington, D.C. was conceived by Major Pierre Charles L'Enfant, an ingenious and temperamental French artist-designer-architect who had served as a volunteer in the American Revolutionary Army. Appointed by President Washington in 1791, L'Enfant envisioned the major features that characterize the heart of the city today: the Capitol and White House as the two main focal points linked by historic Pennsylvania Avenue, the classical architecture, the stately Mall, numerous parks, and the graceful yet efficient system of streets and wide, radial avenues.

Unfortunately, the volatile Frenchman was not permitted to oversee the building of the city, which became the seat of government in 1800. Only a year after his appointment he became embroiled in controversy and was fired, and it remained for others to execute his grand design. During the 19th Century some of his successors departed from the original classical concept, but in the present century an effort has been made to eliminate errors of the past and return to the vision of the man who foresaw the nation's greatness.

The modest origins
of a city of destiny

Pierre Charles L'Enfant

Andrew Ellicott

The site for the capital, settled upon by George Washington, through an act of Congress, was a beautiful, if swampy, area along the shores of the Potomac River. Consisting of about 100 square miles, the region previously had been occupied by Indians, who called it Conocheaque—"Roaring Waters." The boundaries of the city proper within this area were the Potomac and Anacostia Rivers, which formed a Y to the south, east and west, and the present Florida Avenue at the foot of the high ground to the north.

Shortly after actual construction of the capital began in 1792, L'Enfant was dismissed as the result of a squabble with land speculators and the federal commissioners in charge of the project. He was replaced by Andrew Ellicott, a surveyor and engineer, who made only minor alterations in the original plan. As the classical marble buildings rose on the marshy land, and broad avenues and streets were hewn among the forests, the new capital was subjected to a barrage of ridicule and satire. The elegant Capitol was mocked as "the palace in the wilderness," and Pennsylvania Avenue was derided as "the great Serbonian Bog."

As the link connecting the Capitol and the "President's palace," as the White House was then called, Pennsylvania Avenue inevitably became Washington's most important thoroughfare. From a 35-foot-wide roadway, it soon grew to 160 feet in width and a mile in length, lined with Lombardy poplars. In 1805 it became the nation's No. 1 ceremonial boulevard. At that time Thomas Jefferson followed the route for his second inaugural, riding horseback, followed on foot by Congressmen, distinguished citizens, militiamen and musicians. Just south of the diagonal avenue, on a direct east-west axis, was an undeveloped tract that L'Enfant had intended for a mall.

The layout of the city called for square and rectangular grids of streets, broad, radial avenues branching out from parklike hubs *(photo, right)*, and many cheerful little plazas. From the beginning Washington has been divided into four sections (Northwest, Northeast, Southwest and Southeast) by prominent thoroughfares fanning out from the Capitol to the four cardinal points of the compass: North Capitol Street, South Capitol Street, East Capitol Street and the Mall on the west. North-south streets were given numbers, beginning with 1st Street, and east-west arteries were designated by the letters of the alphabet; the diagonal avenues were named after the 13 original states.

In laying out his plan for Washington, L'Enfant had followed the twin guidelines of esthetics and practicality. But some of his successors lacked his vision, and the appearance of the city would soon deteriorate seriously.

48

Grant Circle, a later addition to Washington, followed L'Enfant's ideas.

The L'Enfant-Ellicott plan for Washington *(right, top)* was executed by Ellicott in 1792 and bore only his name. The map at bottom right was made in 1886 and provided for the extension of the city north of Boundary Street (now Florida Avenue). The streets and avenues colored yellow existed at that time, the ones colored tan were proposed, and the sections in brown were to be abandoned.

A mid-century clutter on the Mall

One of L'Enfant's most grandiose concepts was for the development of the Mall. This "Grand Avenue" was to be part of a vast park system, sweeping from the Capitol to the Potomac River, merging with the grounds south of the President's house. At the point where the north-south axis of the President's house crossed the east-west axis of the Capitol, he prescribed a statue of General Washington. But as the city grew, the Mall was neglected and often cruelly violated.

Both nature and man contributed to the Mall's misfortune. One problem was Tiber Creek, which overflowed onto the Mall at high tide. Part of the creek was converted into a canal to control the flooding but it was not entirely successful. Therefore when the time came in the

Two of the eyesores that disfigured the Mall during the 19th Century are shown above. In a sketch of the Capitol *(top)* made in 1858, a polluted canal appears in the foreground. Immediately above is the fortresslike Pennsylvania Railroad Station built on the Mall in 1872.

By 1900 the Mall had reached the deplorable state shown at the right. The railroad tracks can be seen cutting across near the middle of the picture. At the lower right is the massive Smithsonian Institution.

1840s to select a site for the Washington Monument (the proposal to erect a statue had been abandoned earlier), the decision was made to erect it, not at the place L'Enfant had designated, but on a nearby hill safely removed from flooding, thus impairing the relationship of the monument to the White House and the Capitol. In 1847 the Smithsonian Institution was built on the Mall spoiling the broad, unobstructed sweep that L'Enfant had envisioned.

In 1850 an effort was made to beautify the tract. President Millard Fillmore appointed a noted landscape architect, Andrew Jackson Downing, to redesign both the Mall and the White House grounds. Downing, a romantic naturalist, departed completely from L'Enfant's formal design. In the best Victorian tradition he submitted a plan for winding footpaths and carriageways on the Mall and a large open area for military reviews south of the White House. At the end of Pennsylvania Avenue he proposed a triumphal marble arch leading to the White House grounds. The work was started in the early 1850s, and soon thereafter Downing died. The project bogged down and then came to a halt as the nation plunged toward Civil War. By 1872 Downing's plan had been all but forgotten and the Baltimore and Potomac Railroad, later the Pennsylvania, was permitted to build a passenger station on the Mall and lay tracks across it at 6th Street— an esthetic indignity that was to remain until the turn of the century.

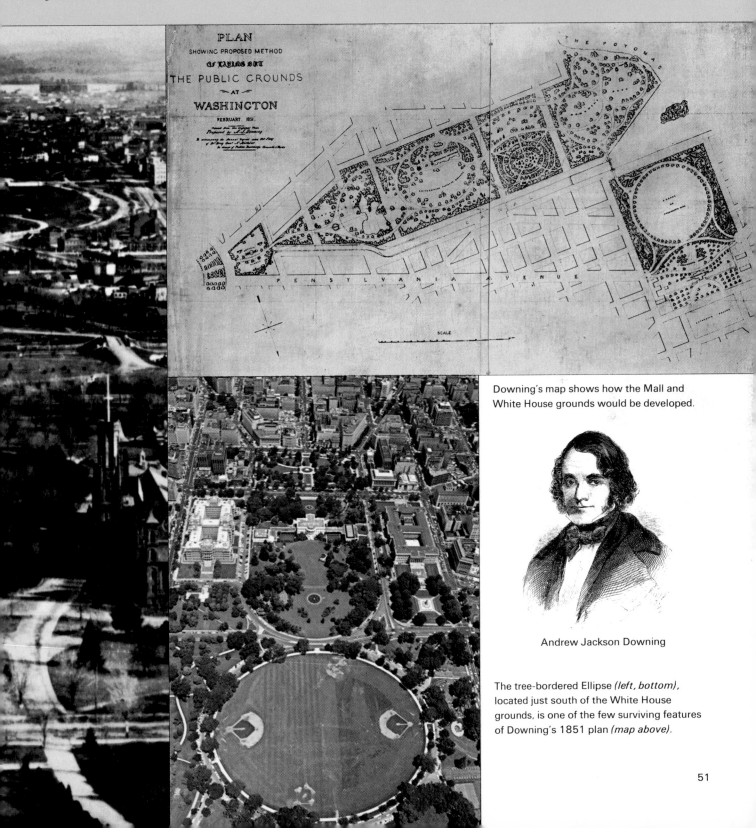

Downing's map shows how the Mall and White House grounds would be developed.

Andrew Jackson Downing

The tree-bordered Ellipse *(left, bottom)*, located just south of the White House grounds, is one of the few surviving features of Downing's 1851 plan *(map above)*.

51

Reviving L'Enfant's original scheme

Senator James McMillan

Daniel Burnham, architect

Charles F. McKim, architect

Fred'k Law Olmsted, landscape architect

Augustus Saint-Gaudens, sculptor

The commission's plan for Union Station included a great plaza *(above)* ringed by classical colonnades and providing an excellent view of the Capitol *(background)*.

In addition to realigning the Mall's axis with that of the White House grounds *(bottom of map)* and extending the Mall to the Potomac, the commission's plan called for parks on the filled-in marshlands along the bank of the river *(upper right)*. The new parks were intended to improve the symmetry of the Mall's borders.

The reaction of some Congressmen to the report is shown in the newspaper at right

By the late 1890s there was dismay among a number of prominent citizens over the increasingly shoddy appearance of the capital. One of the most influential critics was Senator James McMillan of Michigan. A man of tenacity and considerable persuasive powers, he was able to convince Congress in 1900 of the need to set up a commission to recommend steps to restore the District's beauty.

Two architects, a sculptor and a landscape architect, all distinguished in their fields, were appointed to the commission along with McMillan (left). The McMillan Commission began its work by visiting the great European capitals that had inspired L'Enfant. In 1902 the commission submitted its report, which was to eliminate many errors of the past and guide Washington's growth for decades. The primary recommendation was to return to L'Enfant's basic concepts. "The original plan of the City of Washington," the report stated, "having stood the test of a century, has met universal approval. The

departures from that plan are to be regretted and wherever possible remedied."

The commission scrapped virtually all remaining visages of Downing's 1851 plan. Among other innovations, the commission called for the removal of the railroad station and tracks from the Mall and the building of a Union Station at Massachusetts and Delaware Avenues. In front of the station would be an enormous plaza (immediately below), partially encircled by colonnades of classical design and enjoying an unobstructed view of the Capitol. The Mall's axis (left, bottom) was to be shifted so that it formed a right angle with the axis from the White House. The Mall was to be extended to the Potomac River, near which the Lincoln Memorial would be built.

Some Congressmen, appalled by the cost of executing the plan, denounced it (right, bottom), but fortunately there were enough supporters in and out of Congress to bring about its adoption.

THE EVENING STAR, TUESDAY, JANUARY 14, 1908.

SHOWY SHAM, THE CONCOCTION OF A SHAM COMMISSION."
SO CONGRESS CHARACTERIZES PLAN OF SO-CALLED PARK COMMISSION.

Attempt Now Being Made to Gal-
the Project Into the Semblance of
A Tasteless, Decadent, Enormously
sive, Utterly Impracticable Scheme,
Senator Hale Says, "Fell Abso-
Dead the Moment Senators and
sentatives Began to Examine It."

NO. 44—VIEW SHOWING PROPOSED TREATMENT OF APPROACHES AND TERRACES, FORMING A SETTING FOR THE WASHINGTON MONUMENT.

SOMETHING ABOUT
A. J. DOWNING

WHO LAID OUT THE SMITHSO-
NIAN GROUNDS UPON GRACE-
FUL UNDULATING NAT-

Regaining a lost splendor

As a result of the McMillan Commission's studies, Washington took some spectacular strides toward realizing the beauty that L'Enfant had envisioned for the city a century earlier. One of the most dramatic new structures was Union Station, fronted by a broad plaza. (The proposal for an arc of classical colonnades around the plaza was not carried out, however.) By 1910 the old railroad station and the tracks were gone from the Mall, which was transformed into a broad greensward leading to the Capitol. The problem of flooding was solved by diverting the source of the water and filling the Tiber Canal.

As recommended by the commission, the axis of the Mall was shifted, and the Mall itself was extended from the Washington Monument to the Potomac River. The filled-in marshland along the tract was converted into new parklands. The Lincoln Memorial was built at the western end of the Mall on the Potomac, and a beautiful reflecting pool was constructed along the approach to the memorial.

Southwest of the Lincoln Memorial, the Arlington Memorial Bridge

The Federal Triangle, formed by Pennsylvania Avenue *(lower street)*, Constitution Avenue *(upper street)* and 15th Street *(right)*, includes, from le

was erected across the Potomac to Arlington National Cemetery. Later the bridge was adorned with four equestrian statues, one of which is shown in the picture of the bridge above. Designed by American sculptors, the statues were cast in bronze and surfaced in gold by Italian artisans as a gift from Italy to the United States.

On the south side of the Mall, facing the White House across a tidal basin, the Jefferson Memorial was completed in 1942. Constructed of white marble and surrounded by a peristyle of Ionic columns, it conforms with the commission's recommendation to return to the classical style favored by L'Enfant.

Because another recommendation of the commission was followed, the quiet dignity exemplified by the Jefferson Memorial is also found in Arlington National Cemetery, formerly a hodgepodge of irregularly sized and designed headstones and monuments. The commission report stated: "Nothing could be more impressive than the rank after rank of white stones . . . covering the gentle, wooded slopes, and producing the desired effect of a vast army in its last resting place." This effect has been tastefully achieved, and the stones have been complemented with parklike areas and pleasant walks.

In its plan for a logical grouping of government office buildings, the McMillan Commission called for the construction of a monumental complex of structures in the Federal Triangle *(below)*, the area between Pennsylvania and Constitution Avenues along the Mall. Not until 1928, however, did Congress authorize funds to buy all the privately held land in this section. About 85 per cent of the construction had been completed when the Depression of the 1930s halted the work. Although some building was done after that, the job was still unfinished in the late 1960s. Enthusiasm for the existing structures in the triangle has been far from unanimous. Many observers find the buildings ill-matched and unimaginative. But at least one architectural critic has said that when the buildings are "viewed panoramically in the disarming light of late afternoon they are singularly impressive."

ight: Federal Trade Commission, National Archives, Justice Department, Internal Revenue Service, Post Office Department, Commerce Department.

The bright future of Pennsylvania Avenue

As the nation's foremost ceremonial boulevard, Pennsylvania Avenue has been the scene of many stirring historical dramas: inaugural parades, funerals for heads of state, victorious armies returning home, triumphant welcomes for heroes and visiting dignitaries. And yet, for all of its epic moments, the avenue has failed to attain the grandeur worthy of a stage for great human events. In the early 19th Century it housed gambling dens, brothels and a slave mart. In this century the north side has been flawed with dingy buildings, cheap souvenir shops, parking lots, faded hotels and incongruous modern glass structures. On the south side the Federal Triangle has remained uncompleted.

In 1962 President Kennedy, appalled by the avenue's shoddy appearance, appointed the 10-member President's Advisory Council on Pennsylvania Avenue to draft recommendations to improve the area. Two years later the council, headed by the noted architect Nathaniel A. Owings *(far right)*, submitted its plan, initiating a vast project that has since gotten underway. In 1966 Owings combined the Pennsylvania Avenue plan with a Mall Master Plan in the model shown at right. Pennsylvania Avenue will be widened 76 feet and lined with rows of trees, terminating in a spacious plaza to be known as National Square *(top right of model)*. The plaza will have a wide, low fountain as its focal point and enhance the formal entrance to the White House. There will be two smaller plazas, one bordering Pennsylvania Avenue, and the other on the site of the old Post Office building. A six-acre reflecting pool is under construction in front of the Capitol, facing the Mall. The few remaining temporary buildings will be removed from the Mall, automobile traffic no longer will be permitted to cross over it—there will be underground streets—and it will have a wider band of trees and gravel pathways, reminiscent of the renowned Tuileries in Paris.

Following the end of the Civil War, victorious soldiers of the Grand Army of the Republic march up Pennsylvania Avenue *(below)* in May 1865. Ever since, troops returning from war have paraded up the route.

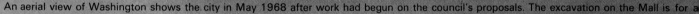

An aerial view of Washington shows the city in May 1968 after work had begun on the council's proposals. The excavation on the Mall is for a

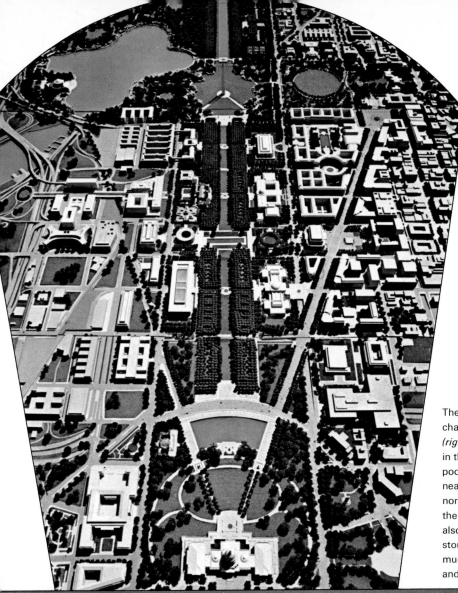

Nathaniel Owings

The model at left shows a number of the important changes that will take place on Pennsylvania Avenue *(right diagonal extending from Capitol at bottom)* and in the Mall *(center)*. In addition to a new reflecting pool in the front of the Capitol and National Square near the White House, a plaza will be built on the north side of Pennsylvania Avenue, directly opposite the National Archives grounds. The north side will also have new arcades, office buildings, hotels and stores. South of the avenue in the Federal Triangle, much of the old Post Office building will be torn down and replaced with a handsome plaza.

new underpass. From the Capitol *(foreground)*, Maryland Avenue leads diagonally to the upper left, Pennsylvania Avenue to the upper right.

Creating the National Center

PART 2: EVOLUTION OF THE CAPITOL

In all the development of Washington, no structure has undergone more changes and enlargements than the Capitol building, the home of the Senate and the House of Representatives and, until 1935, of the Supreme Court. A virtually unending procession of designers, engineers, painters, sculptors and other experts have embellished the structure until today it is a veritable museum of architectural styles—luckily for the most part harmonious.

The building's origins were appropriately grand. On a June morning in 1791, President George Washington and Pierre Charles L'Enfant led their horses up Jenkins' Hill and agreed that it would be the site of the Capitol. The crest of this hill, L'Enfant wrote in his report, "stands as a pedestal waiting for a monument."

The site selected, the government then solicited designs for such a monument. In the spring of 1792 an advertisement appeared in various newspapers announcing a public competition for plans for the new building. To the winner would be awarded a prize of $500

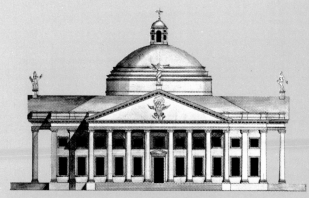

The above design, which included three enormous statues on the building's roof, was submitted by Samuel Dobie.

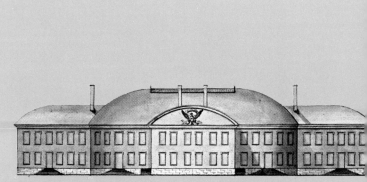

Contemporaries felt that the design submitted by Charles Wintersmith lacked the elegance befitting the Capitol of the new nation.

William Thornton

Praised for its "Grandeur, Simplicity and Convenience" by President Washington, Thornton's design called for a central rotunda capped with a low, graceful dome and flanked by two identical wings, one for the Senate and the other for the House of Representatives. The drawing at right is Thornton's slightly revised version of his first plan; the original design has been lost.

and a piece of property in the District of Columbia. At least 14 plans were submitted (the records are incomplete), but most of them came from rank amateurs, for there were few trained architects in the country at that time, and a substantial majority of the entries were quickly discarded. Even among the designs that remained, none was found wholly satisfactory.

Then, six months after the competition had officially closed, plans were received from William Thornton, a physician, painter and inventor who was also an amateur architect. The design "captivated the eyes and judgment of all," said Secretary of State Thomas Jefferson, himself an amateur architect, and it was quickly accepted.

The construction according to Thornton's plans was completed in 1829, but it proved only the first stage in the evolution of the Capitol. As the nation has expanded, the building that houses its lawmakers has also expanded. And the end is not yet in sight. Today there are plans in existence for enlarging the structure still further.

Étienne Hallet's plan placed second in the competition, and he was chosen to supervise the actual construction according to Thornton's design.

Probably the most ludicrous design was by James Diamond, who capped his building with an enormous weathercock.

Benjamin Henry Latrobe   Charles Bulfinch

The realization of Thornton's design

By 1802 William Thornton's design work on the Capitol was largely completed, and the following year he was replaced as architect in charge by Benjamin Henry Latrobe, who was as much a professional as Thornton was an amateur. Born in England in 1764 and educated at the University of Leipzig, Latrobe had been widely acclaimed in Great Britain—he was Surveyor of Public Offices in London—before coming to the United States in 1796. Latrobe's work was equally well received in his adopted country, where he designed such monuments of American architecture as the penitentiary at Richmond and the Bank of Philadelphia.

When President Thomas Jefferson put Latrobe in charge of the Capitol building, the north wing —designed to house the Senate—had been completed and work had started on the south wing for the House of Representatives. Latrobe completed the south wing to Thornton's design and built a wooden passageway to connect the two buildings. Then, in 1814, British troops invaded Washington and set fire to the Capitol. For the next three years, until his resignation, Latrobe concentrated his efforts on restoring the British-burned edifice.

After a public quarrel with Samuel Lane, the Commissioner of Public Buildings, in 1817, Latrobe was succeeded by the Boston aristocrat Charles Bulfinch, the first native-born architect to take charge of the construction. Under Bulfinch's direction Thornton's design for the Capitol was brought to fruition. Bulfinch finished the restoration of the Senate and House chambers in time for Congress to convene in 1819, and then went on to erect the center section with its low, copper-sheathed dome that he had redesigned.

It took 37 years for Thornton's plans for the Capitol to materialize; stages in the building's development are shown in the contemporary prints above. In 1800, when Congress first occupied the Capitol, it consisted of a single boxlike structure, the north wing *(top)*. By 1814, when the British put Washington to the torch, both wings *(middle)* had been completed and connected by a covered wooden walkway. In the print at bottom, executed in 1826, three years before the building was actually finished, the wooden walkway had been replaced by the Capitol's central Rotunda, and the Capitol looked much as Thornton had envisioned it.

Latrobe's tobacco and corn columns.

A Latrobe mantel (Old Supreme Court Chamber).

Bulfinch's column-enclosed stoves.

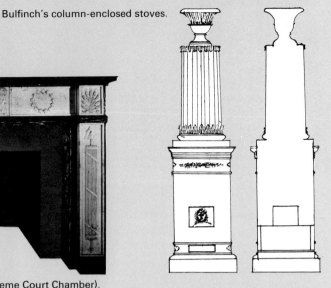

Although Latrobe and Bulfinch made changes in Thornton's plans for the exterior of the Capitol, they did most of their original designs for the building's interior. Among Latrobe's most celebrated innovations were his corn and tobacco motifs, which grace the tops of the columns inside the Capitol. He also designed many of the Capitol's mantels, a number of which are still in existence. One of Bulfinch's most interesting concepts was a heating system: stoves were to be encased in the building's columns. The idea was never carried out, however. Both Latrobe and Bulfinch labored unsuccessfully to correct the faulty acoustics of the Capitol's House chamber *(below)*. All kinds of solutions were tried, from raising the floor to hanging scarlet curtains behind the columns, but nothing worked. The chamber, now Statuary Hall, still exhibits mysterious echoes, but today they are considered a charming curiosity to show off to visitors to the Capitol.

Scarlet curtains, hung behind the columns to muffle echoes in the House chamber, are seen in this 1822 painting by Samuel Morse.

Atop the Capitol dome stands the bronze statue of Freedom, sculpted in Rome by the American artist Thomas Crawford. Wearing a helmet encircled with stars and capped with an eagle's head and Indian feathers, the figure stands almost 20 feet high and weighs more than 14,000 pounds. In her left hand she holds a wreath and a shield, and her right hand rests on the hilt of her sword.

Crawford shipped the plaster model for this statue from Rome in 1858, but violent storms damaged the ship and it had to land in Bermuda, where it was condemned. The model was placed in storage and did not reach Washington for a year. The statue then had to be cast in bronze, but because of delays caused by the Civil War, the figure was not secured to the dome until December 1863.

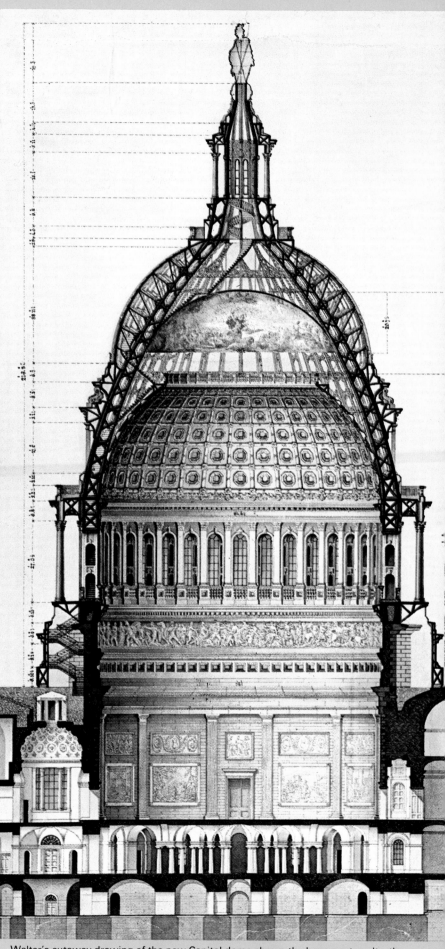

Walter's cutaway drawing of the new Capitol dome shows the basement vaults, the supporting columns and the cast-iron girders that form the curve of the dome.

Expanding the Capitol in troubled times

Thomas U. Walter

In 1850, twenty-one years after the Capitol had been built according to Thornton's plans, Congress decided that it had outgrown its home. Funds were appropriated, and President Millard Fillmore appointed architect Thomas U. Walter to enlarge the building.

Walter served as Architect of the Capitol Extension from 1851 until 1865, and during that time the building more than doubled in size. New chambers for the Senate and House were added to each end of the building, and the original wings became links connecting the additions with the central Rotunda. Realizing that these new wings would dwarf Bulfinch's low, copper-sheathed dome, Walter had it removed in 1855 and began work on the Capitol's present dome, which soars some 275 feet above the Rotunda floor.

Perhaps the most remarkable thing about the enlargement of the Capitol was its near-completion while the Civil War was being fought. In the early days of the war, the Capitol was used as a barracks for as many as 3,000 Union soldiers and later it became a hospital. But work continued during these periods (below). President Lincoln, pleased by the progress, is reported to have said, "If the world sees this Capitol going on, they will know that we intend the Union shall go on."

Constantino Brumidi

Calling of Cincinnatus from the Plow.

Embellishing the Capitol's walls and ceilings

Paintings of heroic size decorate the Capitol's dome, rooms and corridors, and much of the work was done by one artist, Constantino Brumidi, an Italian immigrant whose sole aim in life was, as he said, "to make beautiful the Capitol of the one country on earth in which there is liberty." Several of his paintings are shown on this and the following page.

Brumidi came to the United States from Rome in 1852, when he was almost 50 years old, to escape political persecution in his home country. His reputation as an outstanding artist had preceded him and two years after he arrived he was assigned to decorate the Capitol, then being expanded to about twice its original size. For a quarter of a century, while Presidents Franklin Pierce, James Buchanan, Abraham Lincoln, Andrew Johnson, Ulysses S. Grant and Rutherford B. Hayes carried on the business of government, Brumidi painstakingly applied his brush to the interior of the Capitol.

In 1879, nearly 25 years after he had begun work in the Capitol, Brumidi's chair slipped from a scaffold high above the Rotunda floor and the artist precariously hung from the rung of a ladder for about 15 minutes before he was rescued. The shock of this experience has been blamed for a rapid decline in his health; a few months later he was dead. Brumidi's long labor of love had gone largely unrewarded, and he died in poverty without the recognition he deserved. For 70 years his grave was left unmarked. Finally, in 1949, the 81st Congress voted to erect a monument to show the nation's belated appreciation to this immigrant artist who took pride in signing his work "C. Brumidi, artist. Citizen of the U.S."

A Brumidi corridor ceiling.

Samuel Osgood,
Postmaster General
from 1789 to 1791.

Jefferson and the harvesting painting.

Of the many works by Brumidi that
adorn the walls and ceilings of the
Capitol, the most celebrated is his
fresco *Apotheosis of Washington,*
which covers the eye of the dome
(below). Among other favorites are
Brumidi's fresco *Calling of Cincinnatus
from the Plow* and a medallion head of
Thomas Jefferson above an oil painting
of a McCormick reaper harvesting grain;
both are in the House Appropriations
Committee Room. His medallion
portrait of Samuel Osgood, George
Washington's Postmaster General, is in
the President's Room in the Senate
Wing. On the opposite page is one of
Brumidi's ceiling designs, this one in a
corridor in the Senate Wing.

Apotheosis of Washington (within the dome).

Filling the need for still more space

On July 4, 1959, President Dwight D. Eisenhower ended months of bitter controversy among architects and Congressmen by laying the cornerstone of the east front extension *(dark gold area)* and formally setting underway the first major expansion of the Capitol since Thomas Walter added the new Senate and House Wings and the building's imposing dome nearly a century before. The east front extension, which moved the façade out 32.5 feet, was supervised by Delaware-born J. George Stewart, Architect of the Capitol. His plans had met with violent criticisms from a number of Congressmen as well as from such groups as the American Institute of Architects, who had argued that the proposed changes would ruin the proportions of America's historic monument. (Critics had also

The enlarged Capitol, with its east front extension *(dark gold area)* and the proposed west front extension *(tan area),* is portrayed in the cutaway drawing at right. Also shown are many of the rooms and chambers where the nation's legislative business is conducted, as well as places of historical interest such as Statuary Hall, which once was the chamber of the House of Representatives.

The east front extension added two and a half acres of floor area to the Capitol; the space is used for additional offices, committee and reception rooms, dining rooms, kitchens and entrance foyers. The extension also includes private corridors linking the north and south wings, thus enabling members of Congress to walk between the Senate and House chambers without struggling through crowds of sightseers.

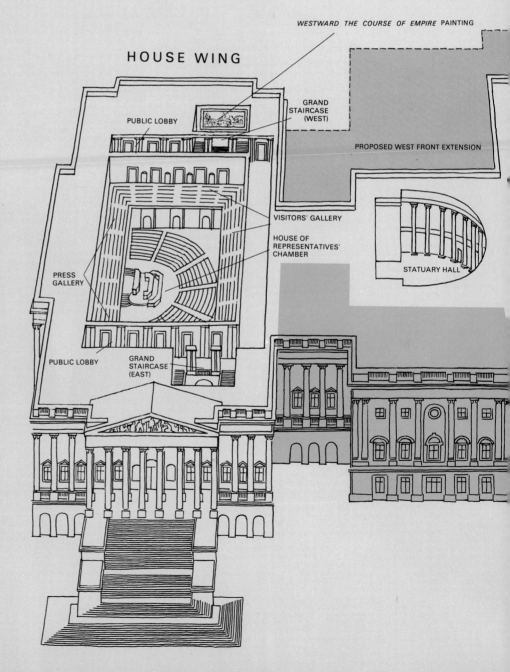

HOUSE WING

WESTWARD THE COURSE OF EMPIRE PAINTING

PUBLIC LOBBY

GRAND STAIRCASE (WEST)

PROPOSED WEST FRONT EXTENSION

VISITORS' GALLERY

HOUSE OF REPRESENTATIVES' CHAMBER

STATUARY HALL

PRESS GALLERY

PUBLIC LOBBY

GRAND STAIRCASE (EAST)

complained that Stewart, a former Congressman from Delaware, was not an architect at all, but an engineer.) Despite the opposition, Stewart's plans were approved by both houses of Congress in 1958, mainly by the efforts of two Texans, Speaker of the House Sam Rayburn and Senate Majority Leader Lyndon Johnson. Because of their support for the remodeling, the new face of the Capitol is sometimes referred to as the "Texas front."

The exterior construction of the east front extension was completed in time for the inauguration of President John F. Kennedy on January 20, 1961. And this may not be the end of the Capitol's face lifting. Congress has already received proposals and cost estimates for extending the Capitol's west front *(tan area)*.

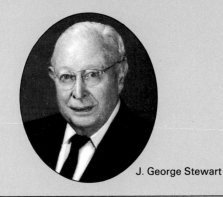

J. George Stewart

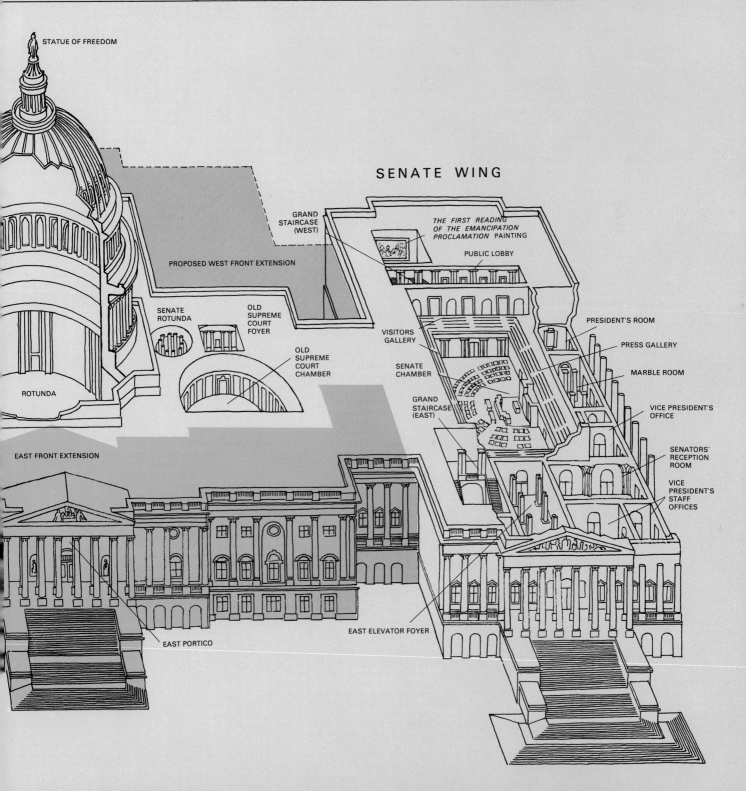

STATUE OF FREEDOM

SENATE WING

GRAND
STAIRCASE
(WEST)

THE FIRST READING
OF THE EMANCIPATION
PROCLAMATION PAINTING

PROPOSED WEST FRONT EXTENSION

PUBLIC LOBBY

SENATE
ROTUNDA

OLD
SUPREME
COURT
FOYER

PRESIDENT'S ROOM

VISITORS
GALLERY

PRESS GALLERY

OLD
SUPREME
COURT
CHAMBER

MARBLE ROOM

SENATE
CHAMBER

VICE PRESIDENT'S
OFFICE

ROTUNDA

GRAND
STAIRCASE
(EAST)

SENATORS'
RECEPTION
ROOM

VICE
PRESIDENT'S
STAFF
OFFICES

EAST FRONT EXTENSION

EAST PORTICO

EAST ELEVATOR FOYER

3

Grandeur and Working Clothes

In 1804 Thomas Moore, an Irish bard visiting Washington, weighed it in the scales of poetic imagination and found it wanting. Annoyed by its muddy and unlit streets and its cheerless boardinghouses, he sneered at

> *This embryo capital, where Fancy sees*
> *Squares in morasses, obelisks in trees;*
> *Which second sighted seers e'en now adorn*
> *With shrines unbuilt and heroes yet unborn.*

Though there was a certain weight to his strictures, Moore underestimated the creative power of the "Fancy" that allowed American eyes to see tomorrow's metropolis in today's swamp. The many squares and obelisks of which he spoke were manifestations of a preoccupation with classic ideas that gripped the generation of Washington, Adams, Jefferson, Hamilton and Madison. They believed that the Greek and early Roman republics had embodied Western man's best political wisdom. The American nation, which would revive such self-governing excellence, should have a capital that

Accompanied by greatness, a boy sits on the marble steps of the Lincoln Memorial and reads about the shrine he is visiting. The classical structure, commissioned **48** years after Lincoln's death, was built on the axis of the Capitol and the Washington Monument.

would evoke the spirit of Athens and Rome—not Caesar's Rome, but Cato's, centuries older and simpler.

It was ever thus in Washington. Someone had a notion of what the United States was all about and tried to embody it in the stones of public or private edifices. Each building and monument on the Potomac's shore inevitably carries the stamp not merely of an architect, but of a particular generation's idea of what the nation should be.

Guidebook tours of Washington are often built around geographical groupings, for the sake of convenience and unblistered feet. On different days the sightseer may "do" Capitol Hill (Capitol, Library of Congress, Supreme Court, the House and Senate Office Buildings), the Mall complex (Smithsonian, National and Freer Galleries), and the White House and monuments (White House, Lafayette Square, Washington Monument, Jefferson and Lincoln Memorials, and, in season, the cherry blossoms). Properly arranged, such packaged tours leave even the four-day visitor time for a foray to Mount Vernon.

The logic of architectural Washington is better perceived, however, if it is considered in chronological clusters. Its original pattern took shape in the neoclassic mind of L'Enfant. He wanted his city to be roomy, well-proportioned and simple. At each end of Pennsylvania Avenue the official residences of Congress and the President would sit like weights on the end of a seesaw, with a square, approximately halfway between them at 9th Street, as the fulcrum. The long sweeps of Pennsylvania Avenue and the Mall were to be generous, but not so much so as to dwarf the structures along and at either end of them. Nor, in turn, should the buildings overwhelm the promenades.

L'Enfant's plan was the precursor of an opening half century of construction in Washington in which buildings followed a tendency to Corinthian, Doric and Ionic columns, severe angles, porticoes and an occasional low dome. The adaptation of classic models was one of the basic influences. One such derivation was the fashionable "Federal" architecture. Its hallmarks were low buildings, commonly of brick, with square and rectangular windows and doorways, often framed in contrasting wood or stone, but very little other outside ornamentation. It was a creation of orderly 18th Century minds in early 19th Century American heads. Both the Federal and neoclassic modes were strongly visible in the first embodiments of L'Enfant's vision of the Congressional and Executive "houses." The designs for both the Capitol and the "Presidential palace" (not called the White House, some historians say, until after 1815) were selected in competition, an appropriately democratic device. The winner of the Capitol contest was a marvelous personification of the Federal outlook, Dr. William Thornton.

Thornton has yet to find his Boswell, but he deserves one sensitive to the peculiar charms of a Renaissance man. Born in a Quaker community in the Virgin Islands, he was educated in England and Scotland and came to New York in 1787 with the degree of M.D. in his pocket (though there is no record of his ever having practiced) and a rather justified notion that he could do almost anything well. He had never studied architecture, but hearing in 1789 that the Library Company of Philadelphia had announced an award for the best design for its proposed new building, he took action: "I got some books and worked a few days, then gave a plan in the ancient Ionic order, which carried the day." Concurrently he also helped the now nearly forgotten John Fitch with the design of the first commercially operated steamboat, which ran on the Delaware for a short period but was abandoned as a nonpaying investment.

Thornton's design for the Capitol in 1792 called for a simple structure of two wings on either side of a central portion that was fronted with columns and surmounted by a low dome. Though now overlaid by nearly two centuries of alteration, it is the foundation of the present Capitol, and it earned Thornton $500 and a city lot. Moreover, he moved to Washington in 1794 and soon was made one of the three commissioners of the capital. In subsequent years he had heated arguments with several successive architects in charge of the actual construction of the Capitol—Étienne Hallet, George Hadfield and Benjamin Latrobe—who, in his view, were changing the spirit of his drawings. When not so engaged he designed private homes in Washington, served as Superintendent of Patents (it will be remembered that it was he who dissuaded a British officer in 1814 from burning down the Patent Office), painted, wrote three unpublished novels, composed *Cadmus; or, a Treatise on the Elements of Written Language* and an essay "on the mode of teaching the Surd, or Deaf, and consequently Dumb to speak," served in societies for ending slavery and "resettling" Negroes in Africa, and was a proponent of a never-established national university. He was also the author of a constitution for a proposed South American nation with a capital near Panama, "where a canal may be made from sea to sea, by locks," an investor in sheep and horse ranches and gold mines, a justice of the peace and a captain of militia.

Thornton's breathtaking pace was not matched by Congress when it came to appropriating money to build his Capitol. The north wing was finished in 1800 and for the better part of a decade housed both chambers of Congress, the Library of Congress and the Supreme Court. The south wing, for the House of Representatives, was completed by architect Benjamin Latrobe in 1811 and was joined to the Senate's home in the north wing by a temporary wooden corridor. After the British-set fire in 1814, work crept on. Not until 1829 did the wings, columns and dome stand out in completed symmetry, and by then architects Latrobe and, later, Charles Bulfinch had added details that blended classical and New World themes. Latrobe, for example, devised marble columns for the Senate wing and topped them not with the traditional acanthus leaves but with ears of corn. Congressmen who passed them every day gleefully called them "corncob capitals." Not long after the "first" Capitol was finished it became clear that the working space of both chambers would have to be enlarged, but the expansion was not undertaken until a second phase of Washington's growth, after 1850.

The first prize for the President's house was taken by James Hoban, an Irish-born architect. His design (said by some to be modeled on the Dublin home of the Duke of Leinster) reflected the Palladian style, then popular in England. The Palladian mode, named for a Renaissance Italian designer, Andrea Palladio, has been described as "characterized by symmetry, monumentality, and an academic use of classical forms." What this means in concrete terms is partially demonstrated by features still visible at 1600 Pennsylvania Avenue—the rectangular shape and symmetrical rows of tall windows, set four on each side of the central entrance and topped alternately with a crescent-shaped or triangular pediment. It is still a simple, clean and handsome building, as unlike the baroque palaces of 18th Century Europe as John Adams, its first occupant, was unlike Louis XVI.

One design that was rejected was submitted under the initials of "A.Z.," who turned out to be Thomas Jefferson himself. Jefferson had a solace available to few other architects in that position. In 1801 he moved into the building designed by his rival and proceeded to make some modifications in it. Even though the building had already been occupied by the Adamses, it was still in a sad condition—only barely ready, cold, cheerless and imparting a certain rueful immediacy to an Adams letter written immediately after he moved in: "I pray Heaven to bestow the best of Blessings on this House." It needed them.

With Benjamin Latrobe's assistance, Jefferson planned for the north and south porticoes, the terraces and other construction. Most of the work was not completed, however, until long after Jefferson had retired and the White House had been partially burned and then renovated. (During its rebuilding, the First Family of James and Dolley Madison spent part of their exile in the Octagon House at 18th Street and New York Avenue, a lovely and still-standing Federal-style home designed by the irrepressible Dr. Thornton.)

The White House gradually underwent interior improvements during the Administrations of succeeding Presidents. Jefferson and Monroe filled it with imported (largely French) furniture, and Jackson installed plumbing; Polk arranged for gaslight, and Millard Fillmore added central heating. By the 1850s the White House was assuming, inside, what L'Enfant had hoped it would have, "the sumptuousness of a palace," and on the outside "the agreeableness of a country seat."

The third and fourth still-existent major buildings of Washington's early years show a continued fondness for antiquity mated to a certain growing

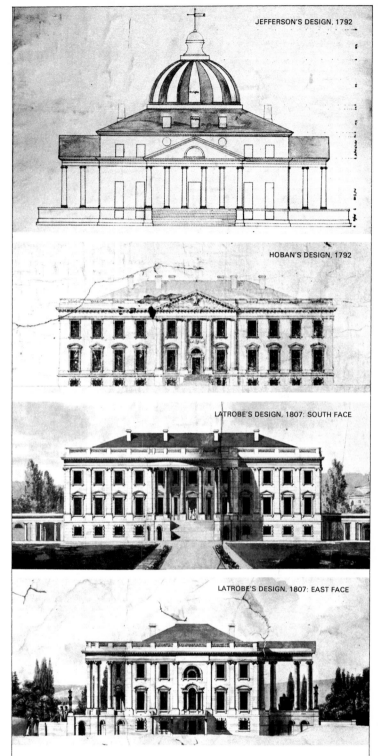

JEFFERSON'S DESIGN, 1792

HOBAN'S DESIGN, 1792

LATROBE'S DESIGN, 1807: SOUTH FACE

LATROBE'S DESIGN, 1807: EAST FACE

How the White House evolved

The White House is the product of several architectural minds, all of them influenced by the Palladian style. In a 1792 contest for its design, Thomas Jefferson was an entrant *(top)*. The winning scheme *(second picture)*, by the Irish-born architect James Hoban, suggests an English country mansion. As President, Jefferson moved into the house in 1801 and, with Benjamin Latrobe's help, began to realize some of his own ideas by making a few additions. Latrobe's watercolor designs show the subsequently added east and west extensions or terrace-pavilions *(third picture)* and north and south porticoes *(bottom)*—all reminiscent of Jefferson's concepts.

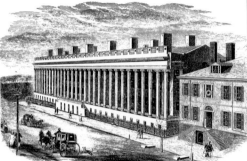

TREASURY DEPARTMENT

WHITE HOUSE

Pennsylvania Avenue

CAPITOL

yen for bigness. In 1836, during a period of booming westward expansion, canal and factory construction, and growing revenues, the Treasury building was begun. Its planner was Robert Mills, the first professional architect born in the United States and a former pupil of Hoban's and Latrobe's. Mills was an exponent of the Greek-Revival style, but he was an expansionist in his own way. He put a row of columns, 36 feet high, on parade on the long sides of the building. Two of the greatest Secretaries of the Treasury, Alexander Hamilton and Albert Gallatin, whose statues are at either end of the structure, would probably have approved of the style but lamented the expense. L'Enfant might have supported the grandeur but would have mourned the placement of the building southeast of the White House, athwart Pennsylvania Avenue at 15th Street. This location forces the avenue to bend sharply north and then west before resuming its course toward Georgetown, but even worse, it blocks L'Enfant's planned view of the Presidential mansion from Capitol Hill. A persistent but undocumented legend insists that Andrew Jackson, in the middle of one of his blazing battles with Congress (which went so far as to vote censure against him once), strode out of the White House, pounded the ground with his stick and gave

a command, in Battle of New Orleans tones, that the Treasury should be placed so as to block the offending legislature from his sight. In 1869 the Treasury building was extended northward to the east-west section of Pennsylvania Avenue that passes the entrance to the White House.

The fourth of the still-remaining old buildings served as the Patent Office for nearly a century; in the 1930s it was taken over by the Civil Service Commission, and in the late 1960s it was remodeled to house the National Portrait Gallery. In L'Enfant's original plans, according to some scholars, the area bounded by Pennsylvania Avenue and F Street and 7th and 9th Streets was to be an open plaza lined with buildings of amplitude, from which one could look to the Capitol on the left, the Executive Mansion on the right, or straight ahead past Pennsylvania Avenue to the green coolness of the Mall. The vision never became reality. Both the avenue and the Mall soon became lined with hotels, hovels and shops. Nevertheless, in 1837, the Patent Office began to rise, fronting on G Street between 7th and 9th. Designed by William Elliot, Robert Mills and others, the building rears porticoed façades that plainly say "I am the Parthenon," but the size of the building belies that claim for the structure as a whole. There was a sweeping

The banished statue

A statue of George Washington, draped in a robe, is another reflection of the capital's early fondness for classicism. In 1832 Congress asked Boston sculptor Horatio Greenough to create a statue of the President for the Capitol Rotunda. Nine years later the marble work, showing Washington draped like a Grecian god, was installed. Later the figure was moved outside to the east lawn *(right)*. In the light of day the public was offended by the statue's lack of clothes, and in 1908 it was hitched to a team of horses *(below)* and carted off to the Smithsonian Institution.

flight of steps on each side of the building, but the one on the F Street side was sacrificed to a new god, the automobile, in 1936, when the steps were shorn off to allow the street to be widened for traffic. The inside of the building is certainly not Greek; its huge interior spaces and vaulted halls show, in the words of architectural critic Wolf Von Eckardt, the "bold and buoyant architecture of a still young Nation feeling its oats."

Less pretentious structures (now gone) on either side of the White House—one of them was in the space now occupied by the north wing of the Treasury building—housed the State, Navy and War departments, reflecting the relative concern of a younger, happier America with making money rather than conducting foreign relations and wars. The departments remained there until after the Civil War, during which Lincoln could—and frequently did—take his hat and walk a few steps to consult Secretaries Seward and Stanton.

By the end of Washington's first 50 years, something approaching L'Enfant's vision was vaguely discernible. The Capitol rose on its hill, and the White House in its park a mile away, both reservedly classic. The Treasury and the Patent Office, though newer and a bit more exaggerated, still fulfilled the idea that the republican virtues of

antiquity had found new embodiment in a New World. The idea could be pushed too far for some, however. Sculptor Horatio Greenough was commissioned by Congress in the 1830s to do a statue of Washington for the Capitol. Not illogically, he produced the Father of His Country as a classic godlike figure, draped in a robe that left him naked to the waist. But Protestant, Anglo-Saxon America was still a long way from unlimited endorsement of Mediterranean customs, even ancient ones. Congressmen could scarcely bear "the nudity of the figure," and after a short time the statue was removed from the Rotunda of the Capitol and placed outdoors, where again people objected to its nudity. It finally came to rest in the Smithsonian Institution.

It may be that more than prudishness was involved in Congress' rejection of Greenough's explicit neoclassic metaphor in stone. A second period of Washingtonian public architecture was at hand, a time of romantic, Gothic and Romanesque modes, following one another in bewildering succession from about 1850 to 1900. The ornate creations of this phase still are prominent in the tourist's Washington. They are witness to what might be labeled "the spread-eagle age."

The dramatic break with the classical style came in 1855, when work was finally completed on the

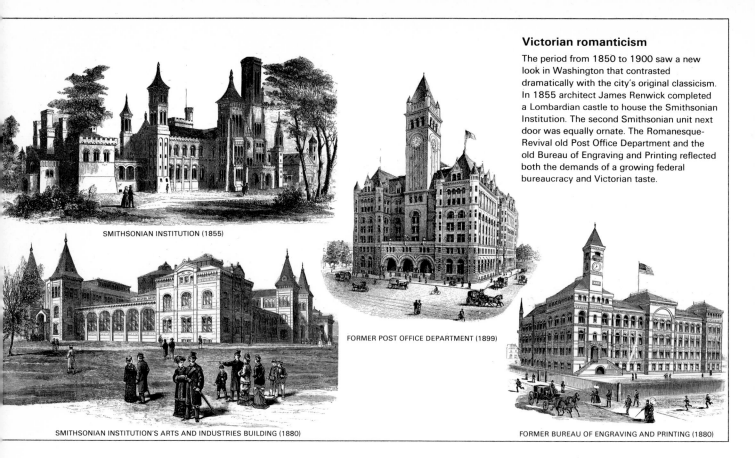

SMITHSONIAN INSTITUTION (1855)

FORMER POST OFFICE DEPARTMENT (1899)

SMITHSONIAN INSTITUTION'S ARTS AND INDUSTRIES BUILDING (1880)

FORMER BUREAU OF ENGRAVING AND PRINTING (1880)

building for the Smithsonian Institution. Its architect, James Renwick, was then in the early stage of a long, profitable career of designing fashionable residences, public buildings and churches, the best known of which is New York's St. Patrick's Cathedral. Renwick's talents for visual excitement were considerable, and the Middle Ages stirred his mind powerfully. He was steeped in a romantic style in stone that was the counterpart of Sir Walter Scott's in prose. Spires and towers were essential to any heroic project he undertook, and he provided many such projections for the Smithsonian. This red sandstone Lombardian castle also boasts peaked belfries, turrets and arched windows. The original Smithsonian building is now an antiquity in its own right, with its own affectionate following. Yet it still contrasts oddly with the green Mall and the white Capitol, almost blushing, as one guidebook says, amidst all that chasteness. It perfectly suited an age that devoured Scott and Victor Hugo, sighed over Longfellow, and dressed its armies, right down to the Civil War, in red sashes and plumes. Later on, Renwick's brain child was joined by similar fancies, such as the old Department of Agriculture building, completed in the 1870s and solidly red-brick Victorian under its mansard roof; the old Bureau of Engraving and

Printing in the 1880s; and the second Smithsonian building, the Arts and Industries Building, done at about the same time. All are "picturesque," a word that Renwick's generation of architects would have taken as a compliment.

The Washington Monument, begun in 1848, belongs to the same surge of capital embellishment. Though it is a starkly beautiful monolith, its design as an obelisk gave fresh meaning to Tom Moore's rhymed fling at America's pretensions to antiquity. Moreover, its original conception was not so pure. Designed by Robert Mills, of the Treasury building, it called for a circular colonnade of a base supporting a platform on which there would be a statue of Washington driving a chariot. The monument had a difficult birth. Private subscriptions flagged after an initial, enthusiastic outburst of gifts from most of the states of the Union and some foreign nations. Then the Civil War interfered. When Congress took over and finished the work in the 1880s, the ornate base had long since been eliminated from the plans, but the shaft's 555-foot reach skyward was welcomed as a symbol of post-Reconstruction America's quest for growth.

Meanwhile, the Capitol underwent enlargement. When Thornton's first plan was submitted there were 15 states in the Union. When his version, more or less, was completed in 1829, there were 24 states and new ones knocking at the door. The total of states reached 33 by 1860, and the U.S. population was increasing by approximately a third every decade. So Congress, in 1850, entrusted to Thomas U. Walter the task of building new wings for its swelling membership. The configuration of Capitol Hill forced him to put them at right angles to the original chambers. They then appeared to him to dwarf the low dome of copper-sheathed wood, and Walter designed a replacement, the present massive dome. Work on it continued right through the Civil War, despite shortages of materials and labor. It was a kind of psychological reassurance to the North that the Union's business would go on as usual.

Walter was something of a neoclassicist *and* an American booster. If domes and columns were good, then a huge dome and a wealth of columns were even better. His creation in cast iron rises nearly 300 feet above ground level. Its base is surrounded by a great row of columns, and it is topped by a slender, colonnaded cupola, above which is poised a statue of Freedom. Executed by Thomas Crawford, an American sculptor then resident in Rome, the statue is unmistakably romantic. Freedom is a woman, and from her feathered and star-encrusted headdress to her flowing, tasseled robe to the hand resting on her sword hilt, she is straight out of a Lord Byron invocation.

Revolutionary romanticism—the worship of Liberty as the quasi-divine spirit working behind the scenes of History—also overflows the inside of the Capitol. Congress commissioned an Italian artist, Constantino Brumidi, who came here in 1852, to execute a painting in the eye of the dome and a frieze around the interior walls, some 60 feet above floor level. Brumidi was a refugee from the unsuccessful Italian effort to set up a republic in 1848-1849. He was devoted to his new homeland, and every day for a quarter of a century this "Michelangelo of the Capitol" devotedly climbed scaffolds and painted his lifework. His death was hastened by the shock of a fall one day, when he barely managed to seize a ladder rung and to hold on for 15 grim minutes until rescued.

Brumidi finished nearly half of the frieze. Whatever the artistic value of the paintings, they are historical works highly expressive of the period of their composition. (The perfect accompaniment to them is George Bancroft's contemporary, chest-thumping 10-volume *History of the United States* published between 1834 and 1874. In it, such

Washington's obelisk

Under construction for 36 years, the 555-foot marble-faced obelisk that rises at the far end of the Mall from the Capitol is a monument to perseverance as well as to the nation's first President. The original design *(top)* by Robert Mills included a "grand circular colonnaded building . . . from which springs an obelisk shaft." But by the time the cornerstone was laid on July 4, 1848, the project was pared to the obelisk alone. Work continued for six years *(bottom left)* and was then halted for a quarter century for lack of funds. Finally, in 1880, work was resumed, and four years later the capstone was set in place *(bottom right)*.

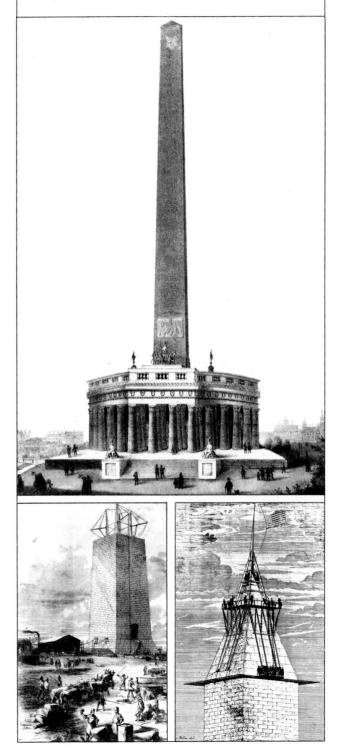

events as the Renaissance and the invention of printing are only minor preludes to the American Revolution's opening battle at Lexington.) In Brumidi's creations Washington is surrounded by 13 female figures representing the original states, and allegorical groups symbolizing Commerce, Mechanics, War, Agriculture, Navigation, and the Arts and Sciences. In the panels of the frieze, De Soto, Columbus, Cortez, Pizarro, Pocahontas, the Pilgrims and William Penn all pose for inspirational tableaux. After Brumidi's death a student of his, Filippo Costaggini, added such other scenes as the death of Tecumseh and the discovery of gold in California. The frieze was not completed until 1953, when Allyn Cox added representations of the Civil and Spanish-American Wars and the birth of aviation. The work is impressive in its heroic proportions. In that way it resembles the four huge historical paintings by John Trumbull and the four by a quartet of other artists hung around the hall below it. And all the artworks resemble the young America that commissioned them.

Pursuing its wartime anxiety to memorialize the nation's historical greatness, however brief, in marble, Congress voted in 1864 to use the old House chamber as a Hall of Statuary. It was to contain two sculptured favorite sons or daughters contrib-

uted by each state. Overloaded floors have since dictated the distribution of some of these statues to other locations in the Capitol. The entire building has therefore become, over the years, a gallery of ancestor-worshiping painting and sculpture. Thereafter, the Capitol stayed essentially untouched until 1959, when the east front was moved out 32.5 feet to enlarge the working space within. It remains a neoclassic project overlaid with generations of growth and swagger.

The climax of the Renwick outlook, if not of his handiwork, came in two post-Appomattox creations. One is the Executive Office Building on 17th Street, just west of the White House. It was begun in the Grant Administration to furnish combined offices for the State, War and Navy Departments, which were swollen beyond any possibility of reduction to prewar proportions. It was completed in 1888. Architect Alfred B. Mullett chose for it a style described as "Second Empire," but it was actually a zesty and not particularly consistent mixture of everything that struck him as attractive: innumerable mansard roofs, dormers, columns, chimneys, pediments and porches. General Grant, observing it after a trip around the world, is supposed to have said that it was the most curious of all the things he had seen. Time has

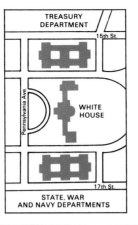

What is now called the Executive Office Building was completed in 1888, and at various times was the home of the Departments of State, War and Navy. Its Second Empire exterior, overladen with mansard roofs and columns, was anathema to early 20th Century purists. They found it out of place as a counterbalance—with the White House as fulcrum *(right)*—to the classic Treasury building. Plans were drawn to sheathe it in a Greek Revival façade *(below)*, but the 1930s Depression forced abandonment of the project. The edifice is now a much-loved landmark.

made it a landmark for which some capital residents have come to feel the affection bestowed on a slightly dotty aunt who still dresses in the manner of Lillian Russell.

About a dozen years after its completion, Mullett's work was matched on Capitol Hill by the Library of Congress. The architects on that job— J. J. Smithmeyer, Paul Pelz and Edward P. Casey —employed a style called Beaux-Arts Classic. The library's great central dome, sheathed in copper, its massive wings, arched portico and cascade of steps are all outward manifestations of an equally spectacular interior ornamentation. Marble floors, monumental vaults, marble columns and staircases, and ornamented galleries combine to give the visitor a sense of being adrift in a *palazzo* fit for an Italian prince rather than a research center for the American people. Yet the painters and sculptors who did the wall decorations and busts and carvings, even the dark wood desks in the huge, octangular Main Reading Room, were convinced that they had reared a temple of learning worthy of a great republic.

Both the State, War and Navy Building and the new Library of Congress represented the final efflorescence of the Gilded Age. They came into being in a day of transcontinental railroads, multi-

million-dollar trusts, cattle and mining empires, armored battleships, skyscrapers, dynamos and transoceanic cables. It was an era in which the United States exuberantly and openly put on the purple of overt colonial imperialism by annexing the Philippines and Puerto Rico. The men who reaped the wealth of the era lived in unabashed, high-hatted enjoyment of their position. Architects built them stately—and very expensive—mansions on such elegant pieces of real estate as Lafayette Square and the stretch of Massachusetts Avenue northwest of Dupont Circle.

Naturally, such an age wanted to house its government as handsomely as its nabobs. The "new" Washington of the 1890s advertised to the world America's acceptance of the greatness that industrial power had thrust upon it. The buildings bracketed in time between Renwick's Smithsonian and the Library of Congress encompass not only space but a point of view as well.

The flourishing of the American historical imagination after the Civil War contributed also to a long Washington boom in outdoor statuary. Many of the monuments found in the parks where streets and avenues intersect are, in fact, dedicated to the war heroes of 1861-1865. General George McClellan is there, as are Winfield S. Hancock, James McPherson, John A. Logan, Philip Sheridan, George H. Thomas, and Admirals Samuel DuPont and David Farragut. Grant has a big memorial between Pennsylvania and Maryland Avenues at the Capitol end of the Mall. It is a lively, though large composition, the second-biggest equestrian statue in the world, depicting the hero of Appomattox surrounded by charging cavalrymen and artillery caissons galloping hell-for-leather into action.

But the look of sculptured Washington is not only martial. Any group that holds a stake in American history, or thinks that it does, and can raise the funds to honor one of its representatives on a public site, can try to secure permission from Congress and, nowadays, the approval of the Commission of Fine Arts. Those who have already successfully done so are numerous. The result is that a stroll around Washington brings on encounters with some predictable marble or metal figures, and some surprising ones, testimony to the many American heritages that come to confluence in the capital. One anticipates John Marshall, but not Blackstone. John Paul Jones is a natural, but Edmund Burke, British statesman and friend of the colonies, is rather unexpected. Bishop Francis Asbury, the father of American Methodism, stands at 16th and Mount Pleasant Streets, not too far

The city's outdoor art

Like a vast outdoor museum, Washington displays a wide variety of monuments and statues that pay tribute to the nation's and the world's famous—and sometimes not so famous—figures. Not counting statues displayed in various government buildings, there are some 70 memorials to people or groups scattered throughout the city. Some of the monuments are enduring works of art; a few are appallingly bad. With no reference to their artistic merit, or lack of it, seven of these tributes in granite and bronze are shown at right.

James Cardinal Gibbons (1834-1921), head of Baltimore's Roman Catholic archdiocese, sits in bronze at 16th Street and Park Road. Gibbons helped found the city's Catholic University.

On the Mall between 7th and 9th Streets, a svelte granite figure holds the wreath of fame over the bronze bust of Louis Daguerre (1789-1851), the inventor of a photographic process.

Taras Shevchenko (1814-1861 professor and poet from the Ukraine exiled to Siberia for his revolutionary activities, is hono by a towering bronze erected in 1964 at 22nd and P Streets.

from where James Cardinal Gibbons upholds the prestige of Roman Catholicism. Ecumenism is recognized this way in America.

So is the power of the ethnic vote. One expects and gets Columbus and those heroes of the Revolution, Thaddeus Kosciuszko and Friedrich Wilhelm, Baron von Steuben, but one may be startled at 22nd and P Streets by seeing Taras Shevchenko, a Ukrainian poet and national leader. Foreign inventors are paid due respects with Louis Daguerre and Guglielmo Marconi. Two physicians, Samuel Gross and Samuel Hahnemann, seem to demonstrate the strength of the medical profession. Joan of Arc, at 16th and Euclid Streets, has somehow crept into the pantheon of the American military men, country lawyers and the businessmen who waxed mighty. It is unusual to find a political boss enshrined, but Alexander Shepherd stands at 14th Street and Pennsylvania, keeping an eye on what happens to his city.

One of the pleasantest statues in town adorns a fountain at 5th and D Streets. It is dedicated to a Pennsylvania lawyer, Joseph Darlington. Instead of Darlington's features, the sculpture simply presents a slender, naked girl caressing the ear of a small deer. If Darlington should ever be resurrected and he decided to run for public office, he would have a substantial bloc of grateful voters waiting.

At the turn of the 20th Century, Washington entered a new 40-year phase of planning and building activity. It represented a return to neoclassicism, but on a scale that tried to mate L'Enfant's ideas of simplicity with the real needs of a capital that now administered the affairs of a nation 76 million strong. The "rediscovery" of L'Enfant began with the 1901 plan of the famed McMillan Commission on parks (*Chapter 2*), which proposed to take his original idea for the Mall and Pennsylvania Avenue as the central axes of official Washington and make it the basis for future growth. New executive branch buildings were to circumscribe Lafayette Square, across the street from the White House. Judicial and legislative structures should frame Capitol Hill. Only cultural and educational buildings should face the Mall itself, and the triangular area between the Mall, Pennsylvania Avenue and 15th Street should be filled with working government buildings, tastefully harmonious in design. West of the White House the Mall was to descend gently around a reflecting pool to a memorial to Lincoln on the shore of the Potomac. A bridge to Virginia would be nearby.

The Park Commission had other ideas, never realized—fountains, terraces and waterfalls at the

Seemingly lost in eternal thought, the brooding bronze figure of Samuel Hahnemann (1755-1843), founder of the science of homeopathy, dominates a small square to the east of Scott Circle.

Memorializing a man who said he had "not yet begun to fight," a 10-foot-high bronze John Paul Jones (1747-1792), naval hero of the American Revolution, towers defiantly over 17th Street.

A gilt bronze nude and a small deer frolic in the middle of a Judiciary Square fountain erected by the city's bar association to honor Joseph J. Darlington (1849-1920), a prominent local attorney.

An equestrian statue in bronze of General John A. Logan (1826-1886), one of the commanders of the Army of the Tennessee in the Civil War, surveys Logan Circle at 13th and P Streets.

foot of Capitol Hill and stone wharves along the Anacostia roofed with boulevards on which river watchers could stroll as in Paris. But the Reflecting Pool and the Lincoln Memorial, the Arlington Memorial Bridge with its guardian equestrian statues, and the landscaped Tidal Basin (part of the park scheme) all survived economy cuts and changing fashions and added to the city's beauty as they were executed piecemeal into the 1930s. More important, Congress kept faith with the essential element in the Park Commission report—that future federal buildings should strive for some kind of unity of design. It was clear, too, that that design should at least have some recognizable relation to the neoclassic style of the city's beginnings.

Certainly the magnificent Lincoln Memorial, one of the most popular tourist attractions in Washington, was especially successful in fulfilling this purpose. Designed by Henry Bacon, the memorial is like a Greek temple with a colonnade of 36 Doric columns supporting the rectangular structure. Daniel Chester French's heroic statue of the President dominates the central area and Jules Gerin's murals the two smaller rooms.

There were esthetic problems, however, with larger structures. It is difficult to reconcile early 19th Century neoclassicism with massiveness, but

a government agency spending millions of dollars annually and employing thousands of workers cannot be housed in tidy little quarters. Therefore it was essential to architects of post-1900 Washington that their buildings convey, both esthetically and functionally, the new reach and complexity of America. So the buildings going up in the era between Theodore and Franklin Roosevelt embodied Greek and Roman columns, friezes and cornices, but often in a magnitude that did not so much suggest the classic world of Pericles as the era of Nero. The old Senate Building and the Longworth and Cannon House Office Buildings are examples of the style, but its outstanding memorial is Union Station, which began operations in 1907. Costing $19 million, this structure was designed by the brilliant Chicago architect and city planner Daniel Burnham. Burnham's legacy to young civic designers was "make no little plans." In the early 20th Century the railroads were at their peak, an incarnation of modern corporate and technological might. Where they entered the American capital, Burnham felt, there must be something breathtaking. So he made no little plans The terminal building has a 760-foot-long interior concourse; an arched roof construction allows this vast space to be free of supporting pillars. Outside, along the

A classic revival

Washington's fling with Victorian romanticism *(page 74)* was followed by a sharp reaction. In the first half of the 20th Century, classicism once again reared its hoary head. When the sheer size of a building did not obscure its purity of line and detail, the result was undeniably elegant. The National Archives, the Supreme Court and the Lincoln Memorial show this 20th Century neoclassicism at its best. However, when a gigantic office warren like the Department of Justice was poured in that mold, the result was less successful. Later attempts to build even larger office buildings produced only classic eyesores.

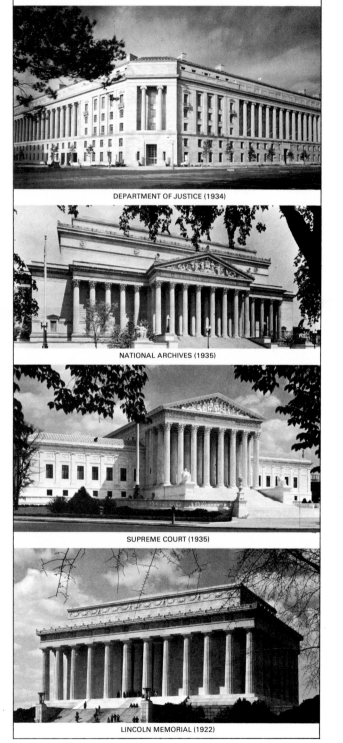

DEPARTMENT OF JUSTICE (1934)

NATIONAL ARCHIVES (1935)

SUPREME COURT (1935)

LINCOLN MEMORIAL (1922)

front, are huge columns topped with massive granite statues: Fire and Electricity, Agriculture and Mechanics, Freedom and Knowledge. The whole creation stands in a great plaza with a fountain memorial to Columbus. Later, Union Station was followed by buildings comparable in spirit—the post office next to it, and the Museum of Natural History on the Mall, finished in 1911.

Construction of the buildings comprising the Federal Triangle was not finished until the late 1930s. Within their clifflike walls thousands of clerks handle the paperwork for the Departments of Justice, Commerce, Labor and the Treasury. A wish for symmetry led to making the cornice levels of these structures identical in height, but the result was, to many observers, an unfortunate, overpowering flatness.

By the 1940s there was a slight retreat from the massive straight-line style of the Federal Triangle. One of the leaders in that direction was John Russell Pope, who received numerous commissions in the New Deal period, among them the National Archives and the Jefferson Memorial. The Archives building is in the gigantic mold, with a vast expanse of steps and enormous bronze double doors. But in the Jefferson Memorial, Pope let his known fondness for pure classic style take over. He gave it a soft rotunda, circularity and columns, which, though templelike, suggest tranquillity instead of majesty.

Other signs of the neoclassic trend were the new Supreme Court and Library of Congress Annex, both large, but essentially chaste and simple. By the time of the bombing of Pearl Harbor in December 1941, Washington's builders seemed to have created a neo-neoclassicism in which the early American spirit was implanted in structures far bigger than the founding generation of the nation could have imagined. Whether America could have both bigness and architectural purity was a debatable subject, but the debate was suspended during World War II.

The argument has, of course, been resumed since the end of the war. The comparatively new working buildings of the government, from the 1941 Pentagon to the white office buildings of Housing and Urban Development (HUD) and National Aeronautics and Space Administration, are essentially utilitarian and therefore huge. Such thrusts toward elephantiasis are always in evidence. Many critics have found the enlarged Capitol and the super-Texan Rayburn House Office Building offensive, though it is always possible that this generation's grandchildren will come to love them as some now love Mullett's Executive Office Building, which seared the eyes of many esthetes of the 1890s. Even the Commission of Fine Arts' plans for a redoing of Pennsylvania Avenue have caused some perturbation. They call for a Versailles-like promenade of trees, fountains and parks in the lee of graceful buildings. But it is not certain whether they leave room for the mundane, everyday life that has surged up and down the avenue, quarreling, buying, selling, shoving, mourning and hurrahing, ever since 1800.

A novel element in the Washington picture is the development of a substantial body of interesting private buildings. The national lobbies, the hotels, the banks, and the communications and other corporations have brought, to Connecticut Avenue especially, the huge glass panels, nests of pre-formed concrete shapes, polished granite facings, long, separating strips of shining steel and other earmarks of contemporary urban architecture. And then there are the rising ranks of apartment houses and the splashes of redevelopment—town houses, restored Federal-style buildings, high rises and shopping plazas—in the Southwest section of the city and also around the Kennedy Center for the Performing Arts, in the Northwest. Tourists do not ordinarily come to see sights like these, but in due course the private Washington may conceivably outshine the public one.

Perhaps in the long run the private and public attractions of Washington can be happily blended. To the southwest of the Capitol the outline of such a city is visible. A brief walk takes a visitor first through the gleaming, modern splendors of the southwest redevelopment, then going eastward he finds a neighborhood of quiet, restored old homes with porches and carriage lamps, and finally he walks north to the white masses of the new office buildings on the Hill itself. If a few parks, some modern schools set in pleasantly landscaped surroundings, and an ever-changing mix of commercial and public buildings in varied sizes and styles were added, it could be a model for an exciting—but human-scale—capital.

But there is the other and glummer prospect, that Washington's fate will be settled by drift, rather than plan, and L'Enfant's lovely conceptions will be lost under towering federal rabbit warrens, creeping slums and all-devouring freeways. Unfortunately, those portents also exist within a few blocks of where the Congress sits. So the city's visual future is uncertain. Whatever happens, nonetheless, Washington will reflect the current generation's thought about its nationhood.

The search for new forms

By the end of World War II, the neoclassic revival had receded, but in seeking new forms federal planners were cautious. The architectural scene began to clear in the 1960s, however. Marcel Breuer's 10-story Housing and Urban Development Building gives massiveness a new shape, while the Federal Office Building Number 6 seeks to camouflage bulk with an airy windowed wall. Where problems of harmony exist—on Lafayette Square the New Executive Office Building dwarfs the historic 19th Century town houses—a solution has been found not in copying old forms but in an imaginative use of an old material, brick.

HOUSING AND URBAN DEVELOPMENT BUILDING (1968)

FEDERAL OFFICE BUILDING NUMBER 6 (1961)

NEW EXECUTIVE OFFICE BUILDING (1967)

Shuttle pilgrimage to the center of power

A measure of Washington's influence over world affairs is the steady stream of people who must travel to the city to visit its myriad departments and agencies. Selling carpet, arranging foreign loans, many come on Eastern Airlines' 8 a.m. Air-Shuttle Flight from New York, which permits a full day's work in the capital. When the 104 passengers on one recent 8 a.m. flight were polled by TIME-LIFE BOOKS, 58 reported they were going to Washington on business involving the U.S. government. Their announced trip plans, given on the next three pages, indicate the tremendous range of the government's day-to-day activities and concerns.

Numbers in red denote persons traveling on business pertaining to some branch of the federal government. Most of the passengers can be seen in this picture. The back section of the plane appears again on the following pages for clearer identification.

1 Gilbert Smigrod, President, Charles Jewelers, Inc., Great Neck, New York, on company business.

2 William A. Hertan, President, Executive Manning Corp., management consultant firm, New York City, on company business.

3 Mary Ziegler, Jarvis School Bureau, Washington, returning from personal trip to New York.

4 Max A. Petrich, Assistant to the President, Karastan Rug Mills, New York City, to see General Services Administration about carpeting.

5 Jon A. Turner, Section Head, Engineering Department, ITT Avionics Corp., Nutley, New Jersey, consulting with Navy Department about new electronic systems.

6 Siguard Eklund, Director General, International Atomic Energy Agency, Vienna, Austria, to see U.S. Atomic Energy Commission and the State Department.

7 Barbara O'Hanley, Air-Shuttle stewardess supervisor, New York City, to observe services provided during flight.

8 Ann Segrave, Leasco Systems and Research Corp., computer systems analysts, New York City, on company business.

9 William Baker, President, Chicago Cleaning Contractors Corp., New York City, on company business.

10 Oscar Dystel, President, Bantam Books, Inc., New York City, to attend meeting of committee advising State Department on foreign library programs.

11 Martin L. Santini, President, Santini Bros., Inc., Maspeth, New York, to represent National Furniture Warehousemen's Association in talks with Army officials to improve moving and storage services for government personnel.

12 Bertram Julien, Sales Director, Air-Tech Industries, Inc., Clifton, New Jersey, on company business.

13 General James M. Gavin, commander of 82nd Airborne Division during World War II, Chairman of the Board, Arthur D. Little, Inc., Boston, Massachusetts, to see John Gardner, head of Urban Coalition, and to visit Army's Office of the Military Historian concerning archives.

14 Louis Prisco, Marketing Manager, General Instrument Corp., Hicksville, New York, to confer with Defense Department on future instrumentation and systems requirements.

15 Dan A. Bruce, attorney for Shell Oil Co., New York City, to attend hearing before Federal Power Commission on natural-gas rates.

16 Michael A. Samuels, Research Assistant, Columbia University's Center for Education in Africa, New York City, to visit Georgetown University's Center for Strategic Studies about Latin-American student problems.

17 Arthur B. Colwin, attorney, New York City, to represent an alien in deportation hearing before Immigration and Naturalization Service.

18 Raymond J. Frisch, President, Wilkinson Publishing Co. Ltd., New York City, on company business.

19 Robert A. Forrest, Vice President, Philip Wechsler and Son, Inc., coffee and tea importers, New York City, on company business.

20 James M. Walsh, Manager, Satellite and Radio Engineering Division, RCA Communications, Inc., New York City, to attend seminar on satellite communications.

21 Tin Win, Design Engineer, RCA Communications, Inc., New York City, for same purpose as (20).

22 Edward M. Smith, M.D., Assistant Professor of Radiology, University of Miami School of Medicine, Miami, Florida, to visit Atomic Energy Commission and National Center for Radiological Health.

23 Edward H. Ginn, National Sales Representative, Marriott Motor Hotels, New York City, on company business.

24 Charles D. Marshall, Chairman, Associated Latin-American Freight Conferences, New York City, to attend hearing before Federal Maritime Commission on regulations governing freight shipping.

25 John P. Landolt, Vice President, International Division, Chemical Bank New York Trust Co., New York City, to confer with Export-Import Bank, Commodity Credit Corporation and World Bank about loans needed for foreign programs by such agencies as Agency for International Development.

26 T. V. Rama Rao, General Manager, Minerals and Metals Trading Corp. of India, Ltd., New Delhi, India, to confer with Commodity Credit Corporation.

27 Edwin A. Locke Jr., President, American Paper Institute, New York City, to attend meeting of Board of Directors of HOPE, a charitable foundation, and to testify before a White House trade committee.

28 Norman R. Roth, accountant for Elliot J. Sachs and Co., law firm, New York City, on company business.

29 A. N. Voripaieff, Regional Manager, A. M. Byers Co., wrought-iron and steel pipe manufacturers, New York City, on company business.

30 Ernest F. Rosenstock, Market Planning Manager, Loral Electronic Systems, Bronx, New York, to attend symposium on military electronics sponsored by National Security Industrial Association in cooperation with Defense Department.

31 Tribeni Prasad Singh, Chairman, Minerals and Metals Trading Corp. of India, Ltd., New Delhi, India, same purpose as (26).

32 James H. Mills, President, Home Facts Research, Inc., Darien, Connecticut, on company business.

33 Henry Z. Walck, President, Henry Z. Walck, Inc., book publishers, New York City, same purpose as (10).

34 Leonard F. Charla, attorney for National Center for Air Pollution Control, Department of Health, Education, and Welfare, Washington, returning from trip to New York City to check on air-pollution controls on imported automobiles.

35 Moses W. Hirschkowitz, Professor of Marine Engineering, U.S. Merchant Marine Academy, Kings Point, New York, to help draft safety codes for merchant ships.

36 Thomas H. Rogers, Vice President, Machlett Laboratories, Inc., Stamford, Connecticut, to attend meeting sponsored by Navy Department to discuss performance and safety standards for X-ray and other radiation equipment used by Navy and private industry.

37 Lester H. Spangenberg, Account Executive, Kayser Roth Hosiery Co., Inc., New York City, on company business.

38 Carlyle H. Jones, Director of Public Affairs, Sperry Rand Corp., New York City, to attend meeting of Public Affairs Council of the Aerospace Industries Association.

39 Russell H. Whempner, Director of Commercial Aviation Sales, Honeywell, Inc., Encino, California, to attend a Federal Aviation Agency conference concerning automatic controls for commercial jets.

40 W. S. W. Edgar, Assistant Vice President, Western Union Telegraph Co., New York City, on company business.

41 Thomas Lamar, Manager, Latin American Stations, Pan American World Airways, New York City, on company business.

42 S. M. Logan, Line Maintenance Manager, Pan American World Airways, New York City, on company business.

43 S. A. Mirkovich, Assistant Line Maintenance Manager, Pan American World Airways, New York City, on company business.

44 John W. McDermott, Business Manager, Public Relations Department, U.S. Steel Corporation, New York City, on company business.

45 Milton Semel, engineer for Kollsman Instrument Corp., Old Bethpage, New York, to visit Night Vision Laboratory, Fort Belvoir, Virginia, and negotiate a contract.

46 Mrs. Roger Leclere, Williamsburg, Virginia, accompanying her husband.

47 Roger Leclere, Vice President and Secretary, Colonial Williamsburg, Williamsburg, Virginia, to meet with Congressmen and government officials on forthcoming bicentennial celebration of American Revolution.

48 Frederick W. Rosenbauer Jr., Assistant Comptroller, Central Railroad of New Jersey, on company business.

49 Frank E. Resnick, Director of Commercial Development, Philip Morris, Inc., New York City, to see former Kentucky Senator Earle Clements, President of Tobacco Institute.

50 Robert J. Krefting, Public Affairs Department, TIME magazine, New York City, on company business.

51 Kennett Hinks, marketing consultant, Ivy, Virginia, returning from New York to attend meeting at Department of Agriculture on selling American foods abroad.

52 David Paget, Assistant U.S. Attorney, U.S. District Court, New York City, to confer with Treasury Department and Justice Department.

53 O. Pruszanowski, System Analyst, American Tabulating Corp., Englewood Cliffs, New Jersey, on company business.

54 Mary Haney, Supervising Teacher of Speech and Hearing, New York School for the Deaf, New York City, to attend conference on new speech-teaching methods, sponsored by Department of Health, Education and Welfare, at Gallaudet College.

55 Lou Wiener, President, Time Saver Food Products, Inc., New York City, to visit Agriculture Department for approval of company's labels on government-inspected meat.

56 Eugene S. Merrill, Vice President, Stone & Webster Engineering Corp., New York City, to testify before Federal Power Commission about rates charged by pipeline company.

57 Bruce Erlichman, Senior Management Consultant, Anathon, Inc., New York City, to confer with Office of Transportation on plans for high-speed train service between Boston and Washington.

58 Austin J. McCaffrey, Executive Director, American Educational Publishers Institute, New York City, for same purpose as (10).

59 William G. Carlson, Deputy Director, Project Operations, Burns and Roe, Inc., consultant engineers, Hempstead, New York, to confer with Army on missile project.

60 Charles L. Ritchie Jr., Trustee and Public Safety Commissioner, Village of Irvington, New York, to attend meeting of International Association of Chiefs of Police.

61 (No information available.)

62 L. J. Burnett, head of Engineering Department, Systems and Management Division, Sperry Rand Corp., Syosset, New York, to confer with Navy on Polaris submarines.

63 Barbara Currier, White House Fellow, Office of the Vice President, Washington, returning from personal trip to New York City.

64 William Derganc, Manager, Infrared Electro Optical Division, Servo Corp. of America, Hicksville, New York, to attend Defense Department meeting on night-combat operations.

65 Stephen C. Brown, Environmental Sciences Coordinator, Tenneco Chemicals, Inc., to consult with Maryland and U.S. health officials about new water- and air-pollution legislation.

66 F. Hastreiter, Field Engineer, R. Hoe & Co., Inc., printing press manufacturers, New York City, on company business.

67 Jack Bryer, Assistant Chief Engineer, R. Hoe & Co., Inc., New York City, for same purpose as (66).

68 Al Gorchoff, Sales Manager, Elm Jay Metal Products Co., Inc., New York City, on company business.

69 Charles Diamond, Vice President, Dyson Shipping Co., Inc., New York City, to confer with representatives of India on shipping matters.

70 Gerald Tischfeld, accountant, Flushing, New York, private business.

71 (No information available.)

72 John Geminder, Manager, Commercial Development, Food and Beverage Department, Charles Pfizer & Co., Inc., New York City, to confer with several government departments on nutritional additives to foods sent to underdeveloped countries.

73 Bernard Feinman, General Manager, Krasner Bros., Inc., buyers of clothing for retail stores, New York City, on company business.

74 John W. Heilshorn, Vice President, First National City Bank, New York City, to visit Office of the Comptroller of the Currency, Treasury Department.

75 Edward J. Smith, Chemical Engineer, McKee-CTIP International, Inc., engineering firm, New York City, to discuss with Department of Commerce clearance for building of small oil refinery plant in the Soviet Union.

76 Thomas C. Palmer, Dean, The Evening College, Texas Christian University, Fort Worth, Texas, to visit office of Urban Coalition.

77 William Jacobs, accountant, New York City, on private business.

78 Victor M. Dagenais Jr., Field Engineer, United Parcel Service, Inc., New York City, on company business.

79 Joseph McClain, Real Estate Representative, United Parcel Service, Inc., New York City, for same purpose as (78).

80 Mark Geier, graduate student, Queens College, New York City, to visit the Department of the Census.

81 Mrs. Ricardo Rey, Lima, Peru, accompanying husband.

82 Ricardo Rey, Rector, University of Piura, Lima, Peru, to visit International Development Association.

83 Sheldon I. Wilpon, Electronic Engineer, U.S. Naval Applied Science Laboratory, Brooklyn, New York, to discuss with Navy officials communications system for deep-diving submarine rescue craft.

84 Milton Adelman, Supervisory Electronic Engineer, U.S. Naval Applied Science Laboratory, Brooklyn, New York, for same purpose as (83).

85 Romney Barnes, Research Assistant, The Economist Intelligence Unit, Ltd., New York City, to get information about iron-ore production from Bureau of Mines, Department of the Interior.

86 Henry A. Freedman, Staff Attorney, Center on Social Welfare Policy and Law, Columbia University, New York City, to attend U.S. Supreme Court hearing on case affecting welfare clients.

87 Joseph B. Bonney, Cargo Container Manager, Weyerhaeuser Company, wood-products firm, Gig Harbor, Washington, to confer with Army about cargo containers.

88 Henry C. Kahler, Flight Operation Specialist, Federal Aviation Agency, New York City, to confer with FAA about short-take-off-and-landing (STOL) and vertical-take-off-and-landing (VTOL) aircraft.

89 Sidney Knapp, Field Sales Manager, Consolidated Cigar Corp., New York City, on company business.

90 George P. Jacobson, General Manager for Transportation, Allied Chemical Corp., New York City, to attend meeting of U.S. Coast Guard's Merchant Marine Council and discuss regulations for transporting hazardous materials by water.

91 Robert L. Mitchell Jr., Secretary and Treasurer, Chlorine Institute, Inc., New York City, for same purpose as (90).

92 Thomas W. Gilbert, Principal Engineer, Maxson Electronics Corp., Great River, New York, for same purpose as (64).

93 T. L. Anderson, Regional Manager for South Africa, Worthington Alco Africa Ltd., diesel locomotive sales, Johannesburg, South Africa, to confer with Export-Import Bank and Department of Commerce.

94 W. C. Ballou, Director of International Sales, Alco Products, Inc., diesel locomotive manufacturers, New York City, same purpose as (93).

95 Joseph A. Gilman, Vice President for Sales, Fashion Fragrances Ltd., New York City, on company business.

96 Eugenio Gimenez, Vice President, Association for the Development of University Education, Lima, Peru, to visit several agencies.

97 Alberto Moncada, Professor, University of Piura, Lima, Peru, for same purpose as (96).

98 Raymond J. Weigele, General Operations Manager, United States Lines, Inc., New York City, to confer with Navy about use of cargo ships in Vietnam.

99 Ivan G. Owen, Comptroller, United States Lines, Inc., New York City, for same purpose as (98).

100 Jerome B. Gordon, Research Associate, Manpower and Population Program, Bureau of Applied Social Research, Columbia University, New York City, to consult with Research Analysis Corp., group sponsored by Defense Department.

101 Charles R. Eubank, Manager of Systems Projects, Bunker Ramo Corp., returning to McLean, Virginia, for Defense Department work.

102 Sidney Rait, President, Ivy Lee Ltd., clothing manufacturer, New York City, on company business.

103 David E. Scoll, attorney for Scoll & Coleman, New York City, to visit Department of the Interior and Congressman on behalf of client.

104 Mrs. Susan L. Jolliffe, McLean, Virginia, returning from personal trip to New York.

In the House of Representatives chamber in March 1965, President
Lyndon B. Johnson addresses a joint session of Congress. Joint
sessions provide a rare chance for the executive, legislative and
judicial branches to meet. Supreme Court Justices take front seats.

4

The Mighty
Federal Arm

"We, the people of the United States," the preamble to the Constitution reads, "in order to form a more perfect union, establish justice, insure domestic tranquillity, provide for the common defence, promote the general welfare, and secure the blessings of liberty to ourselves and our posterity, do ordain and establish this Constitution for the United States of America." Even in the summer of 1787 the objectives described were ambitious for a proposed government whose anatomy and functions could be described in six succinct Articles. These objectives have become no easier of attainment in the ensuing years, and the enormous contemporary apparatus designed for their pursuit would undoubtedly appall the 55 delegates who pieced out the framework of national cohesion in Philadelphia.

Yet for all its mass, the modern federal establishment is an aggregation not of boxes on an organization chart but of people. Every official,

from the President down to the head of an agency stenographic pool, enjoys certain powers whose limits are set both by the Constitution, statutes and precedent and by the resistance of those on whom the powers are exercised. This thrust-and-yield interaction that takes place every day among thousands of public servants is the basic process determining how the government actually works. It is a human acting out of the script furnished by the lawbooks, inexorably modifying the authors' intentions, sometimes in innocence but more frequently with deliberation. It is a drama whose cast —the Washington community—lives in fascinated self-scrutiny. Every morning they pore through *The Washington Post* with the zeal and devotion of a Muslim heeding the muezzin's call to prayer—the heavy brass searching among the editorials for clues of popular responses to policies, lawyers and lobbyists probing for indications of the set of the tides on which their clients' enterprises float, even the lowliest clerks and custodians reading columns like "The Federal Diary," which deals in such matters as pending pay raises and changes in civil service regulations. Drawn to the capital in the main by their own long-standing interest in the arts of rule and persuasion, the members of Washington officialdom remain self-conscious about the quality of their own performances and the public reaction to them.

Power begins with the lawmakers on the Hill. The two bodies whose chambers are on either side of the commanding white Capitol dome are separated by more than a rotunda and the prescriptions of Article One of the Constitution. The 435 members of the House of Representatives, elected every two years, are naturally more anonymous and more vulnerable to changing political winds than the 100 Senators who serve six-year terms. A visit to the House gallery confirms an impression of slightly, but only slightly, controlled disorder; in contrast, the Senate still possesses a rather Augustan aura. The semicircular rows of Representatives' chairs are spaced closely together in a style evocative of a college lecture room. The House chamber is rarely full, and the tourist who hopes to tingle at the sight of democracy in action usually sees only a scattering of men shuffling papers in and out of briefcases, a few chattering clusters in the aisles and a steady flow of traffic through the doors behind the Speaker's rostrum that lead to the lounges. Often enough the Speaker or the Congressman who is substituting for him is clearly paying not the slightest attention to the rhetoric of a member who has been given the floor. During a debate, access to the limited number of microphones, needed to make the legislators audible, is controlled by a manager on each side of the immediate issue. Speaking time is precisely measured and rigorously restricted, and a Congressman who may have just gotten up to cruising altitude with his argument is remorselessly shot down when the clock runs out. It is not a system that invites majestic oratory.

The Senate is less hurried and, as even a casual newspaper reader knows, defends its tradition of unlimited debate with ursine fury. Yet the Senate no longer is a theater of forensic display as it was in the days when fashionable Washington went to hear Daniel Webster. Too much is involved in legislation nowadays for Senators to be blown on or off a course by winds of eloquence. Debate merely formalizes, and votes record, a process of negotiation that is spread over many weeks in committee rooms, offices, corridors and restaurants. Roll calls

in both legislative bodies rarely leave anyone in suspense, and in the House they are a time-consuming chore, avoided whenever possible. (When the bill in question is not one of the major measures of a session, but provides for the construction of a toll bridge or forgives an Indian tribe on a reservation a delinquent irrigation charge, both the Senate and House frequently pass or reject the legislation by voice vote—members merely shout "Aye" or "No" as at a PTA meeting.)

The decline of serious debate in Congress is not necessarily symptomatic of a loss of democratic vitality. The fact is simply that a two-house legislature with a total of 535 members, representing some 200 million people, cannot be a town meeting. Only a fraction of the public business can be dealt with on the floor, and even that snippet cannot be selected by a shouting contest for the attention of the Speaker or the Vice President. It is the standing committees that sift, weigh and funnel proposed actions. They decide what bills get to the floor and in what shape. They can be prodded (but only so far) by a determined President who has patent public backing and good control of his party. Even then, committee chairmen are apt to take their private readings of popular opinion and party need and walk their own paths.

The power of the House committees was recognized as long ago as 1910, when the Speaker appointed their chairmen and members and was thus a virtual parliamentary czar. A revolt of Republican insurgents and Democrats at that time took this power away from Speaker Joseph G. "Uncle Joe" Cannon of Illinois and gave it to the party caucuses. The new practice of following seniority in awarding chairmanships has made many committee chairmen with long terms of service from safe districts (notably Democrats in the South) into important powers in their own right when their party has a majority. They preside over their hearing rooms like feudal lords, with assured tenure and the knowledge that the sponsors of any legislative program must pay appropriate political tribute before the committee will release a bill and permit it to go to a vote on the floor of the House. Autocrats of the Hill, the chairmen are clothed with powers nowhere precisely described in the Constitution. But the lesson that Washington teaches to anyone who examines its daily rounds with care is one well expressed by Douglass Cater, a reporter who has also served as a White House assistant: "American government operates under a living, not a literal, Constitution." It must not be read "the way a hardshell Baptist reads his Bible."

Each Congressman serves on several committees. Aiding him in his committee work and other duties are his Congressional staff members and assistants. He is given a budget for hiring such helpers and may increase their number at his own expense to whatever extent he chooses. They work in one of the five massive office buildings—two for the Senate and three for the House—that flank the Capitol. The size and elegance of a Congressman's office suite depend on his seniority. (The gleaming new Rayburn Building is not for a Representative serving his first term.)

On every Congressman's staff is an Administrative Assistant who, along with other duties, is charged with responsibility for "casework." Casework is Congressional bread and butter, and it is nothing more glamorous than helping constituents transact business with the federal bureaucracy. Civics textbooks do not dignify it with so much as a paragraph. It is, nevertheless, a better indicator of what people and government are to each other than any quantity of academic prose could fashion. On a typical January morning in the mid-1960s the Administrative Assistant to an upstate New York Congressman dealt with some 40 letters. A random sample of their subject matter included an old woman's request for an expedited Social Security check; a parental petition to have a sole remaining son reassigned from combat duty to the United States; queries on how to qualify for government life insurance, Medicare and a pension; a plea for help in getting a European relative over a medical hurdle in the path of his immigration to America; a township's bid for a new post office; a big-city school system's application for a grant from the Department of Health, Education, and Welfare; a church youth group's polite hint that they would like a flag for their meeting room from the Congressman's own hand.

Each request was forwarded to the Congressional liaison office maintained by the appropriate federal agency, and a pleasant note about the action taken was sent by the Administrative Assistant to the constituent. In due time the Congressman's office received an answer from the agency, and another letter was sent to the petitioner offering congratulations, advice or consolation as circumstances warranted.

The Administrative Assistant explained to a visitor that the handling of such matters was not a distraction from the Congressman's work, undertaken to win votes. "The citizen today has no notion of how to get his problems through the labyrinth of the federal government," he said. "Guid-

For most of the period (1903-1911) that Joseph G. "Uncle Joe" Cannon served as Speaker of the House, he dominated the body through his authority to appoint committee chairmen. The House took that power away in 1910 and gave it to the party caucus.

ing him *is* a big part of his representative's legitimate work." And watching the office staff at work—typing, telephoning, dodging streams of visitors and messengers, piling notes between coffee cups and full ashtrays—an onlooker does get a sense of living connection between the faceless millions of the citizenry and their elected servants in Washington. Popular government seems, after all, to have something to do with people.

But popular government also has to do with the structure and personalities of Congress itself, and how successful a legislator is in gaining acceptance of the measures he wants passed is largely dependent upon how well he can function within the established framework. The homework of the lawmaker includes much more than familiarity with the facts of his case, which the Legislative Reference Service will willingly provide for him. He must also establish rapport with the many power centers that can generate unfriendly vibrations. Within Congress itself these will include the leadership of his own party and of the opposition, and individual members, particularly if they are committee chairmen or ranking minority members, whose own interests are affected. The Congressman undertakes much of this spadework with patience and meticulous respect for the necessary courtesies expected by the sometimes leisurely leadership. Master builders of consensus like the late Speaker Sam Rayburn or the onetime Senator Lyndon Johnson cannot be rushed in their work.

It is also necessary for the Congressman to make contact with all the federal agencies and offices that may have a stake in the proposal. A measure involving the control of strikes in the transportation industry, for instance, casts a shadow over the jealously protected "turf" of the Commerce, Labor, Transportation and Justice Departments and a host of independent agencies. The Congressman must have some idea of which bureau chiefs will be affected, how they are likely to react, and what their pipelines are to their own department heads, to the White House, to the press and, most of all, to the key committees.

Then, too, press reaction to his proposal must be screened and the mimeographed releases of lobbies for and against the measure weighed in relation to the handwritten letters from aroused voters at home.

Although the decision to charge ahead, delay or retreat is ultimately his, the Congressman must place heavy reliance upon his Legislative Assistant, who aids him in handling the staggering amount of detail work involved in the passage of legislation. Among other jobs, the Legislative Assistant compresses masses of information into brief memos, uses his contacts in the various departments and on Capitol Hill to remove hurdles faced by the lawmaker's bill, and generally serves as adviser, listener and nursemaid to the harried Congressman. The Legislative Assistant must be unusually dedicated, willing to work with little reference to the clock, to waiting dinners or missed dates. Yet he must be capable of greeting a hometown tourist who drops unannounced into the office as if his visit were an unutterably welcome event.

The reward of these staff assistants is conscious proximity to the action, salaries probably not equal to what they could earn outside the government, and an awareness of contribution. The Congressman who has ideas of doing more than running errands for his constituents faces difficulties enough to begin with. He must balance the demands of conscience, constituency, country and party. In addition, the formidable latticework of Congressional procedure discourages the nonenergetic; it seems designed to prevent legislation. The wonder is that Congressmen do as much as they do, and it would be impossible for them to do anything without their staffs, a fact known to staff members. "Everybody up here," said one Legislative Assistant watching hundreds like him snatch a quick lunch in the House cafeteria, "whether he actually writes the Congressman's speeches or mails out calendars with his man's picture on them, thinks he helps to run the government."

About a mile away from the Capitol (and sometimes it seems to be the world's longest mile) sits the White House, the world's most publicized, peeped at and pictorialized single-family residence. The incongruous marriage of past simplicity and present global involvement that shapes so much of Washington's life flourishes here. The house at 1600 Pennsylvania Avenue remains in theory a private home loaned by the people to their chief magistrate for his use while in office. Time was when any citizen could affirm his share of ownership by dropping in to call on the President at his desk. Those days are gone, but John Doe may still line up with his family in the morning, Tuesday through Saturday, and be shown free through the great rooms of state on the main floor.

But the White House is also the business address of the man who is ceremonially and operatively the top executive of the world's most powerful state. This fact alone makes the Presidential presence in Washington a major force in the city's style. The community is always aware of the might embodied in the office because it is so spectacularly visible. The long, black, chauffeured limousines are constantly pulling into the driveway with their assorted distinguished passengers. The lords temporal of the Congress alight under the handsome portico, as do the chiefs of the Armed Forces, the very biggest wheels of the agencies, the editors, the industrialists, and the political experts whose faces and voices are seen and heard each week on millions of television receivers. With appropriate ruffles and flourishes the diplomatic visitors arrive and run the gantlet of thrusting microphones and cameras. Some of the guests are prime ministers of superpowers, some are the tin-pot kings of exiguous client states carved out of oil-rich sands or strategic jungle. In either case their arrival is an event that sets flags flying on Pennsylvania Avenue and lights the Executive Mansion windows with the blaze of formal dinners.

At any hour, moreover, the President may command attention. Expectancy of his needs dictates the lives of a sizable collection of people. Helicopters must stand ready to whisk him from the lawn of the White House to the Presidential airplane at Andrews Air Force Base on brief notice. Top reporters spend hours in the White House press room waiting hopefully for him to originate a printable item. A technical crew can have him on national radio and television within a relatively few moments. Even without the hard reminder of the ultimate, awesome power of the office—the communications device that can signal the Strategic Air Command to obliterate much of the world—the Presidency overshadows the capital in a way that removes this generation light-years from the March morning in 1801 when Thomas Jefferson walked unobtrusively from his boardinghouse to the Capitol to be inaugurated.

The growth of responsibilities and awesome power of the Presidency over the years is reflected in the ever-increasing number of departments in the Executive Office and in the large numbers of assistants now required on the White House staff. As long ago as 1902 a west wing had to be added to the White House to accommodate the additional clerks and secretaries needed by Theodore Roosevelt. Forty years later, when cousin Franklin lived at the same address, the east wing was built to provide space for the personnel of the recently created Executive Office of the President. This body today includes the Bureau of the Budget, the Council of Economic Advisers, the National Security Council, plus other sometimes overlapping advisory councils and commissions and the hosts of civil servants who keep them operating. Under Johnson the number was about 4,700 and had long since overflowed into the ornate building next door on 17th Street, once home to the State, War and Navy Departments.

Certain agencies of the Executive Office are under the control of the President but beyond his personal supervision partly by reason of their size—the Central Intelligence Agency and the Office of Economic Opportunity, for examples. But the White House corps of assistants itself is a different matter. These are the figures often seen around the President as he goes through his working day—the press secretaries and social secretaries for himself and the First Lady, his physician, his military aides, his personal secretary, his administrative assistants. Despite their sometimes modest-sounding titles, they all have offices, deputies and secretaries in their own right. In addition there are those who go by the catchall title of Special Assistant to the President. Their jobs and their backgrounds are numerous and variegated but boil down essentially to being extra eyes, ears and hands for their chief. Their basic qualification, in the words of an old Washington hand, is "intelligent loyalty plus a feeling that it is thrilling to work fourteen hours a day for the President." They may be veterans of the President's entourage drawn from his own days as a governor or Senator, they may be personal friends, or they may be distinguished men from academic life on special assignment, as were so many of President Kennedy's advisers. They can have a great deal to do with the Presidential image on the Hill or in the press, depending upon their own powers of lubricating friction points between VIPs and reporters and the White House.

The Presidential assistants can rarely hope to be universally loved as life goes on in Washington, however. Inevitably their proximity to the boss provokes jealousy, and their channel to his ear is eagerly sought after by innumerable petitioners. Since they must refuse a vast majority of such requests—their job fundamentally being to relieve the President of burdens, not to bring him fresh problems—they make enemies. A classic case was Sherman Adams, Eisenhower's chief administrative assistant. As Eisenhower was particularly anxious to deal only with issues that had already been prepared for his decision by Adams, the one-time New Hampshire governor got into a position in which he appeared able to determine what questions raised anywhere in the government received White House attention. Some said that this was tantamount to the exercise of the Presidency itself. When Adams was forced to resign by the revelation that he had accepted modest favors from a businessman of questionable ethics—essentially a trivial offense—there was scarcely a mourner at his official funeral.

The Presidential assistants are likely to prove acutely abrasive to Congressmen, particularly to the seniority-rich rulers of special provinces like armed services and foreign trade relations. When a measure of special interest to the President comes before such a committee, it is often the duty of an assistant to call these touchy, independent chieftains to explain how a particular vote would please the Chief Executive. How much pressure the assistant can apply depends on a number of factors, including how many of the lawmaker's political IOUs are held by the President. But whether or not the assistant is successful, he is not likely to endear himself to the legislator.

The bureaucrats toiling for the Executive departments are likely to find the assistants even more vexatious, for the White House personnel must often bring tidings of Presidential impatience with the slowness with which pet projects are moving. It is one of the ironies of the Presidency that, for all its power, it can be the victim of its own bulging complexity. Just as the legislative will of a Congressional majority can be crippled by delaying tactics in the committees, or just as a fully authorized program can be pinched and bruised by the failure of the legislature to provide it with funds, so implementation of a Presidential decision can be retarded by officials whose delaying tactics have been developed by years of experience. A veteran bureau chief can build himself a satrapy into which intruders venture at their own risk. A real expert can muster enough allies in Congress and out to be largely unassailable. No President has the time to pursue his own purposes to final fulfillment through the maze of committees, subcommittees, and departments within departments that honeycomb the Cabinet and the Executive Office. It is a lesson a President soon learns. Political scientist Richard E. Neustadt tells a story of Harry S. Truman, in his last months of office, discoursing from behind his desk on the sad future that awaited his successor. "He'll sit here," said Truman, "and he'll say 'Do this! Do that!' *And nothing will happen. Poor Ike—it won't be a bit like the Army. He'll find it very frustrating.*"

To keep such frustration at the lowest possible level, the Presidential assistant must be on constant call—and that means 24 hours daily within reach of a telephone. He must draft papers, attend committee meetings, absorb for instant retrieval from his head voluminous masses of information (including the whims, peculiarities, marital problems and liquor-holding ability of strategically placed officials), and be able to identify the key log in any jam in a department within his area of operation. And that area may change overnight at the President's request. The President will generally be too busy to thank him for whatever he has done and often explosively critical of what he cannot do. The Special Assistant to the President has what seems to be a dramatic and prestigious official life, but it is likely to be a short and intense one.

Existence is somewhat easier for another handful of men unique to Washington. These are the wise and gray lawyers and ex-officials who have learned their way around, have proved their judgment, and are called on by the President for quick advice or immediate access to past experience or a mission demanding special credentials. They have helped to draft press releases in midnight sessions, and they have dropped whatever business they had on hand to board planes for Moscow or New Delhi, Geneva or Saigon on the strength of a call from the White House. They give this expertise in return for no visible price in titles or salaries, although the prestige they gain may have some effect on their private affairs. One such former adviser, however, said that he doubted his own role as occasional

counselor to Truman, Kennedy and Johnson had enhanced his practice. If he had attempted to use influence on behalf of a client, he avers, he would have destroyed his standing with any President worth helping.

It is ultimately in the anthills of the administrative departments and agencies that the true character of District life is found. As the more than 300,000 civil servants constitute the essence, the soul of the city, so their own ruling preoccupations are molded to the blueprints of their particular bureaucracies. Merely to list the commissions, boards and authorities under each of the 12 Cabinet departments is to acquire an immediate sense of the pervasiveness of government—and of government workers—in the computerized, urbanized, subsidized and relentlessly analyzed society of the late 20th Century. And running down an alphabetical list of the independent agencies—those not under the jurisdiction of a Cabinet officer—awakens echoes of dormant and nearly forgotten historical battle fronts. There is the Atomic Energy Commission, born in the immediate post-World War II quest for the peaceful harnessing of nuclear power; a few names later we are at the Civil Service Commission, fighting the spoilsmen in the 1880s; then on past the National Labor Relations Board

GRADE	SALARY RANGE	OCCUPATION AND AVERAGE GRADE LEVEL			
GS-1	$3,889-5,057	Accountant	GS-11	Internal Revenue Agent	GS-11
GS-2	4,231-5,501	Agricultural Commodity Grader	GS-9	Librarian	GS-9
GS-3	4,600-5,981	Air Traffic Controller	GS-11	Messenger	GS-2
GS-4	5,145-6,684	Archeologist	GS-11	Meteorologist	GS-11
GS-5	5,732-7,456	Attorney	GS-13	Museum Curator	GS-12
GS-6	6,321-8,221	Cartographer	GS-11	Naval Architect	GS-12
GS-7	6,981-9,078	Civil Engineer	GS-11	Park Ranger	GS-8
GS-8	7,699-10,012	Clerk Typist	GS-3	Patent Examiner	GS-12
GS-9	8,462-11,000	Computer Programmer	GS-11	Physicist	GS-12
GS-10	9,297-12,087	Cryptographer	GS-11	Plant Pest Control Technician	GS-5
GS-11	10,203-13,263	Customs Inspector	GS-9	Psychologist	GS-12
GS-12	12,174-15,828	Economist	GS-12	Secretary	GS-5
GS-13	14,409-18,729	FBI Agent	GS-11	Social Insurance Claims Examiner	GS-9
GS-14	16,946-22,031	Fingerprint Identifier	GS-5	Statistician	GS-12
GS-15	19,780-25,711	Fish Hatchery Manager	GS-9	Surveyor	GS-5
GS-16	22,835-28,923	Forest Fire Control Worker	GS-5	Telephone Operator	GS-3
GS-17	26,264-29,764	Game Warden	GS-9	U.S. Marshal	GS-8
GS-18	30,239	Guard	GS-4	Wage and Hour Law Administrator	GS-11

and the Tennessee Valley Authority flavored in name with the 1930s idealism of the New Deal; and, near the very bottom, the Veterans Administration, whose 170,000-man work force and seven-billion-dollar budget are reminders of the wry comment of Mr. Dooley—the creation of newspaper columnist Finley Peter Dunne—on being told that the Spanish-American War was over: "Th' part ye see in th' pitcher pa-apers is over, but th' tax collector will continyoo his part iv th' war with relentless fury!"

Both kinds of agencies—independent and Cabinet-affiliated—deal with aviation and the merchant marine, with banking and irrigation, with railroad labor relations and conservation of timber, with problems of the 19th Century and the 21st— the settlement of Indian claims and the conquest of space. They range in size from the mammoth Defense Department, with more than 1.25 million *civilian* employees around the world, to the Federal Coal Mine Safety Board of Review, which is listed as the employer of nine persons. They can be loosely classed as regulatory (like the Federal Power Commission or the Civil Aeronautics Board), scientific (like the National Aeronautics and Space Administration), economic (like the Federal Reserve System) or quasi-military (like the Central Intelligence Agency). But there is in fact a tremendous overlapping of their functions, which is one reason why an incalculable number of officials spend their time on the mysterious process known as "coordinating."

The huge Defense establishment is the classic example of a department grown into a subgovernment, with a bureaucracy so large and so intricately organized that its denizens more than elected officials determine what gets done. In the late 1960s, Defense was spending more than $75 billion each year on enterprises that, among other things, formed the economic foundations of many communities and vitally nourished a number of universities. The Washington brain box of this leviathan, the Pentagon, is appropriately enormous. Defense public-relations officials like to point out that it is the world's largest office building, has 17.5 miles of corridors, provides doctors, dentists, nurses, chapels, and banking, shopping, and postal services for its nearly 30,000 civilian and military workers, and is equipped with its own bus terminal, heliport, printing plant and typewriter repair facility, plus a section for pulping waste paper.

The size alone of the subgovernment forms a tremendous barrier between the snap of command by officials at the top and the click of execution by subalterns at the bottom. The bureaucracy often fails to get the word—sometimes intentionally. In the Defense Department's particular case, the bureaucracy's power is magnified by the intricacy of command arrangements within the Pentagon walls and the fiercely guarded independence of each of the three services. The Army, Navy and Air Force maintain wholly separate sections devoted to research, intelligence, personnel and procurement, and each section in each service is a sponge of subsections. Anyone who interferes with this independence of operation meets tremendous resistance. The efforts of various Secretaries of Defense to secure better interservice cooperation and economy have been blocked for years, not only by the overt resistance of generals and admirals working in tight formation with allies on the Armed Services Committees and in the defense industries' lobbies, but also by the simple fact that any decision to change procedures must make its way through layers of coordinating committees, review boards and allocations officers, each equipped with the power of obstruction. Nor is this difficulty peculiar to the military. An examination of the problems of the war on poverty in 1966 showed that its various programs were carved up among so many federal departments and agencies dealing with labor, construction, conservation, housing, education and credit—some 21 in all, to say nothing of the role of 50 state, 3,000 county and innumerable local governments—that the hardest task of administration was simply to know where to lay hands on money that Congress had already voted.

Such problems underscore the tremendous importance of the veteran civil servant, the maligned bureaucrat, in the scheme of government. Given the interlocking nature of agency operations, it is inevitable that business proceeds by a process of "moving paper" from in box to in box—initialing, duplicating, buck slipping, reproducing, foldering, filing, verifying, channeling. The federal government spends up to $3.5 million annually on pencils, paper clips and mimeograph paper, and needs it all. Amid these whirring wheels the standout man is the old hand who knows the parts— where messages can be "lost" for weeks, which secretary will get a document in and out of her superior's office quickly, who must be sweet-talked into action, who can be bullied, who is impossible to deal with. Knowledge of this kind can be acquired only through years of experience. Seniority is as precious in the civil service as in the Congressional committee room; it is reflected not only in the pay raises and longer accumulated leaves,

the larger offices and such minor prerogatives as reading the newspaper openly on office time and having coffee brought to the desk, but also in that knowledge which is power. Presidents and their Cabinet secretaries and agency chairmen come and go, but office autocrats stay on, to help or hinder with the process indissolubly linked in the Washington vocabulary with "coordination," namely, "implementation." Speeches and publicized drives are launched from the top, but policy—foreign, military, racial, economic—changes at the pace of the clerks and superclerks in State, Defense, Justice, Commerce and the other departments.

The civil servant's life is ringed by regulations that he has learned to approach with caution and respect, but he is not always a colorless caricature. The differing departments have distinguishable styles. In the cafeterias serving the personnel of the economic organizations (Export-Import Bank, International Monetary Fund, Bureau of the Budget) one may see as many copies of *The Wall Street Journal* as on Wall Street. The attaché case is as much in vogue in the neighborhood of the Justice Department as it once was on Madison Avenue, and the younger lawyers wear their correct suits with just a touch of dash. Those who work for the supersecret CIA or the National Security Agency, in their respective hideaways in Langley, Virginia, and Fort Meade, Maryland, tend to affect a tight-lipped air. They had better: ironclad security regulations are drummed into them from the moment they begin work, and they tend to cluster together at parties so that if beans are inadvertently spilled, they will at least land in a family lap.

Each morning the tides of traffic flow into the parking lots of the office buildings, and the rivers of paper soon thereafter begin their flow from desk to desk. At 5 o'clock, except in certain emergency-oriented headquarters, the process is reversed. The folders come to rest in file cabinets, and the human streams leave the domes and columns and pediments of official architecture behind them and inch home to suburban gardens, tired wives, noisy children and waiting suppers. It seems a shadow show on some days. Yet power is there; shifting, diffuse, now dissolving and now coagulating under the coaxing of experts, but always there. Decisions somehow squeeze through the pores of the system. This fact is what sustains Washington's faith in its own importance and makes aspiring politicians scorn conventional delights and live laborious days. This faith that the chosen few can affect the nation's destiny is the nutriment of the capital's often weary human tissues.

Legislating for the United States

PART 1: THE MEN WHO MAKE THE LAWS

Of the numerous bills introduced in Congress each year, a surprisingly large percentage are formulated by people not in the legislative branch. During the 90th Congress (1967-1968), for example, about two thirds of the major bills that came before Congress were part of the Administration's legislative program, drawn up by staff members of executive departments. Coordinating this effort were the President's Special Assistant, Joseph Califano Jr., and his staff *(below)*. Many of the remaining one third originated with private-interest groups. Both they and the executive branch have lobbyists who press for passage of favored measures placed in the Congressional hoppers. But the final legislative power still rests with the Congressmen. Only they can introduce, pass, change and vote down bills. Some of the key people in this complex process are shown on the following pages.

Photographs by Steinbicker / Houghton

Writing bills for the Administration

Much of the actual drafting of Administration bills is done in the various departments and agencies of the executive branch, each working in its own field. The legislative staff of the Department of the Interior *(left, bottom)*, for example, formulates proposed laws concerned with such matters as Indian affairs and mineral resources. But a central role in the legislative activities of the executive branch is performed by the Bureau of the Budget on behalf of the President. For part of the Administration of Lyndon B. Johnson, the bureau was headed by Charles J. Zwick, shown in the center of the upper group flanked by his deputy, Phillip S. Hughes *(left),* and an assistant, Wilfred H. Rommel. For the beginning of each session of Congress the bureau draws up a budget at the President's request. This budget, which includes estimates of monies needed for forthcoming legislation as well as for existing programs, provides Congress with a comprehensive outline of the President's program. The bureau also reviews requests from the executive departments for legislation not included in the program, and decides whether the proposals are in line with it. The bureau even examines important bills drawn up by individual Congressmen and recommends Presidential support or opposition.

But the Administration's influence—through the bureau—does not end there. For instance, most bills considered by a Congressional committee are sent to the executive departments that would be affected by the measure if passed; and the department's report must then be reviewed by the bureau before going back to Congress. "No" from either can severely handicap the bill, especially if the President's party has a majority in Congress.

"Lobbyists" for the executive branch

Once an important Administration-backed bill is introduced in Congress, two coordinating teams of "lobbyists"—one representing the President, the other the executive department concerned—seek to influence Congressmen to pass it. During the latter part of Lyndon B. Johnson's Administration, liaison between the White House and Congress was supervised by Legislative Counsel Harold Barefoot Sanders Jr. *(left, top)*. Each member of his staff *(left, bottom)* concentrated on either House or Senate measures. Each week Sanders' group discussed strategy with their counterparts from the executive departments concerned with pending legislation.

In addition to attempting to influence individual legislators, representatives of executive departments, often including Secretaries, also testify before Congressional committees on the merits of proposed legislation. Usually the job of preparing the material for this kind of testimony is assigned to an assistant in charge of legislation, who also functions as a direct lobbyist. During the Johnson Administration, the man who held this post in the Department of Health, Education, and Welfare was Ralph K. Huitt Jr. *(right)*, an Assistant Secretary. With the aid of his staff *(below)*, he served as principal adviser to the Secretary in legislative matters along with carrying out his functions as lobbyist. Announced President Johnson just after Huitt's appointment, "We're going to feed him to Congress."

HEALTH
EDUCATION
AND
WELFARE

Representing private interests

In addition to the men and women who seek to influence Congress in behalf of the Administration's legislative program, there are more than a thousand organizations and individuals who are operating as lobbyists for private interests, plus many times that number engaged in the same activity but not registered. (Because of ambiguous language in the law, many actual lobbies, like the National Rifle Association, are not required to register.) The clients of these official and unofficial lobbies range from the wealthy Association of American Railroads to the modestly financed Animal Health Institute. But all are in Washington for a single purpose: to influence legislation.

The five U.S. Chamber of Commerce lobbyists *(below)* are among the most powerful in Washington. Attempting to influence Congressmen directly is only one of their functions. Like most big lobbies today, the Chamber maintains a sizable research staff to provide lawmakers with facts and figures on issues of concern to the Chamber. Because Congressmen often use lobby-furnished data in committee meetings and floor debate, great care is taken to provide accurate information.

Like all registered lobbies, the Chamber representatives must report all monies spent "directly" to influence legislation—from office rent to cab fares. But lobbies that spend money to drum up grassroots pressure on Congressmen or to retain experts to prepare Congressional testimony need not account for such indirect disbursements. According to one study, lobbies spent $18 billion between 1947 and 1964, but less than $100 million (barely one half of 1 per cent) was reported

The busy life of a Congressman

Although the executive branch and private-interest groups may draft proposed legislation and attempt to influence Congress, final power of life or death for any bill still rests with duly elected Senators and Representatives. They can even override a Presidential veto with a two-thirds majority in both houses.

The average Congressman is a hard-working man. Republican Representative Frank Horton *(left)*, from New York's 36th District, for example, spends an average of 80 hours a week at his job. About one third of this time is spent on immediate legislative matters—drafting bills, studying measures before his committees and becoming familiar with bills on which he must vote. Much of the remaining time is used for handling constituents' problems, meeting lobbyists, working on magazine articles and preparing speeches. During an average month while Congress is in session, he makes at least 20 radio broadcasts and another 20 television appearances.

Horton receives an annual allowance of about $95,000 from the government to pay his staff members *(below)*, who not only do routine chores like answering his mail—some 700 letters per week—but, in the case of his Legislative and Administrative Assistants, help Horton in the drafting of legislative proposals. During recent years Horton has introduced some 100 bills in each session of Congress. Even if a bill is first drawn up by a lobby or civic organization, most Senators and Representatives prefer to reword the measure in their own terms. If a Congressman requires additional assistance in the drafting of a bill, he can call on the Office of the Legislative Counsel maintained by Congress and request a new version drawn to his specifications.

The powerful standing committees

Most of the important work in Congress takes place in its standing committees—16 in the Senate and 20 in the House. The two sets of committees roughly parallel one another in areas of responsibility—armed services, banking and currency, for example—and when a Senator or Representative introduces a bill, it is sent for comprehensive study to the appropriate committee in either the Senate or House. The committees are empowered to hold public hearings to evaluate a bill's benefits and drawbacks, and to change the measure in any way they choose.

In general, committees are made up of men with backgrounds or interest in the field in which they will be working, or who come from states most likely to be affected by the bills they study. Thus during the 90th Congress, the Senate Agriculture and Forestry Committee *(right)* included mostly men from farm states under Chairman Allen Ellender of Louisiana *(fifth from right)*.

The chairmen of committees, who can usually expedite or bottle up legislation, are among the most influential men in Washington. Although committee chairmen are theoretically named by the majority party in each house, by ironclad custom the party selects the Senators and Representatives with the longest committee tenure.

One of the most powerful of these men is the Chairman of the House Appropriations Committee, a post held during the 90th Congress by George H. Mahon *(left)* of Texas. His committee reviews the Administration's budgetary requests and can block or trim any appropriations asked for.

The men who guide the legislative process on Capitol Hill and who largely govern its speed, productivity and smoothness of operation are the Congressional party chieftains: the Majority and Minority Leaders in the Senate, the Speaker and Minority Leader in the House of Representatives.

Although both houses of Congress have a high proportion of members who often ignore the policies of their respective parties, the leaders still have considerable power over their fellow legislators. Not only are the leaders the prime voices in making committee appointments—a vital matter to all Congressmen—but in the case of the majority party in the Senate, the head men normally determine the order in which bills come to the floor for debate and vote.

During the 90th Congress, the Majority Leader in the Senate was Democrat Mike Mansfield of Montana *(second from left)*; the Speaker of the House was Democrat John W. McCormack of Massachusetts *(third from left)*. Because the President was also a Democrat, they had the job of getting his legislation through Congress. If a Republican had been President, the task would have been assumed by the Minority Leaders.

During that same Congressional session, Illinois Everett Dirksen *(far left)* and Michigan's Gerald Ford *(far right)* were the Minority Leaders in the Senate and House respectively. A Minority Leader's most important legislative job is to influence the members of his party to vote as a solid bloc and thus improve their bargaining position with the majority. His power is particularly manifest whenever the opposition is divided and the Majority Leader needs his support.

How these political forces contend with each other to arrive at a compromise is described in Part 2 of this essay, which begins on page 109.

The kings of Capitol Hill

Legislating for the United States

PART 2: THE STORY OF A LAW

When a proposed law is introduced in the House of Representatives or the Senate, it faces a long and tortuous journey through the legislative process, a journey often filled with maddening obstacles, frustrating delays and bitter conflicts. The fate of the bill—whether it will be approved or rejected, accepted as written or changed by amendments—is often determined away from the limelight. Although there are frequently exciting happenings on the floor of the House or Senate, much of the important action occurs in Congressional committee meetings, in the offices of influential Senators and Representatives, in the cloakrooms of the two houses, in private conferences between lobbyists and legislators, and between Administration representatives and lawmakers. The actual voting in the House and Senate is often a mere formalizing of agreements reached elsewhere.

The federal legislative process functioned in this typical fashion when Congress was considering the so-called Civil Rights Act of 1968. The original bill, designated H.R. (for House of Representatives) 2516, was introduced in the House on January 17, 1967, by Congressman Emmanuel Celler. Some 15 months later, and after major modifications that vastly broadened its scope, it was finally signed by President Lyndon B. Johnson and became law.

What follows is the story of H.R. 2516's dramatic and key passage by the Senate. It is based largely on reports filed at the time by Neil MacNeil of the TIME-LIFE News Service in Washington.

The original bill. Congressman Celler was acting at the request of the Johnson Administration when he introduced the civil rights measure in the House of Representatives in January of 1967. The primary purpose of the bill was to provide federal protection for civil rights workers who were being harassed in the South. Penalties were prescribed for acts of violence or intimidation employed against "any person because of his race, color, religion, political affiliation, or national origin" while he was exercising such rights as campaigning for public office, serving on a jury, or encouraging or assisting others to exercise those rights.

Compared with other civil rights legislation that had been passed in recent sessions of Congress, the Celler bill was not of major importance, and it aroused no great furor in the House. Trailing nine amendments, none of which seriously weakened it, H.R. 2516 was approved by a 327-93 vote on August 16. Now the measure was sent to the Senate.

If the bill had remained unchanged, it probably would have received more or less routine Senate approval as well. But a highly controversial amendment was to be proposed that would touch off a conflict of major proportions. Other Senate business was to be sidelined for weeks as the battle raged on the Senate floor, in Senators' offices and wherever the legislators came into contact. There were to be internecine fights in both the Republican and Democratic camps; political and personal loyalties would be strained. Opposing lobbies were to match power, and the Administration would use its own leverage.

But there was nothing to foreshadow the coming struggle as H.R. 2516 encountered its first Senate obstacle, the Judiciary Committee. Like all

On January 15, 1968, Richard Russell of Georgia takes the Senate floor to attack a mild civil rights bill, H.R. 2516, previously passed by the House. Majority Leader Mike Mansfield *(right)* and Minority Leader Everett Dirksen *(left)* listen from their seats. Easy passage of H.R. 2516 was expected, but controversial amendments were to plunge the Senate into eight weeks of debate and negotiations.

such committees, Judiciary is empowered to hold hearings, amend a measure or even rewrite it from scratch. But H.R. 2516 experienced little opposition or delay. On November 2 the committee approved the bill with some minor changes. Now a motion could be made to bring up the bill for debate on the floor.

Senator Mike Mansfield of Montana, floor leader of the Democratic majority, took that step on December 15, the last day of the 1967 Congressional session, and moved that the bill "become the pending business for next year." His motion was approved.

When the 90th Congress reconvened on Monday, January 15, 1968, H.R. 2516 was the Senate's first order of business. But this session was brief; only Richard Russell of Georgia and Louisiana's Russell Long, both opponents of the bill, had time to speak before adjournment. For a number of reasons the real debate did not begin until Thursday, January 18.

Long, Russell, Sam Ervin of North Carolina and Florida's Spessard Holland were among a number of Southern Senators who took up most of that session inveighing against the bill.

The next day Senator Ervin proposed an amendment that would have gutted the bill. Now there was fuel for still more speeches by Northerners as well as Southerners, and day after day they went on. Finally on February 6 there was a motion to table (i.e., kill) the Ervin amendment; it carried by a 54-29 vote.

Everyone knew that vast amounts of oratory would still take place—even if it were not listened to—before a vote would come on H.R. 2516, but there seemed little prospect of a major filibuster; the bill was simply not important enough to evoke such tactics. Even the Administration seemed only mildly concerned with the measure.

A new turn. But a bombshell was about to be dropped that would change everything. Immediately after the defeat of the Ervin amendment, Democrat Walter Mondale of Minnesota rose to offer another, this one jointly sponsored by himself and Republican Edward Brooke of Massachusetts. If the Mondale-Brooke amendment were adopted by the Senate and the House concurred, H.R. 2516 would become one of the most sweeping pieces of civil rights legislation ever passed by the U.S. Congress.

The Mondale-Brooke amendment would prohibit "discrimination on account of race, color, religion or national origin in the purchase, rental, financing and occupancy of housing," and provide means for federal enforcement. Unlike Celler's bill, which would have affected the South almost exclusively, the amendment would hit every section of the nation. "Gentlemen's agreements" to exclude Negroes and other minority

groups—unwritten pacts that exist in certain neighborhoods all over America—would not only be invalid but subject to dissolution by law.

This was not the first time the Senate had been faced with a so-called "open housing" measure. In 1966 an omnibus civil rights bill that included an open housing section had come to the Senate floor after being passed by the House. It had been filibustered to death—the filibuster succeeding largely because the Minority Leader, Senator Everett Dirksen, had felt an open housing law was unconstitutional and would not rally Republican Senators in support of cloture, the cutting off of debate. The Administration's own open housing bill had been introduced in the Senate in March of 1967, but it was being held up in the Banking and Currency Committee. To circumvent this roadblock, Mondale and Brooke had simply adapted the wording of the committee-held act to their amendment, thus making sure open housing would come before the Senate as a whole.

This plan for bypassing the Banking and Currency Committee had been put forward by a lobbying organization known as the Leadership Conference on Civil Rights (LCCR), a coalition of 115 national organizations, including the AFL-CIO and the NAACP, that specializes in promoting legislation benefiting minority groups. LCCR officials had been eager to have some open housing measure come before the Senate, even if it failed. They had reasoned that the mood of the Senate must be tested before strategy could be devised in pressing for additional civil rights legislation. In December 1967 representatives of the LCCR had approached several Senators sympathetic to the civil rights cause and advanced the action-through-amendment proposal. Mondale had agreed to introduce the amendment. He had then sought and received the collaboration of Brooke (the Senate's lone Negro member), thus assuring bipartisan support for the measure. Later Brooke and Mondale had called on Philip Hart of Michigan, floor manager of H.R. 2516, to solicit his support. Hart assented, and the three discussed tactics.

The Mondale-Brooke amendment was introduced on Tuesday afternoon, February 6, the day the Ervin amendment was defeated, and released another flood of debate. Ten days later there was still no action, and Majority Leader Mansfield tried to get the Senate off

Seeking support for an open housing amendment to H.R. 2516, Senators Edward Brooke *(left)* and Walter Mondale *(standing)* and an aide meet with Michigan's Philip Hart *(right)* during the Senate's Christmas recess. Hart, who is to be floor manager for the bill, promises his backing.

dead center by moving for a commitment to vote on the open housing amendment on the following Monday. Such a motion requires a unanimous vote. Senator Ervin sprang to his feet. "Mr. President," he said, addressing the presiding officer, "I object." Senator Mansfield repeated his motion. Again Senator Ervin objected. Senator Mansfield then took the only remaining course that could force the Senate to stifle the meaningless debate and bring the amendment to a vote. "Mr. President," he said, "I will send to the desk shortly a motion on cloture."

(The means for stopping debate on an issue did not exist in the Senate prior to 1917. In that year a group of antiwar Senators had successfully held the floor to prevent the Senate from voting on President Woodrow Wilson's bill to arm American merchant ships against German submarines. In a rage, Wilson denounced the group. In response to Presidential pressure and to hostile public reaction, the Senate adopted Rule 22, which provided a procedure for cutting off debate. This rule now requires that the cloture motion be sponsored by 16 Senators and that two thirds of the Senators present and voting approve it. Cloture has never been popular with the Senate, however. In the first half century of Rule 22's existence, cloture was invoked only seven times.)

Later that day, Friday, February 16, Senator Mansfield submitted his cloture motion, signed by 29 Senators. Senator Vance Hartke of Indiana, who was serving as acting President pro tem of the Senate, intoned: "The rule provides that the motion will be voted upon one hour after the Senate meets on the following calendar day but one. If the Senate meets on Monday next, it will be voted on one hour after the Senate convenes on Tuesday."

The first test. At 1 p.m. on Tuesday, February 20, the cloture motion came to a vote. Not even its sponsors expected it to be passed the first time around. This was just a test of strength. If cloture were defeated by a large margin, this would show there was little support for open housing and the amendment might as well be dropped. If the vote were close, then some maneuvering, compromising and pressuring might lead enough Senators to change their votes to gain victory when a second cloture motion came up.

Before the vote was taken, Senator Dirksen rose to speak. Shoulders back, wholly self-assured, Dirksen

said, "I have made it abundantly clear that I should like to see a civil rights bill. I am still in that frame of mind. I trust that before the session of the Ninetieth Congress concludes, there will be a civil rights bill." It was apparent that Dirksen did not mean *this* particular civil rights bill, but that at least he favored *a* civil rights bill. He continued: "And so I fervently hope, Mr. President, that the Senate will not gag itself. I do not want to go home and say 'I gagged myself by my vote.' "

His colleagues were entitled to a wry smile. In the recent history of the Senate the passage of cloture motions had been achieved largely through the efforts of one man—Everett Dirksen. Now, however, ending debate did not suit his purpose. Dirksen had made it plain that he wanted his Republican associates to vote against cloture.

Before the first vote to stop debate on H.R. 2516, Everett Dirksen rises to speak against the motion. "I fervently hope, Mr. President," he says, "that the Senate will not gag itself."

Supporters of the amended bill were not surprised at Dirksen's present tack. They knew he had two major objections to the pending legislation. The first was to a provision in H.R. 2516—the original bill to protect civil rights workers—that gave the federal government immediate authority to enforce the law. The second was to the entire concept of the Mondale-Brooke amendment. Dirksen spoke out on the first point. "The crux of the controversy," he said, is "whether the state shall have the opportunity first to bring an offender to the bar of justice before the long arm of the federal government reaches in." Sponsors of the legislation were not too concerned with this point; some compromise could probably be reached. But the open housing amendment was a more difficult problem. Dirksen had killed the civil rights bill in 1966 because he considered the open housing section unconstitutional.

As the motion for cloture came to a vote, the chamber was hushed. The Vice President came in and took his place as presiding officer. In the nearly packed gallery sat an anxious Clarence Mitchell of the NAACP, who had been working for the bill behind the scenes. The clerk called the roll and the staccato replies came back: "Aye," "No," "No." Mike Mansfield stood at his Senate desk, somber, his arms folded across his chest, as he watched an aide keep the count. But there was never any doubt as to the result —not with Dirksen in opposition. The Vice President read the final count: "On this vote there are fifty-five yeas and thirty-seven nays. Two thirds of the Senators present and voting not having voted in the affirmative, the motion is lost."

Cracking the bloc. Democratic Senator Philip Hart, floor manager of the civil rights bill, was depressed. He and his colleagues, with the aid of the civil rights lobbyists and the President, had gone just about as far as they could go in pressuring the Democrats to vote for cloture. Only Republican votes could save the day the next time there was a cloture motion. On this first vote the Republicans were split evenly, 18 for cloture, 18 against. It was now a question of whether liberal Republican Senators like Jacob Javits of New York and Brooke could crack the Dirksen bloc of conservatives.

On the day after the defeat of the cloture motion, Mike Mansfield took a step that must have puzzled many of the onlookers in the spectators' gallery; he moved to table the Mondale-Brooke amendment. Mansfield did not, of course, want the amendment killed, but he had to learn how much support there was for open housing. If his motion carried, a development few expected, that would end the matter.

But even if the vote were close, the likelihood of the amendment's eventual passage would be slim, and therefore the measure would probably be dropped and all efforts would be devoted to salvaging the original bill. But if the vote against tabling were substantial, then there was reason to hope that, with compromises, some kind of open housing legislation could be passed.

Conservative opponents of the amendment, primarily Southern Democrats and some Midwestern and Western Republicans, supported Mansfield's motion. But those favoring civil rights legislation, including an open housing provision, voted solidly against the proposal to table. This time the vote was 34 for and 58 against tabling. Clearly a substantial majority of the Senate favored open housing, even though that majority was not enough to force the Senate to halt its five-week debate.

(It should be noted, however, that more Republicans voted against tabling the amendment than would have voted for its adoption in its present form. Backstage, Republican defenders of the bill had had to promise that if the tabling motion were defeated, the open housing amendment would be softened before it actually came to a vote.)

Mansfield then made an all-important move: he sent in a new cloture motion. So another try at ending debate would be made. The vote on it was scheduled for Monday, February 26.

During the long weeks of debate on the civil rights legislation, there had been considerable backstage effort to effect a compromise. Much of the action centered on Dirksen. The Illinois Senator supported the concept of legal protection for civil rights workers, but he wanted primary responsibility for enforcing the law given to the states; only if they failed to act should the federal government be empowered to step in. There was little discussion about the Mondale-Brooke amendment. Dirksen seemed flatly opposed to any open housing law.

On Wednesday afternoon, the day that saw the defeat of the tabling motion and the introduction of Mansfield's new cloture motion, Dirksen received a telephone call from Attorney General Ramsey Clark asking if he could come by and have a talk with the Senator. Indeed he could, Dirksen said. Others would

"It depends on how all-inclusive you made it [an open housing amendment], on what you excluded," Dirksen tells Attorney General Ramsey Clark *(right)*, who represents the Administration. It is Clark's first hint that Dirksen, who has previously opposed open housing, might now compromise.

also be coming later. In Dirksen's special "hideaway," a room off his Minority Leader's office in the Capitol, there was a scheduled 5 p.m. meeting between a battery of Justice Department lawyers, Dirksen and the Senator's staff lawyers, familiarly known as "Dirksen's Bombers." Together they planned to make another attempt to hammer out a compromise on H.R. 2516. Clark came ahead of time, however, arriving at 4:20 p.m. "Well, Ramsey," Dirksen said, indicating stacks of civil rights drafts on his desk, "it's right here before me. I'm trying to plow through on some compromise that will be fair to you and everybody else." The two talked for some time, and then Clark asked the Senator how he felt about the open housing amendment. Dirksen's reply astounded the Attorney General.

"It depends on how all-inclusive you made it, on what you excluded," the Senator said. "For instance, if it did not apply to an individual . . . I have a house and you want to buy it and I don't want to sell it to you. That's one situation. When it's handled by brokers and agents—they operate under a license of the state—it's a different picture."

One could almost feel the earth shifting. There was

no mistaking Dirksen's intent; he was talking compromise, across the board. He waved at the Justice lawyers who by now were assembling in the hideaway: "They're laboring to find a compromise just as we are. All hands are on the pump handle now."

Talking compromise. One of the few persons in Washington who would not have been startled to hear Dirksen indicate a change of attitude on open housing was Howard Baker, Republican Senator from Tennessee and Dirksen's son-in-law. In early February, Clarence Mitchell and other LCCR lobbyists, along with Senators in the civil rights bloc, had had a number of talks with Baker about supporting open housing. Baker, a fairly liberal Southerner, had been sympathetic. He had then brought up the matter with Dirksen and, during several conversations, had learned that his father-in-law was at least willing to consider some kind of open housing legislation. On the day before the Dirksen-Clark meeting, Baker had called Dirksen and said that he had an idea for a compromise amendment. "Do you have it on paper?" Dirksen had asked. Baker had said "No," but had added that he would have a draft by the next day. Baker had worked all night drawing up a substitute measure. Shortly before 3 p.m. the next day, about an hour and a half before Clark arrived, Baker had been on his way to Dirksen's office. En route he had passed Mitchell in the Senate subway and had waved the new amendment in the lobbyist's direction to indicate that work on the bill was moving ahead. When Baker had delivered the measure to Dirksen, the Illinois Senator had read it and said it was a good starting point for talking compromise with the civil rights bloc.

Word that Dirksen was changing his position on open housing spread like wildfire through the civil rights camp. Northern Democrats and liberal Republicans alike were excited, yet nervous. They feared that Dirksen might back away and become intransigent. To avoid any boat-rocking, they agreed to keep absolutely quiet about the new turn of events and about the negotiations underway.

On Monday, February 26, Mansfield's second mo-

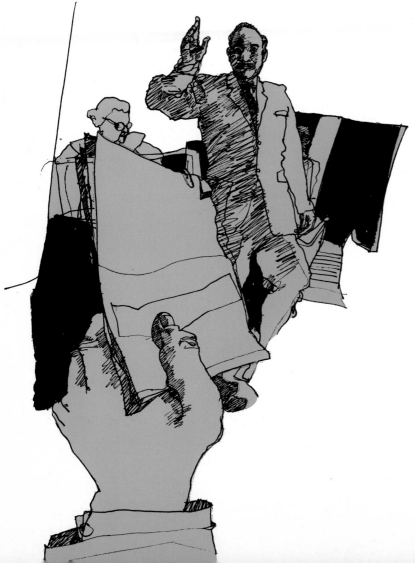

In the Senate subway *(left),* Senator Howard Baker gestures with a draft of the open housing proposal he will show Dirksen, and NAACP lobbyist Clarence Mitchell waves back.

In Dirksen's office suite, Senators, their aides and Justice Department lawyers work on the compromise bill. Dirksen *(center)* tells Clark *(left)* and Brooke that Mansfield is concerned about the Senate schedule and that the new measure must be ready for introduction early that afternoon.

tion for cloture came to a vote. The vote failed, as expected—56 in favor to 36 against, six short of the two thirds needed—but that mattered little now. Negotiations were well underway between liberal, pro-open housing Senators and the conservatives who wanted the Administration's bill toned down—chief among them Dirksen. Knowing this, Mansfield was sure to introduce still another cloture motion once a compromise had been worked out.

The bargaining in Dirksen's office was now centered largely on open housing. The civil rights bloc of Javits, Brooke, Mondale and Hart pressed for the most comprehensive coverage possible. Dirksen, Baker and Roman Hruska of Nebraska wanted to limit the scope of the legislation. Dirksen insisted on the right of the homeowner to choose his buyer if the services of a real-estate broker were not used. But when a broker entered the transaction, Dirksen said, the circumstances changed. He was licensed by his state and therefore could be obliged to adhere to open housing legislation.

Negotiations continued through Tuesday, February 27, and into Wednesday. There was urgent need to reach agreement. Mansfield wanted a bill by Wednes-

day; other Senate business needed attention. He planned to introduce another cloture motion and vote on it that week, on Friday, March 1. Wednesday in Dirksen's office was the most hectic session of all. Down to the wire, a group that included Baker, Attorney General Clark, Javits, Mondale, Hart, Brooke and Hruska, plus their legislative assistants, was piecing together the final draft of a bill that would be a substitute for both H.R. 2516 and the Mondale-Brooke amendment. (Because the new measure was a substitute and not a wholly new bill, it would continue to bear the designation H.R. 2516.) Most of the provisions of the new measure, including the section on open housing, had been agreed upon, and it was now only a matter of couching them in legal terminology. The conference table was strewn with papers, the Senators' aides were cutting and pasting together previous drafts of the bill and scribbling changes in the margins, and Dirksen was striding in and out, insisting that he have the bill in hand by 2 o'clock to be certain there would be time to introduce it that day. But it was after 3 p.m. when the new draft was ready, a collage of old bills and proposed amendments strung together, occasional passages inked out, proof-

Senate Legislative Clerk Edward Mansur begins reading the compromise bill. The text consists of parts of other bills, with scribbled additions and inked-out passages.

readers' marks dotting the pages. Dirksen took the draft and headed for the Senate chamber.

The Senators in the civil rights bloc were, of course, aware that the Dirksen bill would be introduced that afternoon, and Mondale and Brooke were happy to withdraw their own open housing amendment to make way for the compromise. As soon as Dirksen arrived with the substitute measure in hand, Mondale rose and was recognized by the chair. Remarking that a breakthrough was imminent, he said he would move to table his own amendment. Senator Brooke, adding words of praise for Dirksen, concurred. The Southerners, who had had Dirksen's support until now in their opposition to the civil rights bill, were visibly shaken.

Mondale's motion carried easily: 83 "Yeas" to five "Nays." Now the way was cleared for the compromise bill. It was 4:16 p.m. and the chair recognized Dirksen for his big moment.

"Mr. President," Dirksen began, "I submit an amendment in the nature of a substitute." At this point, because of their anger over Dirksen's shift, the Southern Senators resorted to petty delaying tactics. Usually the Senate gives its unanimous consent to dispense with the reading of an amendment, since the full text appears the next day in the *Congressional Record*. But now, when permission to do so was requested, Albert Gore of Tennessee objected. And when the clerk had been reading for a brief period, Senator Holland of Florida asked that he go more slowly. More than an hour went by before the clerk finished reading the patched-together measure.

Then Dirksen was again on his feet, this time to explain his astonishing about-face on open housing. His voice was deep as he stood in the Senate center aisle, hands in his pockets, his body in a half-slouch. "It will be an exercise in futility," he said, "for anyone to dig up the speech I made in September 1966 with respect to fair [open] housing. . . . Mr. President, there are only two categories of people who do not change their minds in the face of reality. One group is sacredly embalmed in the last resting places of the country and could not change their minds. The other group consists of the recipients of the many problems in the field of mental health that have committed them to institutions, and they are not competent to change their minds. But other than that, one would be a strange creature indeed in this world of mutation if in the face of reality he did not change his mind." Presently he submitted a motion for cloture "signed by forty-eight members of the Senate which includes myself and the Majority Leader."

As the Senate adjourned for the day, a favorable vote on cloture now seemed a foregone conclusion. But Dirksen was taking no chances. That evening he was busy lining up Republican votes. It was not long until he realized that he was in serious trouble.

Flood of telegrams. The real-estate lobby, strongly opposed to open housing, had been relatively moribund during the long weeks of debate on the Mondale-Brooke amendment. There had seemed little chance of its ever coming to a vote since Dirksen, a known opponent of open housing, would not support cloture. But when the lobby had learned of Dirksen's plan to submit a compromise bill that would include open housing provisions, there had been a call for help to real-estate men all over the nation.

Telegrams from real-estate brokers to their respective Senators reached flood stage on Wednesday night and continued on Thursday. "Stand firm in opposition," demanded the brokers. Their tone was one of outrage. Such messages were having an especially powerful effect on the very men Dirksen needed to give him a large Republican pro-cloture vote.

Dirksen also learned that he had used bad judgment in introducing his cloture motion on Wednesday, immediately after submitting his compromise. It meant the vote to close off debate would take place on Friday. The new measure was lengthy and complicated and had far-reaching implications, and many Senators felt it deserved a longer period of consideration. Dirksen himself was to add fuel to this particular fire.

Alarmed by the growing opposition he was encountering, Dirksen went to the Senate floor on Thursday afternoon to make what he described as "modifications" of his compromise. Exempting from

coverage all one-family houses financed by the Federal Housing Authority and the Veterans Administration, they would substantially reduce the scope of his original open housing section. Senator Baker, Dirksen's son-in-law, went even further with an amendment to exempt one-family houses sold through real-estate brokers, a change that would, by Mondale's estimate, eliminate some 29 million houses from coverage by open housing provisions. The civil rights bloc, not knowing of the trouble Dirksen was having lining up Republican votes, was outraged.

Dirksen and Baker tried to defend their pullback by arguing that they did not understand that the final compromise agreement of Wednesday afternoon included the coverage they now wanted to eliminate. It was a specious argument that not only infuriated liberals like Javits and Hart, but hurt Dirksen's cause in another way. In effect, Dirksen was confessing that he himself did not know what was in the bill he had offered, and yet he was demanding from his colleagues an almost immediate vote to end debate. This would further weaken his appeal to his reluctant cohorts for support of his cloture motion.

As soon as the session ended, the now thoroughly worried Dirksen resumed his quest for Republican votes. He spent more than an hour fruitlessly trying to corral Clifford P. Hansen of Wyoming, and he had no more success in a later talk with South Dakota's Karl Mundt. Mundt said he would vote for the bill itself if it ever came to the floor, but he would not join Dirksen in supporting cloture. Jack Miller of Iowa was another on Dirksen's list. Miller seemed amenable, but he refused to give a flat commitment until he had discussed the matter with the senior Iowa Senator, Bourke Hickenlooper. As it turned out, Hickenlooper not only refused to join the cloture forces but took Miller with him. There were many more turndowns than Dirksen had anticipated.

Probably the most painful blow of all was dealt by Nebraska's Roman Hruska, a close personal friend of Dirksen's and a collaborator on the compromise bill. The two men met in Dirksen's office hideaway on Thursday evening and, over drinks, Dirksen used his considerable persuasive powers on a reluctant Hruska. Finally Dirksen put the question. "Will you give me your vote?" Hruska sadly shook his head. He was, he said, philosophically opposed to cloture.

But despite the disappointments, the situation was not entirely bleak for Dirksen. He managed to get a

In his office hideaway, Dirksen *(foreground)* urges Nebraska's Roman Hruska to vote for cloture and thus clear the way for a roll call on the compromise bill.

commitment of support from George Murphy of California, who had voted against cloture in the past. The Minority Leader also elicited a promise to vote "Yea" from Carl Curtis of Nebraska, even though Hruska refused to go along.

When Dirksen tallied the "Yea" votes on Thursday night, he found he had a total of 64. He assumed there would be four absentees during the next day's session. With 96 Senators present, the 64 would give him exactly the needed two thirds to invoke cloture. But Dirksen decided to try for one extra vote for insurance. He talked with Frank Carlson of Kansas, who reluctantly agreed to support the motion if his vote were needed—but *only* if it were needed.

The third attempt at cloture began at 11 a.m. Friday morning. Early in the roll call there was evidence that the civil rights bloc would suffer a stunning defeat. Such Senators as Curtis, Miller and Murphy, who had promised with varying degrees of firmness to support the Dirksen motion, voted "Nay." Carlson abstained from voting the first time around to see if his vote would be needed. Albert Gore of Tennessee, who had twice before supported cloture, now voted "Nay." He explained that he wanted more time to study the Dirksen open housing amendment. Democrat Joseph Tydings of Maryland, a sure vote for the pro-cloture camp, arrived too late to be counted. Carlson, seeing that his vote would not change the outcome, voted "Nay." Dirksen's count of the previous evening, 64 to 32, proved well off the mark. The actual tally was 59 "Yeas" to 35 "Nays," far short of the required two-thirds majority.

Dirksen and his allies were shaken. They were not yet ready to run up the white flag, however. "I underestimated the basic resistance to open housing," Baker said soon after the vote, "but I'm still convinced something can be done."

By midafternoon Friday, March 1, the pro-civil rights forces were rallying. Without hesitation, Mansfield introduced another cloture motion that would be up for a vote on the following Monday, and the Democrats belatedly moved to gather their maximum strength. There had been so much confidence in Dirksen's ability to muster the requisite number of votes that the Democrats had not made an all-out effort with their own troops.

Frank Church of Idaho and Gale McGee of Wyoming were campaigning in their respective states and had not been present for the Friday roll call. They were urged to be on hand for the Monday vote and they pledged their presence. A reverse kind of pledge was sought from such other Senators as E. L. Bartlett of Alaska, Carl Hayden of Arizona and Howard Cannon of Nevada who, for political or philosophical reasons, would not support cloture. They were asked to be absent when the roll call was made on Monday, thus making the two-thirds majority easier to achieve.

Meanwhile, the Republicans were not idle. Carlson repudiated his pledge to support cloture if his vote meant the difference between success and failure of the motion. Dirksen got wind of the disaffection and put pressure on him. "Frank," Dirksen pleaded, "I need you." Carlson came back to the fold. Mundt, however, again turned Dirksen down, reaffirming that he was for open housing but against cloture.

Joining forces, Brooke and Javits tackled Gore and succeeded in bringing him back to his former pro-cloture position. Cannon and Bartlett, who had earlier been asked only to be absent for the roll call, were also induced to become active supporters of the debate-ending motion. "I felt agonized," Bartlett said, "because I'm against cloture and for civil rights. If I were responsible for the death of the civil rights bill—well, I couldn't abide that."

A last-minute plea. On Monday morning, March 4, the Senate chamber had the electric quality of a Broadway theater on the opening night of an important production. The vote was already underway and the outcome very much in doubt when Iowa's Jack Miller came in. Brooke, who was standing at the Republican cloakroom door, stopped him to make a last-minute plea. "Jack," Brooke said, "why don't you come with us?" Miller replied that he would vote for cloture if the Dirksen amendment were softened even further. Brooke hurried to Dirksen's side, exchanged a few words and then talked with Javits and Hart. All three agreed to the proposal.

The clerk had almost finished the roll call. Miller went to his desk, was recognized by the President of the Senate and voted "Aye." Dirksen now walked up the aisle and signaled Carlson that his vote was needed. Carlson stood up and voted "Aye." Bartlett, who was waiting in the Democratic cloakroom until he determined that his vote was needed, now walked quickly down the aisle, whispered something to Mansfield, and then voted "Aye."

The galleries burst into applause. They knew what Bartlett's vote had meant. Other Senators crowded around Bartlett, thanking and congratulating him. The presiding officer gaveled for order and then announced: "On this vote, there are sixty-five yeas and thirty-two nays. Two thirds of the Senators present and voting having voted in the affirmative, the motion is agreed to."

Following the passage of the cloture motion, the Senate spent a week tinkering with the Dirksen compromise. During that period, 25 major amendments were approved and 13 rejected. Among those that were voted down was Baker's motion to exempt from open housing coverage all one-family houses sold through real-estate brokers. This proposal had been considered the biggest threat to the substance of the original Dirksen measure. As finally passed, the open housing provisions would take effect in three stages and would cover about 80 per cent of the nation's houses by 1970. Two wholly new elements were added to the Dirksen bill: antiriot provisions and legislation to protect the Constitutional rights of Indians. The provisions in the original H.R. 2516 that protected civil rights workers from violence and intimidation had been incorporated into the compromise measure and emerged with no major changes. Finally, on March 11, the Senate passed the substitute H.R. 2516 with amendments by a vote of 71 to 20.

Now the bill went back to the House of Representatives. There it encountered some strong opposition and was bottled up in the Rules Committee for nearly a month. But partially because of the popular outrage over the assassination of civil rights leader Martin Luther King Jr., on April 4, the committee released the bill and on April 10, 1968, it was passed by a vote of 250 to 172. The next day the President signed the measure, making it the law of the land.

EPILOGUE

Ironically enough, on June 17, 1968, the Supreme Court, basing its decision on an 1866 Reconstruction law, ruled that discrimination in the sale or rental of *all* housing was illegal. This ruling did not make the open housing section of H.R. 2516 meaningless, however. Under the 1866 law, a court can issue an order barring discrimination, but there is no clear provision on whether or not the injured party can recover money damages from the offender. H.R. 2516 is specific on this point. The injured party can recover not only actual money damages but punitive damages as well, i.e., a fine, levied against the offender, of up to $1,000. The 1968 civil rights law also empowers the U.S. Attorney General to initiate legal action in an area where a pattern of discrimination exists. In short, H.R. 2516 put teeth into the 1866 legislation.

"Bob" Bartlett of Alaska is congratulated by Philip Hart *(left)* and Mike Mansfield *(right)* after casting the deciding vote for cloture. Now the Senate can pass the civil rights bill.

Washington newsmen relax and swap political gossip in the White House Press Lobby, their haven from the hectic pace around the President. When a story breaks, however, they must be prepared, on short notice, to follow the President anywhere on earth.

5

Persuasion and Politics

On a day when ideas simply will not come, a desperate political cartoonist may yield to one of the moldiest clichés of his craft and portray the government as the ship of state and the President as the captain. Anyone familiar with the workings of government in the city of Washington can only smile wryly at this bit of imagery. The master of a vessel is never required to convince his officers of the soundness of his decisions, and the officers, in turn, have no need to justify their orders to the crew. But no President of the United States and no group of lesser public servants could ever run the country on this simple command-obey basis. Persuasion is the indispensable tool on all levels of policy making and policy execution. Furthermore, it works in more than one direction. It is, of course, the only tool available to private citizens, whether special-interest groups, the press or individuals,

who hope to influence the course of government. Persuasion may take the form of intellectual argument, horse trading, the promise of reward, or the covert or bald threat of political reprisal, but persuasion is still the force that makes things happen.

Part of the persuasion process takes place within statutory channels, as when the President urges support of his legislative program in his State of the Union message and in other official communications to Congress. Sometimes the persuasion is not truly official but is still in public view, as when an officeholder utilizes the press to explain and win support for his policies. Often the persuasion is equally public but flows in the opposite direction, as when the communications media flay the President or Congress or both to bring about a desired result.

But most of the persuasion in Washington is

done behind the scenes in a wide variety of settings, both official and unofficial. For public servants, persuasion is a vital tool used to keep the machinery of government in operation. For the city's army of lobbyists, it is a career. Journalists, the target of much persuasion, also in turn persuade the public and thus influence the politicians.

The place where persuasion occurs may be the President's office, where the Chief Executive is meeting with Senate leaders of both parties to gain bipartisan support for a treaty with the Soviet Union; the Congressional cloakroom, where some genteel logrolling is taking place; or an office in the State Department, where the representative of a foreign power attempts to have an import quota liberalized. It may also be as private as a rich woman's dining room, for the art of persuasion as practiced by public servants, lobbyists, newsmen and other interested parties is not restricted to a 9 a.m. to 5 p.m. schedule. Washington's social life is an important part of the persuasion process, and therefore a potent factor in government itself.

Though the capital's social life is intertwined with governmental operations, its significance has probably been exaggerated in the public mind, thanks largely to the many novels, plays and movies dealing with life in Washington. In such fictional accounts, there is a kind of stock scenario, played in a setting of Washington's dining and drawing rooms. The basic theme was established in Henry Adams' anonymously published novel of 1879, simply and ironically entitled *Democracy;* variations, in print and on the stage and screen, have been employed ever since.

The cast of characters includes one or more rich hostesses who are unencumbered by visible husbands and who gather under their chandeliers an assortment of figures little changed from Adams' day to that of Allen Drury and Gore Vidal. One or more of the following are always on hand: (1) a naïve and well-meaning Congressman or government official, armored in noble purpose; (2) a corrupt and weary Congressman or official, in rusty armor dented by the hailstones of reality and compromise; (3) a powerful businessman or foreign agent promoting an undertaking bad for the public but gorgeously fattening for him or his government; (4) a strong but ambition-driven would-be President, showing a glossy reputation but hiding some secret vice or scandal; (5) an amused, ironic but impotent commentator—a diplomat, a newspaperman or an old Washington socialite, living on coupons, good taste and low expectations.

All of them pursue, use and freely comment on one another. Conversation in the parlor (or, in recent works, in the bedroom) is the inexhaustible fuel of the plot. However events turn out, the implied message is the same: the interplay of influential Washingtonians at leisure affects the decisions of government itself. What is agreed to in a Cabinet meeting or on Capitol Hill Tuesday afternoon had its origins Saturday night over the terrapin Maryland and its nurture in golf-club locker rooms and boudoirs on Sunday.

Such a picture is not completely false, but it is distorted. True, Washington's social reality does encompass plenty of private, afterhours politics. Persuasion and the weighing of arguments do not automatically cease when the sun drops behind the hills of Arlington. But while transactions among those with power and those with petitions do take place in a variety of out-of-office settings, the social world is only one of them.

Some basic points must be borne in mind. First, Washington parties and dinners are no longer the lengthy, slow-paced happenings of Henry Adams' day. If they are to include the town's top men, they begin promptly at 8 or 8:30 and end at 11 sharp. In today's Washington, any morning can see the launching of a crisis. No one with a finger on the switch can be prepared to meet destiny if he is half-asleep or suffering from a hang-over. Key officials, in fact, miss many an already-cooked private dinner, either because a late meeting holds them or because they are airborne on short notice, en route to avert a coup in Bangkok, a strike in Detroit or a bank failure in Montevideo. Conversations among the mighty, therefore, are provisional at best and have only a short time in which to flow and sparkle even when they do take place.

Secondly, Washington society is not really ruled by the preferences of clever hostesses. The ladies are only as good as their own or their menfolks' connections. In other cities, social life is a great ship floating nightly to nowhere on tides of wine; in Washington the compass is set by power. The ladies issue invitations on the basis of who is important in the man's world of big government. The rating of a hostess will depend upon how many men of real weight and distinction she can gather together.

But real social "clout" in Washington is finally measured by proximity to the President of the United States. The capital may not be, as a reporter once called it, "a city of toadies," but the First Family is the sun and all others are planets. The hostess with a White House "in" is the one whose parties are best attended. Presidential friendship is more precious than gold (which is necessary to shine in society but not enough by itself to make a social success). The President's social life—part of his process of persuasion—begins with the Chief Executive's own formal entertaining routine, which is a compromise between the requirements of Old World court etiquette and the personal style of the man who holds the highest office.

Each White House "season" is punctuated by a number of state dinners. They are held, by historic precedent, for such worthies as the diplomatic corps, the Cabinet, the Supreme Court, the Vice President and the Speaker of the House. Nowadays the jet-age procession of visiting heads of state has created an extra set of formal happenings. The guests are ranked in an order rigidly determined by protocol—Cabinet members in order of the establishment of their departments, Congressmen by seniority, governors in order of their states' admission to the Union, diplomats by length of service and so on. The White House Social Office and the State Department's Division of Protocol hold long, serious conferences over such matters. These officials are aware that everyone is familiar with the rules of the game, and a misranking will be universally recognized and deeply resented.

Following the official guests at a White House dinner come the private citizens who have earned the magic token of a Presidential request for the pleasure of breaking bread with them. Some are old acquaintances. Others are party leaders or prominent men in the worlds of business and communications. Since the 1930s there has been a goodly number of entertainers who, later in the evening, perform for the republic's royalty. In 1967, for example, Carol Channing low-noted through a swinging "Hello, Dolly!" when President and Mrs. Johnson entertained the Vice President, the Speaker and the Chief Justice. Richard Kiley sang selections from *Man of La Mancha* when the President of Italy was guest of honor, and Tony Bennett crooned that he left his heart in San Francisco to Japanese Prime Minister Eisaku Sato. Some guests are chosen especially for foreign visitors, like fruits in season or the formal gifts of "native production" exchanged between heads of state. For Italy's President Giuseppe Saragat the list included many successful Italian-Americans, among them jockey Eddie Arcaro and Joseph N. DePaola, the President of the Journeymen Barbers, Hairdressers and Cosmetologists International Union of America. Prime Minister Sato, a baseball fan like many Japanese, met Bob Gibson, an American Negro from Omaha who pitched the St.

Louis Cardinals to a 1967 World Series victory.

The diners are made thoroughly conscious of the special nature of the occasion. As they arrive—punctually—military aides usher them to the reception line. The Marine Band may play softly in the background. The brilliant draperies of the Blue, Green, Red, East and State Dining Rooms and the gleam of vermeil flatware and historic china set off the chiffons and satins of the ladies and their white- or black-tied husbands. From a butler the guest receives a card bearing his table number and the name of his dinner partner. The menu will offer expertly prepared seafood, lamb, beef or veal, followed by inspired creations of pastry, cream, fruit and ice. The wines are carefully chosen (in deference to the political importance of such grape-growing states as California and New York, they will be domestic vintages) and the overall effect is sumptuous. No recent First Lady has matched the austerity of Mrs. Rutherford B. Hayes, who ran a temperance White House and was known to official Washington as "Lemonade Lucy." And no modern President need fear the fate of Martin Van Buren, who lost the 1840 election partly because of charges that he dined undemocratically on French cuisine washed down with champagne.

The "embassy circuit," where representatives of foreign nations carry on part of their duties of persuasion, sounds more glamorous than facts warrant. To drink well at diplomatic functions is not difficult. There are scores of embassies in town, and there is always a national holiday, a royal birthday or a new staff arrival to honor. Almost anyone with a valid excuse for interest in the host nation—a student, teacher, businessman or journalist—can be bidden to the celebration. The drawback is, however, that embassy entertaining is, in one reporter's words, "more formal and less operational" than most. And few such functions include a formal dinner: only people of the eminence of Senate Foreign Relations Committee members are quite sure of gourmet dining at the expense of another sovereign power.

The lowest in prestige—but possibly the best-attended—capital social affairs are the hundreds of banquets and receptions given annually by commercial, industrial, civic and fraternal organizations that wish to raise funds, make contacts or justify their own lobbying budgets. Every Congressman's mail bulges with invitations to these affairs. A banquet given by an important group like the Women's National Press Club will attract senior Senators, even Majority Leaders and the Vice President to the speakers' table. A dinner of

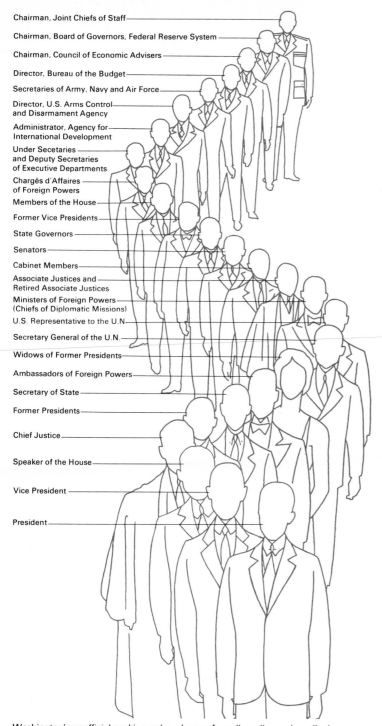

Chairman, Joint Chiefs of Staff

Chairman, Board of Governors, Federal Reserve System

Chairman, Council of Economic Advisers

Director, Bureau of the Budget

Secretaries of Army, Navy and Air Force

Director, U.S. Arms Control
and Disarmament Agency

Administrator, Agency for
International Development

Under Secetaries
and Deputy Secretaries
of Executive Departments

Chargés d'Affaires
of Foreign Powers

Members of the House

Former Vice Presidents

State Governors

Senators

Cabinet Members

Associate Justices and
Retired Associate Justices

Ministers of Foreign Powers
(Chiefs of Diplomatic Missions)

U.S. Representative to the U.N.

Secretary General of the U.N.

Widows of Former Presidents

Ambassadors of Foreign Powers

Secretary of State

Former Presidents

Chief Justice

Speaker of the House

Vice President

President

Washington's unofficial pecking order—known formally as "precedence"—is reshuffled periodically in *The Social List of Washington, D.C.* to keep the city abreast of just who gets to sit "above the salt" at dinner, and in what order. The list's editor, Carolyn Hagner Shaw, tries to keep up with the times in each edition. For example, as peace and international cooperation have become more fashionable in recent years, the heads of the U.S. Arms Control and Disarmament Agency and the Agency for International Development have moved up 25 steps to positions 20 and 21. In positions that can be filled by several people, Mrs. Shaw supplies rigid rules for sorting them out. Former Presidents, for instance, are ranked according to who was in office first. Ambassadors are ranked according to who first presented his credentials, a rating system that also applies to Ministers of Foreign Powers who are Chiefs of Diplomatic Missions (a diplomatic post different from ambassador). Although this list of precedence is invaluable for most of the city's hosts and hostesses—from lobbyists to Congressmen's wives—the White House uses its own official order of protocol supplied by the State Department and kept secret.

the National Egg Council, on the other hand, may draw only a few Congressmen from poultry-raising states. But there is always at least one such function scheduled as any night falls on L'Enfant's city; gastric juice and oratory that is meant to be persuasive are bound to be flowing in the capital somewhere. Merriman Smith, an experienced correspondent, reports that almost any reason will do for a party in Washington—the introduction of a new product, the preview of a movie, the appointment of a corporate executive—and that "a man with a clean shirt and halfway presentable suit, but known only to God and his landlady, can remain well-fed and moderately drunk six nights a week at the better hotels."

Really important receptions, however, will attract high officials and especially Congressmen, who sometimes stop at several in an evening. There are two reasons for following this trying schedule. First, Congressmen cannot easily make contacts at leisurely midday lunches as do private businessmen. Secondly, in the crush it is acceptable to speak to an industrialist or his attorney without the suspicion that might shadow an office visit. Hence, in one writer's phrase, the cocktail glass becomes an instrument of government.

It is hard to say just how *much* government. Policies are not made with drinks in hand, but the ingredients of policy are more than working papers and staff reports. The afterhours talk of Washington is political talk in the broad sense—talk that may not change minds but that opens avenues, establishes communication and creates the climate of action. No one of significance in Washington can dismiss this opportunity. Beneath its shiny surface, official social life conceals a constant, edged competition for advantage. The man who is not "in the know" will be quickly outmaneuvered. That is why Supreme Court Justice Felix Frankfurter, in his pre-Court days of teaching at the Harvard Law School, told his students to follow the society pages if they wanted to understand capital politics fully. Social news often reflects political feuds, alliances and ruptures, and invitations and omissions can prefigure important governmental trends.

Although much of the entertaining in Washington is still done by those professional persuaders, the lobbyists, society pages rarely take note of these parties, perhaps because such affairs have ceased to have much significance for either the hosts or their guests. The modern lobbyist practices persuasion under different circumstances. This is a marked change of tactics from those of the lobbyists who brightened, if they did not uplift, the

Washington scene during the younger days of the republic.

Lobbying was not a subtle art in the 19th Century, and elaborate dinners, vintage wines, attractive and cooperative girls, and out-and-out bribes were among the means of persuasion regularly used on Senators, Representatives and other officials by the men who hoped to influence legislation or secure government contracts for their clients. Scandals periodically blistered Congress over the purchase of legislators' votes and governmental favors by the lobbyists for railroads, land companies and steamship lines. Walt Whitman raged that "lobbiers" were "the lousy combings and born freedom-sellers of the earth."

This description would scarcely seem to have fitted the king of the Washington lobbyists in the late 1800s, Samuel Ward. Son of a distinguished family, brother of Julia Ward Howe, who wrote "The Battle Hymn of the Republic," Latin scholar, mathematician, poet, musician, gourmet and bon vivant, Ward was one of the most famous hosts and most influential men in the capital. "Dined with old Buchanan [President James Buchanan] last night," he wrote in one letter to his sister Julia. "Last Sunday General [Winfield] Scott, Senators Crittenden, Gwin, Latham and John Van Buren dined with me and sat at table until 11 o'clock." ("The way to a man's Aye," Ward once observed, "is through his stomach.")

Rich clients showered money on him to represent their interests in Washington. A fee of $50,000 was reportedly paid to him for securing certain tariff legislation, and on another occasion he spent an estimated one million dollars to get a mail subsidy for a patron; what his fee was for this task is a matter of conjecture. Although he was summoned before a Congressional investigating committee in connection with the mail subsidy, Ward stoutly maintained he had never paid a bribe. And perhaps he never did. Strict moralists, however, might have raised their eyebrows at some of his admitted tactics. One client offered to pay Ward $5,000 if he could keep a certain unfriendly legislator from attending a Congressional committee meeting. In a letter to his friend Henry Wadsworth Longfellow, Ward explained that he earned the fee by arranging to have the Congressman's boots mislaid "while I smoked a cigar and condoled with him until they would be found at 11:45."

Lobbying in Washington is much less colorful today than it was when "bribes, blondes and booze" were among the lobbyist's most effective weapons. But in terms of number of special-interest groups represented and of money spent—a billion dollars annually, according to one House committee—lobbying has never been more flourishing.

Present statutes require the registration with Congress of any person "who shall engage himself for pay . . . for the purpose of attempting to influence the passage or defeat of any legislation by the Congress of the United States." It is estimated that there are now well over 1,000 individuals and organizations so registered and actively operating, outnumbering the combined House and Senate membership by more than 2 to 1. But these acknowledged special-interest representatives are only a small part of the true and total lobby. The law demands only that those whose "principal purpose" is that of persuasion of lawmakers put themselves and their expenditures on record. Public-relations men, attorneys and company technical specialists who sit down to reason together with Congressmen, regulatory commissioners and purchasing agents do not appear on the roll of lobbyists. Washington newsman James Deakin estimates that there are eight to 10 actual lobbyists for every legislator. Nor does the public account book of lobbying expenses include the cost of advertising and public-relations campaigns to sway public opinion in home districts or contributions to individual and party campaign funds. These costs far outstrip the relatively small sums reported for "direct" lobbying expenses—usually the payroll and overhead of a Washington office.

Some but not all lobbying is imperial in scale. Certainly the numerous associations listed in the Yellow Pages of the Washington telephone book include a number of names instantly recognizable as representing well-heeled backers: the Association of American Railroads, the American Medical Association, the U.S. Chamber of Commerce, the National Association of Manufacturers, the AFL-CIO, the American Trucking Associations, the American Petroleum Institute. They hire for part-time or full-time work some of the most distinguished attorneys and former government officials in Washington and are prize examples of the term "special interest." But such small-budget organizations as the American Council on Education, the American Association for the Advancement of Science, the Business and Professional Women's Foundation, the NAACP and the United Nations Association are also lobbies, although not necessarily on the registered list. No matter how noble their purposes, they, as much as the well-bankrolled, are engaging themselves "for the purpose of attempting to influence . . . legislation." The national government's various departments themselves maintain Congressional liaison offices, which are in effect lobbies, and a few states and municipalities have also opened Washington offices that house de facto lobbies. Lobbying, in short, is another of those indispensable, extraconstitutional functions of government that leave their imprint on the Federal City.

Such being the case, a great share of the lobbyist's work, like all the labors of Washington, is neither sinister nor high-minded. Nor even pleasurable. Much of the entertaining by the major lobbyists at the city's expensive hotel dining rooms is undertaken neither for enjoyment nor in the hope of buying, with veal Prince Orloff and Courvoisier, an enlarged import quota or a tax reduction. Often the primary purpose of entertainment is not to persuade but to maintain liaison and perhaps to pick up information that will be of value to the lobbyist's employer. UPI correspondent Merriman Smith goes so far as to suggest that a topflight lobbyist earns most of his keep by attentive listening and intelligent reading.

But neither is this the entire story. Eugene Thoré, the president of the Life Insurance Association of America, which is keenly interested in the wide span of federal activity affecting currency and banking, has another view. Thoré believes that a successful lobby has three functions. First, it acts as a link between government and industry, keeping each informed of the other's intentions. (Ideally it should educate corporation presidents with a built-in fear of "creeping socialism" to the inevitability of big government and "bureaucrats" to the minimum requirements of the profit system.) Secondly, it maintains information necessary for both purposes in as up to date a condition as possible. And only lastly does it seek to affect lawmaking, and then not always by buttonholing legislators, but also by meticulous fact-finding. Communication, intelligence, as well as persuasion; these are the jobs. And research—lots of research. Much of a lobby's work consists of preparing testimony for the industry's spokesmen before Congress or federal agencies. A crack staff of diggers is necessary—in the Life Insurance Association's case, numbering many lawyers, economists and actuaries. A lobby's overall reputation will depend more on the quality of its information than of its whiskey. Legislators often rely on lobby-furnished data, and hell hath no fury like a Senator who produces inaccurate information in floor debate and is caught at it. Thoré has said that he felt he had arrived when Wilbur Mills, the tough chairman of the tax-writing House Ways and Means Committee, publicly declared: "You can rely on information the life insurance people give you."

From the offices of the Life Insurance Association, backed by the billions of the country's top financial institutions, to the small headquarters maintained at 1310 19th Street, N.W., by the University of California is a long distance economically. Yet Mark Ferber, representative of the Golden State's system of higher education, tends to second the insights of Thoré. Ferber's office is near "Egghead Row," a stretch of Massachusetts Avenue near Dupont Circle that is the site of such brain-heavy conventicles as the American Association for the Advancement of Science, the American Association of University Professors and The Brookings Institution. He himself is a relatively young Ph.D. in political science who says smilingly that Washington is to political scientists what Mecca is to Muslims. And his concept of lobbying is shaped by a scholarly interpretation of life in the United States. He believes that we now live in a "brokerage state," its people linked by job, residence or other factors in large aggregations, often several at a time. (An auto worker, for example, is involved in the fate of a union, the transportation industry and the city of Detroit.) These power blocs all make claims on government. The public official is the broker who mediates and arranges deals among them. The lobbyist not only presents the case of his interest group but furnishes the information supporting final judgment. There are, Ferber recognizes, self-serving lobbyists who try to profit at the expense of the vast, undifferentiated public of consumers and taxpayers. But lobbying is neither always nor exclusively a matter of campaigns by the pressure groups against "the public." Lobbying, he says, often pits one pressure group against another, each representing a different segment of public interest. Ferber, who spends more time in monitoring the flow of federal dollars from numerous agencies into California colleges than in "influencing legislation," sees himself as one of many voices suggesting to the public patterns of investment in learning.

There are enough problems still involved in lobbying to furnish plenty of material for crusading books and articles. Candor in disclosing financial support, ethical limitations on "persuasion," keeping the general public represented and equalizing the weight of various interests are only some of them. But no one doubts that the lobbyist, who appeared almost at the birth of the republic, will remain on the scene. So long as American government remains government by persuasion, he will be a powerful force in its First City.

The reporters of Washington are also part of the community of influence and persuasion, a testimony to the power of the word over men's minds. The Washington correspondent is a man or woman who endures uncertain hours, tedious delays, frequent inconvenient travel, and the pressures of hasty composition in return for a front-row seat on the national and international scene and the ego nourishment of seeing his words in print or of reporting before a television camera. In the late 1960s there were nearly 1,600 reporters in the capital, representing some 1,300 newspapers, magazines, radio and television news bureaus, and newsletters. (More than 100 foreign newspapers were among those represented, as well as more than 350 journals concentrating on business, labor, educational and other specialized affairs.) The reporters have their own totems and tattoos of office —in the galleries and lounges reserved for them in the Capitol, in the alacrity with which visiting dignitaries hasten to speak before them at the National Press Club, and in the special travel and other accommodations provided for them by the sweat of press secretaries' brows. This deference stems from the tremendous sensitivity of governing politicians to the matter of image. Politicians are anxious for coverage and exposure, the reporters yearn for news, and on the surface nothing would seem easier than an exchange on approved free-market principles. In fact, however, the giving and getting of Washington news is a complex, subtle and sometimes even stealthy process, thanks to its close involvement with the exercise of power.

To begin with, the good reporter does more than simply record hits and errors. He must also be diligent in digging out news that officials may now and then wish to conceal. The reporter's technique of extraction must be deft and flexible; it can even verge on the unethical. Drew Pearson, who has made a career of muckraking, receives much of his information from government employees. His clamorous revelations have earned him a good income, some libel suits and displeasure in the very highest circles. (Harry S. Truman himself referred to Pearson as an s.o.b.) But the exposés have also been of public benefit. It was Pearson who revealed that Connecticut Senator Thomas Dodd had misappropriated campaign funds for his personal use —one of many similar Pearson disclosures. Less well known than Pearson is I. F. Stone, the leftish, eloquent editor of an independent news weekly, whose effective unveiling of governmental inade-

quacies is achieved by a more tedious method; he grinds tirelessly through mountains of official documents, finding in them the small but immensely meaningful facts that official press releases hide, deny or distort.

Sometimes getting a Washington story simply requires unabashed brass in the presence of official majesty, like that of reporter Clark Mollenhoff, who was once told by the then Secretary of Defense Robert McNamara that he was monopolizing a press conference, having already asked three questions. "You dodged three times," answered Mollenhoff coolly.

Sometimes a shrewd reporter applies a bit of what Stewart Alsop calls "paleontology"—the power to construct a whole animal from a few bits of bone. As an example he tells how Murrey Marder and Chalmers Roberts of *The Washington Post* unearthed the story that, during the 1962 Cuban crisis, Khrushchev sent a message to Kennedy offering to remove Soviet bombers from Cuba in return for an American guarantee of noninvasion. Marder dug out the first fragment. At a diplomatic function he encountered Presidential assistant McGeorge Bundy, who told him that something hush-hush was in the wind. Next Marder ran into George Ball, at that time Under Secretary of State, radiating a contented "top secret" expression. Marder knew that Ball had been working on the problem of the Soviet bombers in Cuba, and from his appearance the reporter chanced a guess that an offer of removal had been made. Back at his office Marder enlisted Roberts' aid, and they telephoned a number of State Department and White House officials, asking in each case: "What was in the message from Khrushchev to Kennedy about the Il-28s [the Russian planes]?" After several tries they got a shock: "For Crissakes, how did you know about *that?* I can't tell you what was in that message." They had three fragments and their story of the Soviet proposal. When it ran, Bundy called up—somewhat nettled—to round it out by revealing the conditions that had been attached.

The able newspaperman does not confine himself to digging for secrets; he also knows enough to let some alone. Douglass Cater, longtime Washington news editor and a White House aide to President Johnson, has said that a reporter "can choose from among the myriad events that seethe beneath the surface of government which to describe and which to ignore. He can illumine policy and notably assist in giving it sharpness and clarity; just as easily, he can prematurely expose policy and, as with an undeveloped film, cause its destruction." When the reporter's aim is illumination of policy rather than its destruction, his inquisitiveness is welcomed—and satisfied—by Washington officials.

The official, in turn, needs the press to explain himself to the voters and prepare them to accept policy decisions still "in the oven." When newsman and official meet in give-and-take exchange on the direction of events—discussing not simply what happened but why and what the significance is—the public is the listener and final judge of the discourse.

The classic form of the engagement is the press conference. The President, Congressional committee chairman or Cabinet officer stands in a glare of television lights and expounds in response to questions. He must keep his best foot forward and be wary of quick and quotable statements that can make trouble. (In a 1950 press conference, for example, President Truman gave a mistaken impression that the use of atomic weapons in the Korean War was under consideration. He created a brief but convulsive international panic before clearing the record.)

"Press conference" is a tough game, enjoyed by few. A better dodge for attempting to control the climate of opinion is the "background interview," in which top officials talk to a select and private group of newsmen, often with the pleasant accompaniment of food and drink. The custom is fairly old but it did not come into frequent usage until the 1940s. The aim of the "backgrounder" was to provide important members of the press, mainly columnists, an inside look into the government's thinking—a kind of key to making sense out of the "hard news" released from day to day. The quid pro quo was that nothing said should be attributed to any individual and the newspapermen should expound any views presented as their own. The purpose of this plagiarism by consent was to protect officials from public responsibility for what they uttered, since a public man often needs to be highly discreet in expressing his private opinions. Later, as more newsmen joined the backgrounder audiences, the nonattribution rule had to be modified because bread-and-butter reporters, unlike columnists and editors, are rarely allowed to express opinions in their stories. Washington news releases thereafter began to erupt with such nebulous neologisms as "sources close to the Administration" and "highly placed officials," imparting a slightly whispery, spiritualistic character to the day's tidings.

Yet the official using the background interview

to impart information needs his anonymity, for when he is identified, dismaying things can happen. In 1955 Admiral Robert Carney, then Chief of Naval Operations, was a member of a high-level group favoring military action against Communist China. During a backgrounder held in the spring of that year, the admiral said that the Formosa Strait islands held by the Nationalist Chinese were in imminent danger of attack from Red China. *The New York Times* headlined the story: U.S. EXPECTS CHINESE REDS TO ATTACK ISLES IN APRIL; WEIGHS ALL-OUT DEFENSE. President Eisenhower, who did not anticipate any such military action in the immediate future, promptly directed James Hagerty, the White House press secretary, to hold his own backgrounder and repudiate the story. Three days after the first story had appeared, the *Times*'s headline was: EISENHOWER SEES NO WAR NOW OVER CHINESE ISLES. When Carney was later revealed as the source of the original story, the Administration forced his early retirement. It is a risky thing in Washington to ride one's own trial balloon.

If the press conference is the formal method of getting political information to the public, and the backgrounder the informal way, the "leak" is perhaps best styled the Machiavellian technique. There are accidental "leaks" by careless public figures, of course. But there are also deliberate "leaks," whereby an official confides in a willing newspaperman in full knowledge that his "secret" will shortly be on the wires, working its influence for good or evil, while he can affect innocence of the results.

A Congressional committee, meeting in executive session that supposedly guarantees secrecy for all testimony, is often a prime source for such stories. A confession of possible error by someone from the Administration may prompt a committee member of the other party to leak the story to a reporter with the hope of embarrassing the White House. Or the circumstances may be reversed. An important witness may give testimony that unexpectedly supports an Administration position, and a member of the President's party may relate the matter to a friendly newsman who will protect the anonymity of his source. The offices of the Executive branch are also notoriously plagued by leaks. Often the story comes from a subordinate who is unhappy with the unpublicized actions or nonactions within his department. If the information is sufficiently explosive, it will lead at least to a spirited defense by the department head and possibly a change of policy, his resignation or even a Congressional investigation. Any or all of these results can provide highly prized grist for the news mill.

A public figure who is seeking an audience for his views can also hope to reach the country through participation in one of the panel interviews that have become a feature of Sunday television programing. (In the late 1960s the three best known were "Meet the Press," "Face the Nation" and "Issues and Answers.") The television audience itself is rewardingly large—"Meet the Press" attracts as many as 10 million *aficionados* to its weekly political bullbaiting—and in addition, newspaper editors often pick up quotable items from the programs for their Monday editions. In the first few months of 1966 twelve statements made on "Issues and Answers" received headline play on Monday. Correspondent Merriman Smith declares that "members of the Cabinet, Congress and the diplomatic corps fight to be interviewed," which is something of an exaggeration. It is nonetheless true that an articulate Senator or Secretary, able to handle himself under fire, can make such a television show a launching platform for favored viewpoints. This is why it is alleged that many public men keep Sunday free until late in the week, and there are rumors that blandishments and threats are sometimes used to secure an invitation to appear on a given program. Lawrence Spivak, the producer of "Meet the Press"—and also a panelist whose insistent, irreverent voice has been lancing political hides for years—declares that "we have made it very clear that we won't yield to pressure of that nature." To some extent, the chances of invitation depend on the burning questions of the week rather than on the status of the guest. During a week of rioting on a university campus, the president of the stricken institution is a better catch than a touring prime minister or a governor with Presidential possibilities.

At the bottom of the persuasion-through-media ladder is the lowly but straightforward news release, one species of the voluminous documents that government offices generate like fruit flies. Every Congressman's assistant prepares for press distribution daily mimeographed handouts detailing the works and wonders of his employer. Every government department has public information officers whose job is to explain the ways of the agency to the taxpayers and, even more important, to justify them. Every Washington correspondent finds his mailbox literally stuffed with releases from these 3,000-plus "briefing" officials. No proliferation treaty among officials limits the number of releases, and so they are deployed without mercy. One columnist has noted that he is Stop 304 on the Department of Agriculture's distribution list, and each morning he finds a large Manila envelope on his desk, crammed with news hot from laboratory and barnyard. "One morning the eye-opener might be a proposal to allocate seventy-seven per cent of the filbert crop to in-shell markets," he says. "The next morning it might be a discussion of the effects of artificial lighting on young laying hens. If I am really lucky, it will be a report updating the epic struggle to sterilize the male screwworm fly."

Through the mountains of papers, the trivia and truth spilling from the chutes of the government's information machinery, the wary reporter treads his way. He may dream, at the press club bar, of surviving to become a pundit like Walter Lippmann or a White House aide like Cater. Or, when the pressures mount, he may consider the attractions of working in public relations or of teaching journalism. But while he remains on the job, he shares with the lobbyists and the highest officials a persistent, itching need to be in the know—and to be one of the persuaders. He must not lose his detachment, but he must stay at root as curious as any town gossip, lingering wide-eyed and open-eared at the common well.

Perhaps the village analogy is finally what best illuminates the extragovernmental relationships in Washington. Allowing for a total of 535 Senators and House members, a like number of key Executive officials, and 1,000 apiece of significant reporters and lobbyists, the action community numbers fewer than 5,000. World capital or not, it is a small town. At the top of the centers of influence, official and personal relationships can no more be sundered than in Podunk. A single stone thrown into the pond rocks everybody's boat.

A correspondent of *The Times* of London tells an illuminating story. At a dinner party one fall evening in 1962 a number of officials and newsmen were gathered together. Unknown to most of them the Cuban missile crisis was unfolding. As the evening went on, the telephone began to ring. With each ring a diner was called to the phone and then there was a quick apology and a departure. Finally no one was left but the women, a little handful of the men not in government or journalism, and the empty chairs, the untouched glasses, and stillness and fear.

The correspondent told that story to an acquaintance and then turned to him with a twinkle. "Now, in what other American city, I ask you, could that happen?" Then he thought for a while and added: "What opera could beat it?"

6

Suddenly a City

Psychologically, Washington may be at the center of the United States, but geography set it near the southern end of the great, smoke-palled megalopolis that unrolls its concrete length down the Atlantic Coast southward from Boston. One American in every five lives in this urban cluster, whose central cities shoot out suburbs toward each other like tendrils that clasp and devour the dwindling open spaces. Washington shares the problems of this massive "Boswash" complex: air and water pollution, transportation arteries burdened to the collapsing point, the mass migration of the middle class to suburbia, and in the older areas of the central city, the taint of poverty, decay, de facto segregation, inadequate housing, sick schools and a climbing crime rate.

Nevertheless, Washington is not quite like the other cities of the megalopolis. It is set apart, for better or worse, by particular circumstances, one of them its relative youthfulness as a metropolitan center. New York, Philadelphia and Boston are among the cities whose experience with the immi-

Winter-bare trees stand above a crumbling fence and dilapidated house in a 1944 photograph taken not far from the Capitol. This site is now covered by landscaped grounds camouflaging two underground garages, a result of a city-wide renovation program.

grant, the slum, the epidemic, the ward heeler, and the hard-squeezing power or streetcar company dates back to the mid-19th Century. Such cities have long known sin on a big scale. But Washington drifted tranquilly into the 20th Century untouched by many of the massive problems peculiar to a metropolis. That background of innocence left it poorly prepared for its later burst of growth, particularly the hyperactive-pituitary onrush toward gigantism of the decades since World War II.

It is estimated that the population of the Washington metropolitan area is growing by 100,000 a year. In 1968 it was home to more than 2.6 million people. Like a blinking, head-shaking Rip van Winkle, sleepy little Washington has become the heart of the nation's eighth-largest urban concentration. But there is more. In its surprised encounter with modernity, the city itself has some special handicaps. At their root is a fact of population revealed in one stunning statistic: more than 60 per cent of the 811,000 residents of the District of Columbia proper are Negroes. In the whole metropolitan Washington orbit the ratio of black to white Americans is only about 1 to 5. But with the exception of Newark, New Jersey, the capital is the only major U.S. city with a black majority.

From this reality grows a number of interlinked

consequences making up a chain that binds the arms of Washington. The first, probably, is its other overwhelming peculiarity, namely that the city has not had an independent government for about a century. There are a number of historic reasons unconnected with race for this denial of self-rule to those who live in the federal shadow. But no honest observer can overlook the truism that probably the most powerful barrier to creating a free Washington today is the fact of the black majority: Negroes could dominate the city if they chose to vote solidly by race. "Lord, help us if those niggers ever get home rule"—the outburst of one suburbanite to a *Washington Post* reporter—is an unspoken thought in the minds of many of the Congressmen who hold the key to the District's future.

Congress has, however, bolstered local administration of the problem-ridden city. Pressure from President Johnson and others led in 1967 to modification of the old three-commissioner form of government, which was replaced with a new system calling for a single commissioner (plus a deputy) and a nine-member council. But the new officials, like the old, are appointed by the President and must be confirmed by the Senate. Their plans and, what is more vital, their budgets must still be approved on Capitol Hill, where the sounds of urban revolution have yet to become deeply alarming.

In other cities, similar sounds usually bring forth leaders ready to cope with their causes; a mixture of selfish interest, civic tradition, paternalism and *noblesse oblige* customarily involves "old families" in house cleaning and humanizing the cities their fathers built. Washington is not in this fortunate position. Congressmen, who come and go as the political winds blow, feel no such dedication to the nation's capital.

Washington's difficulties boil over the District boundaries, too. Metropolitan dilemmas cannot be unraveled without the cooperation of the state and county governments whose jurisdictions cover the suburbs. This headache, familiar enough to most big cities, is the more painful for Washington because its hinterland is divided between Maryland and Virginia, both with legislatures unusually sensitive to Southern, rural viewpoints.

Thus Washington suffers from twin handicaps: the one, unique to the city, of living under a kind of absentee landlordism, since Congress is composed mainly of nonpermanent residents; the other, common to most large cities, of having to deal with other governments that often have interests conflicting with those of the urban center.

Given this doubly difficult situation, one can build a series of pessimistic propositions: Washington is convulsively growing and in need of attentive government; it is, however, largely black and, in effect, a colony; it gets, in consequence, neglectful government. There is one offsetting factor, however. Washington *is* the capital, it *is* a national showcase, and thus there is a more or less constant country-wide nagging at Congress to improve the place. As we have seen in Chapter 3, the lawmakers tend to respond with alternating periods of intense activity and stagnation. If they were ever prodded hard enough and long enough, Washington might be allowed to achieve its potential and become a wholly beautiful, civilized city.

The best place to begin the study of metropolitan Washington's problems is at the center, in the Congressional committee rooms from which the city is actually ruled. The District Committees of House and Senate are the city's formal power sources. They number on their rolls many conscientious students of local affairs, but the seniority system awards the chairmanships to men with long tenure, usually legislators from safe districts—generally rural and conservative. In the 90th Congress the chairman of the eight-man Senate District Committee, which rules the nation's ninth-biggest city, was Senator Alan Bible, who hails from Nevada, 47th among the states in population. Presiding over the 25-man House District Committee, which, with the Senate Committee, makes the laws for a city with nearly half a million Negroes, was John L. McMillan of South Carolina.

Many experts, however, felt that the most important overlord of Washington in the 1960s was neither of these men, but rather the chairman of the Senate Appropriations Committee's Subcommittee on the District of Columbia. He was Senator Robert C. Byrd of West Virginia. A devout Baptist, a country-dance fiddler, a onetime Ku Klux Klan member, Byrd embodied all that is respected by many West Virginia voters. He worked conscientiously at his task, poring for hours over the budgets prepared by District officials and holding lengthy hearings at which he was an absorbed listener and sometimes the only committee member present. But he was convinced that ambition, self-reliance, abstemiousness and family responsibility are the cornerstones of American greatness, and he was therefore a potent foe to what he considered "excessive" expenditures for Washington's welfare programs, which minister primarily to the needs of black Washingtonians lacking those traditional virtues.

True to his roots, Byrd saw urban disruption, unemployment and crime as inherently racial. Like most who share his outlook, he made exceptions for "deserving" Negroes. He was also generous—at least within the limits of an inadequate budget—with the mostly Negro school system, seeing education as the key to advancement. But his mind marched undeviatingly along a row of logical milestones: if most Negroes are poor and "shiftless," they and their white counterparts are questionable material for self-government. Since his arrival in the Senate in 1959, Byrd has fought all home-rule bills brought before that body. He was once described as "a kind of latter-day Horatius, holding the bridge against the invading hordes of infidels, mostly black."

To cast Byrd as the villain in an old Washington drama of the Hill versus the city would be a ridiculous oversimplification, however. He happens, nonetheless, to symbolize a basic weakness of Congressional rule. The tasks of urban government, complex to begin with, are even more tormenting when proposals in areas as diverse as garbage collection, liquor taxes, police procedures, traffic control and smoke abatement must be gotten through committees of busy, nonresident and often old-fashioned legislators. Even well-intentioned Congressmen have on their minds problems that they consider more urgent.

The new commissioner-council government given to Washington in 1967 must continue to operate within this enclosure of Congressional authority. It was installed by President Johnson with his characteristic sense of political imagery. He chose as commissioner a 52-year-old Negro expert in housing matters, Walter E. Washington. At the White House swearing-in ceremonies Johnson pointedly referred to his choice as "Mayor" Washington and almost immediately afterward abolished the post of Adviser on District Affairs in his own administrative family, conveying a clear impression that the Mayor would have direct access to the President to confer on the city's problems. In recognition of the District's black majority, the council also had a Negro majority. The first five Negro members were carefully chosen from among those with long experience in administration, but several of them had enough of a record of civil rights activism to pull the sting of comments like that made by a local black militant, Julius Hobson, about the Mayor—that he was "tasteless, colorless and odorless." The deputy commissioner was

MATTHEW GAULT EMERY   WALTER WASHINGTON

Washington's last elected mayor was Matthew Gault Emery, a New Hampshire-born stonemason who helped build both the Capitol and the Washington Monument. Republican Emery, who ran as a reformer, got needed votes in 1870 by promising Negroes "a fair share of the patronage." But by 1871 the debt-ridden city government had been placed under federal control and it has never been returned to the voters. In 1967, to meet growing demands for home rule, President Lyndon B. Johnson appointed housing expert Walter Washington as District Commissioner, with orders to "act just like the elected mayor." "Mayor" Washington became the first Negro ever to head a major American city.

white, as was the first chairman of the council, John W. Hechinger.

As head of this balanced-ticket team, Walter Washington flung himself with alacrity into dramatizing the new frontier in capital city government. He took as his model New York's John Lindsay, whom he admired and for whom he had been working when tapped for the new position. "My blood is out in the streets of this city," Mayor Washington said, and he took to walking the shabbier of those streets, as the former commissioners had not done. He urged the respectable citizens who came to hear him at various club luncheons to join him in the fight for a better city. He appointed 21 nationally known urban experts to analyze the District's problems and make recommendations. He made himself as visible as an oldtime precinct captain at picnics and jazz concerts and told the audiences: "I want you people to have a feeling of joy about living here."

But the fact remains that he and the council had neither a true voting constituency nor an independent budget. Walter Washington's Washington depended for its future not so much on his efficiency in the District Building, the structure on 14th and D Streets, N.W., that serves as a city hall, as on his persuasiveness in the House and Senate Office

Buildings. Rule takes effect, as elsewhere in Washington, not according to what the rulebook says, but in response to the manipulative skill of leadership in extracting (and combining) bits and pieces of power from their hiding places in the Congressional structure.

The first budget prepared by Walter Washington asked for about $580 million. Of this sum, Congress would contribute no more than $70 million, a limit preset by earlier vote. This could cause little surprise, however. In effect, the city's largest employer and property owner, the U.S. government, is tax-exempt, and Congress decides the size of its share of the annual expense kitty. Congress further complicates Washington's financial problems by severely limiting the kinds and rates of tax that can be levied on the city. Always sensitive to the pressures of District merchants and real-estate men, many legislators fight hard against increases in local taxation. The merest suggestion of a payroll tax on commuters provokes not only predictable rage from Marylanders and Virginians but anger from their representatives and their representatives' friends on the Hill. The District has no Congressmen to argue on its behalf. As a result of such factors, Washington's proposed budgets are usually slashed.

Even if a payroll tax were passed, many Washington suburbanites would be unaffected because they no longer work in the central city. The movement of many high-level agencies, such as the Bureau of Standards, the Atomic Energy Commission, the Naval Ordnance Laboratory and the National Institutes of Health, to out-of-city locations has meant more than the exemption of certain Saturday crab-grass fighters from the daily struggle to get downtown. It has accelerated the exodus of middle-class citizens from Washington proper and disrupted life both in the city and in the countryside. While Washington is being made into a powerless ghetto, its suburbs are becoming a kind of superuniversity community: a concentration of residents who are overpowering in their level of education and their per capita income. A Montgomery County, Maryland, housewife recently observed that almost half of her neighbors held either medical or other doctorate degrees.

These invasion forces of lawyers, economists, social planners and other professional intellectuals bring to their new home counties a passion for public improvement and a background of activism. When they encounter the deep-set conservatism of oldtime Potomac countryside residents, the meeting of political temperature extremes generates intense storm activity on a wide front. Coalitions form and are thunderously disrupted. The suburban governments improve schools and services and make other advances on an irregular basis, depending on who has won the recent elections—"progressive" elements or "conservatives" devoted to yesteryear's principles and tax levels. The mix varies from town to town and from year to year. National issues are dragged into the various contests. With California-like abandon, the campaigns mix Birchite and New Left viewpoints on race, education, peace and sex into discussions of new playground sites or zoning ordinances. The added attraction (and distraction) in such places as Arlington or Bethesda is that many of the combatants are busy, between bouts, in running the nation.

Having no elective government, and having lost so many of these gifted and informed activists, the city cannot benefit from this kind of political give-and-take in its municipal affairs. Without the power to reward or punish at the polls, residents can only be petitioners who may be noticed or ignored according to Congressional whim.

The public schools in particular have suffered from this political impotence of Washingtonians. The inadequacies of the school system are felt almost wholly by Negroes; more than 90 per cent of the 150,000 pupils and 75 per cent of the 6,400 teachers are black. The situation would almost certainly be improved if Washington were self-governing. Not only do Negroes constitute a majority of the population, but if they had any real voice they would have no trouble producing effective leadership; Washington probably has a higher percentage of well-educated, affluent Negroes than any other major city in the United States. More than an eighth of the city's black adults have been to college, one third of the families have incomes of more than $8,000 per year, and more than a third of the Negro families own their own homes.

These are the kinds of citizens who might be expected not only to want a good school system but to see that they got it. That they have not been able to do so is the result partly of their lack of political power and partly of their own social and economic success. There are several Negro societies in Washington. First, there is a kind of Mayflower-descendant class, stemming from those freed slaves who established themselves financially more than a century ago. Its members live expensively, privately and well. A group of distinguished Negroes who have achieved the summit of the political elite —the topmost Negro appointees in the nation— make up another category. Successful professionals

ROBERT C. WEAVER   BENNETTA B. WASHINGTON   EDWARD W. BROOKE

An academy for excellence

Before the Supreme Court outlawed segregation in public schools in 1954, Washington's most renowned public school exclusively for Negroes was the Paul Laurence Dunbar High School, shown at left with three of its most distinguished graduates. Dunbar was founded in 1870 as the Preparatory High School for Colored Youth—one of the first publicly supported high schools for Negroes in the country—after a bill proposing integrated schools was defeated in Congress. The object of the school was to prepare students for college, and in this it succeeded admirably. Many of Dunbar's graduates have achieved public acclaim, including Dr. Robert C. Weaver (Class of 1925, named Secretary of the Department of Housing and Urban Development in 1966), Dr. Bennetta B. Washington (Class of 1933, in 1964 named Director, Women's Job Corps, Office of Economic Opportunity) and Edward W. Brooke (Class of 1936, in 1966 elected Senator from Massachusetts).

—lawyers, doctors, professors at Howard University, librarians, principals, high-level career civil servants—comprise still a third group. Many of these "arrived" Negroes live in handsome older suburbs within the District line, some have settled in new high-rise apartments segregated only by expense, and a few—aided by suburban liberals and local open-housing laws—have even penetrated potentially hostile Maryland and Virginia.

But the presence of a substantial number of affluent, well-educated Negroes has not substantially eased the school crisis. For Negro families with money have chosen in heavy numbers to enroll their children in private schools. Their flight from the public school system, combined with that of whites—many of them, admittedly or not, escaping the impact of school desegregation since 1954—has gripped Washington in the cruel cycle common to so many cities. The families with the knowledge and power to exert influence for better schools withdraw their sons and daughters, leaving the inner-city classrooms to those children who are most in need of special attention but whose parents are the least likely and least able to exert influence to get it. Deterioration sets in quickly, driving away all who can escape and feeding on itself.

In Washington, deterioration has gone far. In 1967 a large-scale study, commissioned by the city's Board of Education and headed by Professor A. Harry Passow of Columbia University's Teachers College, revealed that education in the District was "in deep, and probably worsening trouble." On standardized reading tests, only 26 of 130 elementary schools showed their sixth-grade pupils to be reading at or beyond national norms—and 15 of those 26 were in the Northwest, the whitest and wealthiest area of Washington. Only four of 11 high schools delivered reading scores at or above the national level. Students in only *one* high school performed that well in mathematics. One Washington high school, Dunbar, formerly top-notch (*see above*), rated in the bottom 8 per cent in the U.S. in both reading and mathematics levels.

The schools that did the poorest were, predictably, in the neighborhoods with the lowest median income and the fewest average years of parental schooling. The low-rated schools were assigned fewer of the small number of well-trained white teachers and more of the poorly prepared graduates of Southern colleges of education. These schools were generally forced to get by with textbooks years out of date and held together with string. Pupil quotas for many of the schools exceeded classroom space by 250 to 500 bodies. They also had a daily absentee rate of 15 to 20 per cent, shakedowns of students by other students, even beatings and knifings of teachers and pupils. This was the learning environment.

The Passow report called for new and daring improvements, among them decentralized school boards elected by local communities and the recruitment and training of idealistic white teachers who would regard assignment to slum schools as opportunity and not punishment. But what the system needed desperately, to make *any* ideas work, was money. It was not forthcoming. Mayor Washington's first budget included a proposal of some $110 million for the schools, but he reached that figure by slashing away almost $20 million in new school construction proposed by his planners. Even Senator Byrd objected to this, but his solution was not to increase the overall budget but to take the money from still another sector: social-welfare programs that Mayor Washington wanted to save.

Senator Byrd himself was no spendthrift on school construction, though he was more liberal in this area of public investment than in others. Still, in the first seven years of his tenure as chairman of the Senate District Appropriations Subcommittee, Congress appropriated only some $127 million for school building, repair and modernization, or about $18 million a year, a sum hardly enough to keep up with obsolescence, let alone underwrite expansion. Furthermore, what money there was had a way of finding a path to the better schools. The Northwest's Woodrow Wilson High got nearly $1.5 million in 1967 to add to its library, gymnasium and classrooms. Anacostia High, in a run-down neighborhood and 554 pupils overloaded, received $98,000; a projected $1.23 million in construction funds for the school was deferred by Congress.

Other scars of financial neglect pockmark Washington. Its public housing projects are, in some places, dirty, deteriorated, garbage-littered and vandalized. The District's building-code enforcement procedures are slow and inadequate. Its refuse collection is arthritic in many areas of the city. Its jail is not only an anachronism but a sin against humanity. Its courts are overtaxed with the cases generated by a rising crime wave that has terrified merchants, taxi drivers, late-working women, and others who must be abroad at night in poorly lit and poorly protected neighborhoods. Congress spastically reacted to this problem in 1967 by passing a District crime-control measure permitting the police to arrest, hold and question suspects without formal arraignment for as long as three hours. But it did not add any financial provision for solving a police manpower shortage of some 10 per cent in an authorized force of 3,100, a shortage caused in part by poor working conditions. Congress was not ready to spend its way to a modern law-enforcement program in the city whose chief end is the making and interpreting of laws.

Congress undoubtedly reflects the mood of the nation's taxpayers, who show little enthusiasm for walking the hard and costly road of urban modernization. To chant the depressing litany of Washington's shortcomings, after all, is simply to identify it as one more sick city among others. But Washington is not merely another city. The particular sting of its dilemmas is in the awareness that it *is* the capital and that money *is* spent freely to enhance its beauties for the eyes and photographic lenses of the tourist. In the Southwest and on the site of the Kennedy Center for the Performing Arts and elsewhere in the sightseer's Washington, lovely works of architecture are rising (along with others not so lovely) on footings of federal dollars. On the drawing boards is a grand design for a rehabilitated Pennsylvania Avenue, broader sidewalks refreshed with parks and fountains, blazing in season with flowers. L'Enfant, one feels, would have liked the general idea if not each detail.

But in Anacostia, only a few minutes from where the new Pennsylvania Avenue will glisten, a bitter store owner said that the President and the First Lady should see this forgotten part of Washington. "Let them come out here without their Secret Service guards. Let them come out and see what Washington's really like." What Washington—all of Washington—is really like is depicted in part by the Passow report on the city's sick school system. And the report reminds readers that the tourist's city, the exciting, power-hungry city of brainy, successful men enjoying the game of making history and managing empires, is only part of the national capital. If America's capital is to be something special, then *all* of it must be, and not the little spotlighted circle on public view. Would-be urban reformers in Washington might well take their cue from a passage in the Passow report that goes beyond the framework of education for one generation's children in one community. Congress, said Passow, "must help make it possible for Washington to become the Nation's laboratory for the creation of a model for urban school systems and its show place to other countries of how America's goals and values for equal opportunity can be attained."

One gets the feeling that Major L'Enfant would have liked that, too.

The faces of
black Washington

Arthur Carver, 11, comes from a fatherless slum family *(pages 146-147)*.

The Negro is as much a part of Washington as are Congress and the Washington Monument. Negroes make up more than 60 per cent of the city's 811,000 residents and more than 90 per cent of the children in its public schools. In no other American city have Negroes attained such predominance and developed so complete a social and economic structure.

At the top is a wealthy, well-educated upper class comprised of families that have been in Washington for generations. Many of them can claim distinguished ancestry in two races, and at one time light skin was a requisite for being a part of the group. Below this peak is a large and growing middle class of doctors, lawyers, university professors, high-level government officials, businessmen, merchants, civil service employees, secretaries and skilled workers.

But it is at the very bottom of the social and economic structure that the majority of Washington's black population can be found. Many of them, like the unsmiling boy at left, live in desperate poverty in the city's sprawling ghettos. There are more than 36,000 Negro families in Washington with incomes of less than $2,874 per year—the officially calculated poverty level. Negroes make up most of the estimated 122,000 unemployed—or underemployed—and most of the 34,000 who survive on public assistance (i.e., relief).

The faces of black Washington pictured on the following pages represent not only a sampling of the city's Negro population but the backgrounds, attitudes and aspirations that make the nation's capital a land of economic opportunity for some but a prison for many more.

Photographs by Evelyn Hofer

her Andrew Trent, 58, was born and educated in Boston and holds a master's
ee from New York University. He decided to come to Washington in 1940 when
as unable to get a job in the Boston schools. Even in the nation's capital he had to
as a mailman for six years ("In those days it was a good thing") before being hired
ach in a segregated Negro school. Now a Latin teacher at integrated Western High
ool, Trent lives with his wife—who is also a teacher—in an attractive integrated
hborhood of middle-class homes in Northeast Washington. Each summer he
hes special classes in English to high-school seniors, like the ones at left, who failed
ourse in the regular school term and who must now get passing grades in order to
uate. In these predominantly Negro classes "most of the kids read on an eighth-
e level," says Trent. "English is a foreign language to them."

College students Carol Brooks *(foreground)* and Marjorie Booker
are members of Alpha Kappa Alpha sorority at predominantly
Negro Howard University in Washington. Carol, who comes from a
middle-class home in Fort Worth, Texas, turned down offers from
two "white" colleges to attend Howard because "I wanted to be
with black people." An English major, she likes Washington and
might remain after graduation if she can find a job. She believes
that Howard students are now "more aware, and not satisfied with
the status quo." But Marjorie, a native Washingtonian whose
father is on the faculty of the prestigious Howard Medical School,
is less enthusiastic about remaining. "I intend to stay for a while
after graduation," says Marjorie, a French major who would like to
be an interpreter, "but I wouldn't want to live here."

The Reverend Earl L. Harrison has spent 38 years as minister of
Shiloh Baptist Church in Northwest Washington and has seen his
former congregation scatter as the neighborhood deteriorated into
a riot-torn slum. There has been talk of moving the church out of
the area, but Dr. Harrison believes that it should remain and work
"to overcome the enmity between the affluent, the semi-affluent
and the poor." The church has bought and renovated some slum
buildings and supports a number of community activities, including
downtown "excursions" for children who have never been out of
the ghetto. But Dr. Harrison is concerned about the inability to
"cool" the militancy of young Negroes. "As we come into
possession of the things we fought so hard for, the younger
element seems to turn around and destroy them," he says.

A soda-fountain manager, Carrie Tindall was born on a farm near Arvonia, Virginia, and came to Washington in 1947, joining a sister and a brother who were already working there. She was a cleaning woman at the National Gallery of Art and a housekeeper for former Senator James H. Duff of Pennsylvania before going to work as a drugstore waitress in 1958. She is married but has not lived with her husband for many years. Now 40 years old, Mrs. Tindall supports a 17-year-old son who wants to be a "star singer" despite his mother's wish that he go to college and then on to medical school. A daughter, age 19, whose husband is serving in the Army, also lives with her. "I don't like Washington," says Mrs. Tindall. "My life has been very, very hard here. The [Negro] areas aren't nice any more. I'd like to leave, but not to go back to Virginia. I kind of like Pennsylvania. All I want is for my children to have a better life than me."

Furniture-store worker Joseph Walker, 35, shown here with his wife and eight of their 10 children, ages 3 to 19, makes $85 a week. Born in Washington, he left school at 15, was married and a father at 16. He has always had trouble finding steady employment and once held 13 jobs in a single year. "A job is a job, as long as I get money to feed my family," he says. "Without education, you don't get nowhere in this city." With frugal budgeting the Walkers manage to support not only their own family but also Mrs. Walker's invalid father, the child of 16-year-old Michael Walker *(top, right)* and the child's mother. "I'm not going to see anyone hungry," says Mr. Walker, who has long been promised a larger apartment in the public-housing project where his family is squeezed into four bedrooms. Mrs. Walker not only manages to make ends meet but is an active volunteer worker in 10 community organizations.

Lawyer Charles Duncan and his wife, Dorothy, dressed in evening clothes in front of their home in Northwest Washington, represent the new aristocracy of black Washington, which no longer adheres to the color caste system. Duncan, a graduate of Dartmouth and of Harvard Law School, had a successful law practice in Washington but now devotes full time to his job as District Corporation Counsel, i.e., attorney for the city government. His wife holds a teaching degree and also studied at Harvard. Commenting on the old "light makes right" social standard in the Negro community, Duncan says, "We Negroes were victimized by the reverse of 'black is beautiful.' But that's all changing now."

Barber Joseph Swann learned his trade in the Army during World War II. After the war he left his native North Carolina to find work and stopped off to visit his mother and sister in Washington. He has been there ever since. "Washington is a different world from North Carolina," he says. "It's larger, more money circulating, the schools are better." The father of five children, Swann has owned his own shop for eight years in Northeast Washington where there was extensive rioting in 1967. "I wasn't surprised by the riots," he says, "but I didn't think there would be all this burning. The store right next to me would have been burned out—he's a Jew—but I told them not to. I wasn't frightened of them burning me."

These four angry youths, standing in the doorway of a youth center in the Anacostia
section, are linked by bonds of frustration and hate with thousands of ghetto Negroes.
All are school dropouts (40 per cent of Washington's Negro children fail to finish high
school), all have poor employment records, all blame the white man for their troubles.
"The purpose of the riots was to let black people tell 'whitey' how much we hate him,"
says Hezekiah Carter, 22 *(second from left)*. "We should exterminate all white people,"
says Melvin Brown, 21 *(second from right)*. Herman Harris, 22 *(far right)*, adds: "We
need to stop 'whitey' from running into the ghettos and telling us how to run our lives."
All long for the goals listed by Harold Wood, 19 *(far left)*: "I want a job I can go to every
day. I want a decent home in the black community. I want my son to have a college
education. I want security for myself and my family."

Social leaders Mr. and Mrs. Robert Grayson McGuire (both in their fifties), seated on the patio of their house in Washington's exclusive "Gold Coast," are members of a small group of wealthy, well-bred Negroes who form the traditional upper crust of Negro society in Washington. McGuire's maternal grandfather was in the first graduating class at Howard University and his paternal grandfather opened one of the first Negro drugstores in Washington. Mr. McGuire's family goes back four generations in the city. The owner of a well-known funeral home established by his father in 1912, Dartmouth-educated McGuire is able to move easily between the upper levels of both black and white society. He has served as president of the city's Urban League, is on the board of Washington's National Symphony Orchestra and holds a medal from Pope John XXIII, honoring him for his work in Catholic organizations.

Unemployed Mary Carver, 36, supports herself and her six children—ranging in age from 5 to 11—on an allowance of $200 a month from her husband, who is serving with the United States Army in Vietnam, and from whom she is legally separated. She pays $80 for a slum apartment that was so infested with rats, roaches and flies that the board of health sent in an exterminator. ("The dead rats sure do stink up the place.") After paying for electricity and gas she has little money left for food and clothing. "I've thought about moving," she says, "but any place I can afford don't want all these children." Mrs. Carver, who never finished high school, has applied for a job as a hotel chambermaid but cannot go to work until she finds someone to look after the children. "This area is so rough I'm afraid to leave them with just anybody. You can't walk the streets at night around here. I worry about the kids all the time."

Economist Andrew Brimmer, a member of the Federal Reserve Board, is one of an elite group of Negroes who have attained high positions in the federal government as Presidential appointees. A 42-year-old native of Louisiana, he is a graduate of the University of Washington, studied in India, holds a Ph.D. from Harvard and was an Assistant Secretary of Commerce. "I have been in Washington longer than any other place," he says, "but I find it difficult to become part of the community." One reason is that, although he helped shape the federal antipoverty program and has been active in programs designed to aid Negro businessmen, Dr. Brimmer avoids local civil rights involvement. "I am not an action man—a marcher or a speaker. I am a researcher and scholar. I try to keep my public life separate from my private life."

Printer Johnnie Richard Thornton, 28, is an apprentice in the Government Printing Office. When he finishes he will be making close to $10,000 annually—enough to give him middle-class status. Thornton grew up in a ghetto called Cow Town in the northwest part of Washington and attended Phelps Vocational High School. His parents were separated, and his mother worked in a laundry to support four children. Now Thornton lives in a racially mixed neighborhood and his three sons attend parochial schools—where they are taught by Negro nuns—"because they are better schools and have better discipline." Mrs. Thornton, a teacher, is studying for her master's degree. "Washington is a good place for Negroes," says Thornton. "There is still a lot of prejudice, but these little things will change. They have to."

The pool players shown below are slum-born young men who still have some hope that education may be the key that unlocks the ghetto. Sylvester Simpkins, 17 *(far left)*, Ronnie Jones, 16 *(second from left)*, and Phillip King, 17 *(second from right)*, are high-school students; Cornell Jones, 19 *(far right)*, is a high-school graduate. The most determined of them is Albert Rogers *(center)*, a 23-year-old Navy veteran now in his third year at the District of Columbia Teachers College. He says, "I realize in this white man's world you need at least an M.A. to get what the white man gets with a high-school diploma. But I want to be a teacher so I can straighten out some of the wrongs being done here."

Charles Pugh, 23, shown at right with his wife, Merlean, 21, and their son, Carlos, 1, came to Washington from his native Mississippi after graduating from Jackson State College in 1967 and now holds a good job as a budget analyst for the Labor Department. The Pughs have no relatives in Washington and moved there strictly for the career opportunity it presented. Pugh experiences less personal discrimination than most Negroes in Washington, but he is acutely aware of the situation in the ghettos. "When people have nothing and are forced to live in miserable conditions," he says, "they have no choice but to try to break out any way they can—to tear down and burn the invisible wall."

7

A Concentration
of Learned Men

When comparisons are cultural and not political, not even the most ardent American patriot would rank Washington, D.C., with the storied capitals of Europe. The Left Bank of the Seine is—or once was—alive with the artistic rebels of Paris. (On the Potomac's left bank there may be picturesque eccentrics, but most of them are members of the United States Congress.) Vienna is better remembered in history for Mozart and Freud than for Franz Josef and Metternich. Rome lives in the minds of men for the splendor of its paintings, sculpture and architecture, not for its mad emperors and strutting dictators. Ask an educated person to say what the word "London" brings to mind, and Shakespeare, Hogarth and Dickens are as likely to emerge as are the names of the kings and ministers of English history.

But Washington is another story. Few distinguished American poets have let their minstrel raptures swell there. No modern novelist of national stature lives there. If one did, he would have to mail his manuscripts to New York for publication,

The Main Reading Room of the Library of Congress, with its curving file cabinets and alcoves filled with reference works, is only a small corner of the complex that houses probably the world's finest collection of books and pamphlets—more than 14 million volumes.

even as the hopeful writers of Terre Haute or Little Rock must do. Washington has as yet no major resident opera company, and its symphony orchestra, the National, though competent, is not ranked as outstanding.

There is a single theater that shows touring Broadway plays and two resident professional companies. The National Ballet Company, which gave its first performance in 1963, is also located there. As for art, while Washington's distinguished museums display some of the finest works of the past, the city has no academy of design presently incubating the top painters, architects, designers and sculptors of tomorrow.

Summing it all up is the absence of an intellectual "heart" to Washington in the form of a great university such as Harvard, Columbia, Yale or Chicago. In a recent survey the American Council on Education asked some 4,000 scholars at more than a hundred universities to name, in order, the best graduate faculties and programs in their specialties. The result was a professional bluebook of universities in 29 disciplines. Of Washington's five graduate centers, three made the lists. George Washington and Catholic University were each "Acceptable Plus" (below the top ratings) in three fields and Georgetown in only one. American University did not make the list at all. Howard was not considered in the survey because of the small number of graduate degrees awarded.

Despite its shortcomings, Washington is not, of course, a cultural wasteland. In addition to being one of the nation's major art centers and the site of what may well be the world's finest and most extensive modern library—the Library of Congress— the capital probably offers a more substantial and varied musical fare than most American cities of comparable size. Yet, especially in recent decades, Washington has *seemed* culturally underprivileged. What makes the inadequacies loom large is the astounding concentration of intellectuals now to be found in the city, the very people who normally demand a full cultural life. Washington today is a kind of national campus, crowded with specialists in nearly all fields of learning. The government has sought the services of experts in the past, but never before in history has almost every federal department been so dependent upon the spectrum of talents in the academic community.

There are, first, the offices that manage economic and social programs, ranging from such veteran bureaus as the Departments of Agriculture and Treasury through relatively recent regulatory bodies like the Securities and Exchange Commission and the National Labor Relations Board down to newcomers like the Office of Economic Opportunity and the Department of Housing and Urban Development. The diverse and exacting operations of the offices managing foreign and domestic banking and trade, the budget, aid to education, and other aspects of the federal investment in national growth constantly require the services of men and women with highly specialized skills and information. Each year sees these agencies sending notices and representatives to campus placement offices, attempting to lure holders of degrees in economics, sociology, statistics, law, business administration and other fields to the capital.

Then there are the scientific agencies, many now tied closely to the military establishment. The Naval Ordnance Laboratory, the National Bureau of Standards, the Goddard Space Flight Center, the National Institutes of Health, the Weather Bureau, the Atomic Energy Commission, the Coast and Geodetic Survey, and the Naval Observatory are among those doing their part to maintain the bull market for science specialists.

The major intelligence agencies, CIA and the National Security Agency, employ numerous experts in languages and mathematics whose operations would dazzle the public if they were not kept

BRAIN-TRUSTER RAYMOND MOLEY CONFERS WITH PRESIDENT ROOSEVELT.

in the dark wrappings of security. The experts are both civilian and military. One veteran of World War II still recalls with a twinge a chastening moment in 1942 when he was assigned to one of the military predecessors of NSA (which specializes in work on codes and ciphers). Exultant in the possession of a new B.A. degree, he treated his fellow privates with gentle condescension until one memorable lunch in the mess hall. There he discovered that all of the men spooning up stew at his table were also college graduates and that six had made substantial progress toward master's and doctor's degrees.

All the aforementioned agencies are oriented toward applied knowledge, but there are also two gigantic Washington institutions formally dedicated to general scholarship: the Smithsonian Institution and the Library of Congress. The huge, sprawling Smithsonian—the "octopus on the Mall," as one author recently called it—was founded in 1846 thanks to the $500,000 bequest of James Smithson, an English chemist, who wanted his name perpetuated in the New World to avenge snubs he had received in the Old because he was illegitimate. The institution's mission is "the increase and diffusion of knowledge among men," and it works at it steadily. It is best known for its museums and gal-

A mecca for eggheads

Although intellectuals have played important roles in Washington since the earliest days of the republic, it was not until the Administration of President Franklin D. Roosevelt that large numbers of highly specialized academics were openly encouraged to come to the capital. The movement began in 1932 with the assembling of a three-man group of economic advisers, headed by Columbia University law professor Raymond Moley *(left)*, that became known—and often maligned—as the "Brain Trust." "We were freaks," recalls Adolf Berle Jr., another of the original Brain Trusters. "A politician who talked to a professor in those days kept it a deep, dark secret." But the investment in intellectual brainpower produced not only the revolutionary social welfare and economic programs of the New Deal era, but a World War II scientific harvest that included advances in atomic energy, radar and antibiotics. Not until the Administration of John F. Kennedy was another Chief Executive to make such widespread use of intellectuals in government. In the campaign of 1960 Kennedy drew heavily on Harvard, his alma mater, for such key advisers as historian Arthur M. Schlesinger Jr. *(right)* and economist John Kenneth Galbraith. After Kennedy's election a graduate degree became a more important qualification for high office than membership in the Democratic Party. It was part of the Kennedy legacy that in 1968 four of President Lyndon B. Johnson's 12 Cabinet members were former college professors.

SPECIAL ASSISTANT ARTHUR SCHLESINGER SHOWS KENNEDY HIS NOTES.

leries, which display the bric-a-brac it has acquired in almost a century and a quarter. Mark Twain once called the Smithsonian "the nation's attic." But the objects viewed by the public give no idea of the extent of the Smithsonian's active role in science. Under its jurisdiction are the National Zoological Park, the Science Information Exchange, an astrophysical observatory, a radiation biology laboratory and a tropical research institute. Its anthropologists, ethnologists, archeologists, ornithologists and astronomers have tracked orbiting satellites and dug for prehistoric pottery; they have collected birds from all over the world and studied the properties of cosmic rays.

The Library of Congress, too, is one of the intellectual wonders of the globe. Its collections in the late 1960s were numbing to list—nearly 14 million volumes and pamphlets, one of the world's greatest collections of newspapers, some 28 million manuscripts, three million maps, more than three million volumes of music and individual scores, some 185,000 phonographic discs and tape and wire recordings, 1.8 million photographic negatives, prints and slides, 86,000 reels of motion pictures, and about 380,000 reels and strips of microfilm. Special subdivisions—music, Slavic languages, Orientalia, science and technology (to give

only a partial list)—not only house these treasures but are the home bases of resident and visiting research scholars who are busily classifying, applying and extending the knowledge that the subdivisions encompass.

Washington also houses a number of distinguished private research organizations. One of the best known is The Brookings Institution, founded in 1927, which conducts inquiries into problems besetting national policy makers. Its experts issue a stream of studies and publications indispensable to top officials. John F. Kennedy, shortly before assuming the Presidency in 1961, thanked the institution for a series of meticulous briefings on government operations and public-policy problems that it had delivered to him and his advisers that helped him effect a smooth transfer of power. His gratitude for what he apparently considered a personal favor was embarrassing to the carefully nonpartisan directors, who had stood ready on request to provide the same service for Kennedy's Republican opponent, Richard Nixon, had he won the election.

Brookings stands in a neighborhood—the blocks around Massachusetts Avenue between 15th and 20th Streets—that also houses, in handsome new office buildings, the staffs of the American Association for the Advancement of Science, the American Council on Education, the National Education Association, the National Geographic Society and The Johns Hopkins School of Advanced International Studies. Inevitably, the section is coming to be known as "Egghead Row." When its inhabitants feel the need of a review of the literature in their specialties, they can turn to numerous other intellectual centers, the more than 300 private and public libraries in the District of Columbia and its immediate environs. In these specialized collections they can bone up on almost anything: admiralty law, Africana, agricultural engineering, Aramaica, cryptography, epidemiology, geodesy and geophysics, Jewish literature, Kiplingiana, labor economics, neurology, patrology, petrology, philately, Shakespeareana, urban redevelopment, venereal disease, wildlife conservation, wood-products utilization, and zoology. Many of these collections (including those belonging to lobbies) are the largest and best of their kind in the world.

In addition to the constant stimulation provided by the large resident colony of highly trained experts, Washington's intellectual life is further enhanced by the numerous transient specialists in the city on any given day. Among the passengers landing at National Airport each morning are professors in every field from Arabic literature to zoology. For a daily consultation fee, they help to plan everything from language courses for the armed services to sanitation systems for Asian villages to urban psychiatric clinics, aviation safety programs and census questionnaires.

Such visitors rarely remain more than a few days at a time, and jet transportation has tended to make their stays even briefer while increasing their number. A staff member of The Brookings Institution observes: "Whatever may be on the government's mind, it can have a panel of experts on the subject assembled in virtually a day and have them back in their labs and offices in Cambridge and Berkeley before the coffee in the half-empty cups on the conference table is cool." In this way policy makers, in effect, use the country's pool of erudition without adding to the permanent federal payroll.

Thus Washington is a constantly functioning center for applied studies in every branch of learning. Given this atmosphere, it would seem that the local institutions of higher education should be among the very best in the country. Yet the curious truth may be that the sheer mass of brain power assembled in the District of Columbia helps

to account for the relative weakness of its universities, and thus paradoxically detracts from the District's permanent status as a cultural center. Washington, host to the nation's most learned men and women, is itself a campus with which the universities cannot compete.

Of the five District universities (not counting the University of Maryland in suburban College Park) the oldest is Georgetown, the senior Roman Catholic institution of higher learning in the country. It was founded in 1789 by the first Roman Catholic Archbishop in the United States, John Carroll of Baltimore, as an academy for preparing young men to study "with Advantage . . . the higher Sciences." It has since grown into a university whose schools of law, medicine and foreign service have achieved some note. A century after the founding of Georgetown, the Catholic University of America opened its doors in Washington with the aim of keeping Catholic scholarship abreast of contemporary graduate study.

George Washington University, located in "Foggy Bottom," grew out of Columbian College, an academy begun in 1821 after long prodding by patriots who wanted the capital city to develop a national university. Among its backers was the Father of His Country, who left 50 shares of stock in the Potomac Canal Company to help launch such a project. The college struggled through almost a century of sluggish growth, acquiring graduate divisions, and gained its present name in 1904. In recent years it has had a large population of part-time and evening students.

In this respect George Washington resembles American University, a neighboring and closely comparable school. American was officially founded in the 1890s under Methodist auspices but did not really begin significant operations until about the beginning of World War I. At first it offered graduate programs in downtown buildings, but today it is gradually selling its mid-city facilities and moving their programs to a handsome campus in the upper Northwest section of the city. Thus, in the view of one local educator, it is moving away from urban involvement to become one more middle-class residential college.

Howard University, the most interesting of the District schools, is a direct product of the Civil War. It is named for General Oliver Otis Howard, the head of the Freedmen's Bureau, the federal agency created to rehabilitate the slaves liberated by Union arms. It opened its doors in 1867 to give both these newly freed Negroes and the prewar "free colored" society a ladder to higher learning.

Its first schools were devoted to liberal arts, medicine, pharmacology and religion, and it gradually built faculties of law, fine arts, music, engineering and architecture, dentistry and social work. Howard, which continues to receive an annual federal appropriation of several million dollars, prides itself on being the elite of Negro institutions of higher learning and attracts many nonwhite students from all over the world, as well as a number of whites. Though it is a great incubator for the black bourgeoisie, Howard has stirred to the winds of Africanism and black nationalism from time to time and sent militant reformers, Stokely Carmichael among them, forth from its halls.

Taken together, the District universities represent much diligent effort but only spotty academic achievement. They are low among the recipients of government grants for research—another significant measure of how reviewing committees of experts rate schools—and their part-time programs to satisfy the hungers of government workers for professional advancement are essentially ventures in middle-class adult education. Furthermore, these private colleges have largely failed to meet the educational needs of low-income city students. Partially to fill this gap, Congress in 1967 finally authorized a Federal City College, slated to offer both a two-year junior-college course and a four-year liberal arts curriculum with low tuition.

One of the ways in which the District's very nature sustains the inadequacies of these schools is illustrated in the library situation. None of the institutions has the kind of comprehensive library that marks a great research center. Their students and professors, it is assumed, will use the magnificent collections in the government's libraries, which it would be expensive folly to duplicate. However sound the logic, many academics feel that, in the words of a onetime dean at George Washington, this policy is like building a house without a bathroom because the nearby city hall has splendid free public toilets. A professor whose academy sends him through traffic jams to pursue Truth is not likely to develop great institutional loyalty, and if he gets an offer from a good non-Washington university he may be strongly tempted to leave. If he is at all given to activism, he may prefer to work for the government itself. Those professors who remain on Washington campuses may feel with some justice that they are still some distance from the academic peaks. Thus, without academic excellence money is not attracted, and without money there cannot be the enticements—in salaries, benefits, leaves, research assistance, and facilities—that beckon excellence. The Washington universities, for the most part, train their enrollees gamely but without sparks. They are outclassed not only by other campuses, but by the federal behemoth itself.

An occasional fantasy of non-Washingtonian professors is to build an imaginary capital university staffed by the world's greatest part-time faculty—practicing experts in every public art and science, lecturing weekly from their store of fresh experience. Unfortunately, there are probably too many hitches for the dream to come true, even given the will and leadership. The top bureaucrats simply cannot count on enough freedom from office crises to plan on meeting classroom commitments at regular intervals, and lesser civil servants giving an occasional course would be no improvement on settled professors. Part-time faculty members, moreover, lack time for the telephoning, base touching, conferring and memo writing that are required to maintain high levels in appointing professors and fellows. Thus the institutions of higher learning in Washington continue to exist in a kind of twilight zone between the rays cast by the richly endowed private centers of learning and the publicly owned universities.

In contrast, Washington's museums are bathed in the brightest sunlight. The great National Gallery of Art has 30,000 works, their nucleus being a collection donated in 1937 by the Pittsburgh millionaire Andrew Mellon, who was Secretary of the Treasury under Harding, Coolidge and Hoover. The National Gallery was opened in 1941. The Corcoran Gallery of Art, founded in 1859 by a prosperous Washington banker, Philip Corcoran, houses a fine group of American paintings, plus an impressive number of English, French, Italian, Flemish and Dutch 17th-to-19th Century masterpieces originally accumulated by the Montana mining baron and Senator, William A. Clark. The Phillips Art Collection, in a red brick townhouse near Dupont Circle, is rich in Klees, Picassos, Van Goghs and other rare canvases. The Freer Gallery was founded by Charles L. Freer, a successful freight-car manufacturer, and opened in 1923. Given by him to the government, it is (like the National) under the jurisdiction of the protean Smithsonian Institution. It houses, in its pleasant white building on the Mall, a world-renowned assemblage of Oriental art objects as well as some notable American paintings.

Washington is a good town for looking at beautiful pictures. It is significant, however, that the museums were built on two pillars: the generosity

The National Gallery's benefactors

BARON DUVEEN, ANDREW MELLON AND TITIAN'S *VENUS WITH A MIRROR*.

JOSEPH WIDENER AND REMBRANDT'S *LADY WITH AN OSTRICH-FEATHER FAN*.

SAMUEL H. KRESS AND BELLINI'S *PORTRAIT OF A CONDOTTIERE*.

LESSING J. ROSENWALD AND A WATERCOLOR BY WILLIAM BLAKE.

CHESTER DALE AND DEGAS' *MADAME RENÉ DE GAS*.

The National Gallery of Art was proposed in 1936 by financier Andrew Mellon, then Secretary of the Treasury, to house what he hoped would become "a great national collection." Today it exhibits masterpieces bequeathed by some of the country's most prominent collectors. The nucleus of the gallery's collection is Mellon's gift of 126 paintings and 26 pieces of sculpture, gathered largely with the aid of international art dealer Baron Joseph Duveen. By the time the National opened in 1941, it had added more than 450 works of art donated by philanthropist Samuel H. Kress. By the late 1960s the gallery had more than 30,000 paintings, sculptures and other items. The major contributors were the five collectors shown above with examples of their legacies.

of rich men and the willingness of Congress to allow the government to accept, house and administer their gifts. Comparable support for the other arts has not been available until quite recently. Washington's sole legitimate theater, the National, sustains itself by showing either "pre-New York" or "post-New York" plays, that is, tryouts in various stages of crudeness or road-company versions of established hits. Arena Stage, in a handsome but relatively small building in the Southwest redevelopment area, plays to full houses an excellent repertory-in-the-round of the classics from Molière to Anouilh. But these two, plus the Washington Theater Club, which presents a fair number of experimental plays, are virtually the beginning and end of professional theater in Washington. In symphonic music and dance, the National Symphony and visiting ballet companies perform in Constitution Hall, a somewhat bare auditorium owned by the Daughters of the American Revolution. The resident National Ballet Company generally uses Lisner Auditorium in the George Washington University neighborhood. Professional concert bureaus also book visiting artists into Lisner and Constitution Hall during the regular season, and in the summer into the Carter Barron Amphitheatre, an outdoor stadium in Rock Creek Park. The offerings are essentially those provided in cities like Cleveland, Detroit, Atlanta or Seattle.

But there are important supplements to this somewhat meager fare. For all Washingtonians, rich and not-so-rich, who care for the arts, government itself—sometimes with the help of private funds—provides a meaty and varied bill of fare. This includes some of the best chamber music in the world, played by visiting artists in the Coolidge Auditorium of the Library of Congress on Thursday and Friday nights from October through April. Stradivarius instruments, on loan from the library's rare-instrument collection, are often used. Tickets are usually free on a first-come, first-served basis, and it is worth noting that first come means promptly at 8:30 a.m. on the day tickets are available, when a line begins to form. Except in summer, there are also free chamber-music concerts on Sundays in the National Gallery, the Corcoran and the Phillips.

For more popular tastes, the Armed Forces bands play concerts the year round. In summer these are often held at the Watergate, where the Potomac slips past the Lincoln Memorial. The musicians' stage is a barge anchored in the stream and most of the audience sits on stone steps on the bank. Adventurous music lovers rent canoes and moor themselves to rock gently in the tide for the duration of the concert. There are also frequent summertime band concerts in the impressive setting of the Capitol steps, and in wintertime, more prosaically, at various government department auditoriums scattered around the city.

Washington has its art-film houses, as varied as the Biograph in Georgetown, a remodeled auto showroom that cheerfully combines a highly informal atmosphere with movies by Bergman and Antonioni, and the Plaza Theater, near Dupont Circle, which offers the now almost obligatory paintings and free coffee in the lobby. But on any given night the movies must compete with a mammoth schedule of poetry readings, lectures, recitals, and educational films at the Smithsonian, the National Gallery, the Library of Congress and other government centers. The films range from scenes of Sumerian antiquity to the life and habits of seals.

All of these attractions make for a pleasant, moderately well-rounded cultural life in Washington, but many of them are duplicated—and sometimes bettered—in big cities all over the country. Why is Washington, with its high percentage of intellectuals, not a truly great cultural center? Part of the answer is found in history. The great capitals of Europe—Paris, London, Rome, Vienna—grew naturally with their respective countries and became their largest cities with all the cultural amenities that great metropolises of the world usually offer. Washington was created to fill a single need; except as the seat of government, it has no other purpose.

As a result of this artificial formation and single role, the city never became home to a sizable number of rich, old families who took pride in their community and underwrote opera houses, great symphony orchestras, ballets and theaters. Further, most of the people who come to Washington, even those who are destined to live there for most of their lives, tend to feel like transients. The winds of change blow constantly over the Potomac; a new Administration, a reduction in staff, a defeat at the polls or a reassignment to a new post are just a few of the always possible developments that make it difficult for public servants to achieve a sense of permanence in the capital. Given this lack of roots, comparatively few people are eager to become patrons of local cultural projects, to sell tickets, raise money and do all the other tasks that are routine for the upper and upper-middle classes in many cities.

Perhaps the need for a fuller cultural life would outweigh the feeling of transiency if the nation's capital were, say, in the middle of Kansas. Washington, however, is located some 200 miles from New York. To hear great opera and symphonies, to see the finest modern and classical ballet, to enjoy the best the American theater has to offer, a Washingtonian, even in the past, had only to travel a few hours by train. Today, with fast and convenient jet shuttle service, a trip from Washington to New York takes no longer than a drive from the far suburbs to the center of town. Why, then, struggle to expand and improve the corner grocery store when an excellent supermarket is only a short distance away?

Congress, too, has been a factor in Washington's relatively slow cultural growth. Although the House and Senate have provided the maintenance and sometimes the housing for gifts of great art from rich men, the legislators have only rarely been disposed to lay aside their parsimony and pour tax dollars into such folderol as dance, theater and music. In the last few years there have been signs of change. Congress *did* vote in 1958 to establish a center for the performing arts in the capital. Named for John F. Kennedy in 1964, its majestic structure, large enough to contain nine Lincoln Memorials, was designed by Edward Durrell Stone. It is intended to house a symphony hall seating 2,750, an opera house with a capacity of 2,200, a theater for more than 1,150 spectators and a multipurpose theater for 500. Foreign countries have been donating furnishings, among them chandeliers from Ireland and Norway, Italian marble, a hand-woven silk curtain for the opera from Japan, bronze panels for the main doors from Germany and furniture for the foyer from Denmark.

While it is gratifying to think of the Kennedy Center as the spark for a cultural explosion in Washington, it is possible to see it in a less rosy perspective. The Center may simply be another large, inanimate element in the grand design for a new kind of imperial Washington, whose landmarks are the enlarged Capitol, the Texas-sized Rayburn Building and the proposed new Pennsylvania Avenue, treed and fountained like Versailles.

In any case, much more than elaborate buildings for the performing arts are needed if Washington is to become, like London, Paris and Rome, a cultural as well as a political capital. Most of all, creative, talented people are necessary to bring life to the structures, and at present there is little to entice artists to make the city the center of their careers. Thus the cultural paradox will probably remain.

8

A World Capital

Between the city of Washington and the rest of the world in this final third of the 20th Century there is a close, vital, responsive relationship, born of mutual need and concern. The threads of interdependence are woven daily in committee rooms on Capitol Hill, in the White House, in the concentric corridors of the Pentagon and at the conference tables of the State Department. The pattern begins to take firm shape when Congress makes appropriations—either generous or frugal—for the U.S. military establishment and for foreign aid. Thereafter, the various Executive decisions follow with their consequences. Military bases are opened in a European nation, and its ruler is strengthened as dollars surge into its economy; this has happened in Spain. A project for American assistance in building a vital dam is canceled, and an underdeveloped nation turns toward Moscow; this has happened in Egypt. A small state's air force receives a shipment of late-model United States equipment, and its neighbors reflect anew on how far they dare push their quarrel with it;

Plush carpets and paneling enhance the reception area outside the office of the Secretary of State. From here the Secretary directs a department of 27,000 employees in the U.S. and abroad, and coordinates the work of such agencies as the Peace Corps.

this has happened with Israel. The word from Washington changes history.

The converse is true as well. In darkened Washington, important officials are wakened from dead-of-night sleep to be told of trouble developing for the United States somewhere on the earth where there is still daylight. The president of a Latin-American nation is ousted, and the next time there is a confrontation with the Soviet Union in the U.N., a voice—and vote—friendly to the United States may be missing. An African nationalist leader starts a revolt; villages burn, and the United States stands at a crossroad of decision—intervene and be branded "imperialistic," refrain and risk the establishment of a government ideologically oriented to Moscow or Peking. A coup deposes a Greek government, and America must react in the knowledge that the balance of power in the Mediterranean may hinge on the reaction. Wherever natural and civil calamities, political whirlwinds or death rearrange worldwide lines of economic and political force, official Washington is involved in a problem.

Few involvements have begun with less promise of deepening. John Adams, the first President to reside in Washington, had said in 1783 that "after a very few years" it would be "the best thing we can do to recall every Minister from Europe and send emissaries only on special occasions." In 1801 Adams' Presidential successor, Thomas Jefferson, echoed the same idea: "We wish to let every treaty we have drop off without renewal. We call in our diplomatic missions, barely keeping up those to the most important nations. There is a strong disposition in our countrymen to discontinue even these; and very possibly it may be done." The step was not taken, but the support given to the diplomatic establishment was grudging at best. Andrew Jackson's Secretary of State angrily complained to his chief that diplomats were popularly "considered as favorites, selected to enjoy the pleasures of foreign travel at the expense of the people" and lived in a "continued scene of luxurious enjoyment." Accordingly, the Secretary noted, public support for diplomatic expenditures was nonexistent.

In their turn, European envoys to the Yankee capital in the early years were rarely men of eminence at home, and the assignment was regarded as tantamount to exile. Not until the 20th Century did men of genuine distinction begin to appear in the embassies and to give evidence of relative satisfaction with their appointments. A landmark was the appointment of James Bryce as British Ambassador in 1907. Lord Bryce, a distinguished scholar, had earlier written a two-volume, highly sympathetic study of the United States entitled *The American Commonwealth*, and he joined a diplomatic colony whose members were slowly learning a new respect for the energies of the United States.

But a comparable interest in and understanding of other nations was not widespread in the United States. As late as the early 1940s, isolationism was still a potent force in American life, despite—or perhaps because of—the nation's 1917-1918 adventure in world conflict. The weight of isolationist tradition thrust heavily against whatever tendencies toward a cosmopolitan outlook Washington might develop. Then globalism was thrust on the capital by World War II. That cataclysm ended with the collapse of a Western Europe that had been the center of power of 19th Century Western civilization. The defeated and victorious countries alike were in ruins, economically bankrupt, convulsed with the revolutionary social pressures generated by years of depression and wartime frustration and denial. The European empires in Asia and Africa were also in long-delayed nationalist explosion. Out of stark, brutal necessity the leadership of the non-Communist world was taken over by the United States. After World War II it was the United States that undertook the rearmament

of Europe and the economic rehabilitation of much of the world. The Marshall Plan, Point Four, the North Atlantic Treaty Organization, American involvement in the Korean War, the regional mutual-security pacts in Asia and elsewhere—each was a step, however reluctant, to the assumption of worldwide authority and responsibility.

As billions in aid funneled from the American taxpayer through the United States government to a ravaged world, "little Washington" was transformed. "The center of decision," noted one journalist, "shifted abruptly from the stately, elegant and ancient capitals of Paris and London to the almost provincial, suburbanite atmosphere of Washington." A British observer expressed disbelief. "Can this . . . really be the capital of the world?" he asked rhetorically. "Certainly away from the government buildings and the marble memorials there is nothing at all to suggest that this is anything but a small, sleepy, Southern town."

Small town or not, it was and is a community transformed by its formidable international burdens. The embodiment of that big change is visible in a variety of patterns, people and places. One is the huge, tabular, white Department of State building fronting on C Street in the neighborhood known as Foggy Bottom. It is still often called "New State," though its first section was built in the 1940s (a large addition was completed in 1960). Symbolically, the "Old State" Department home—the Victorian pile across from the White House that is now the Executive Office Building—housed its bureaucrats in a setting of shuttered windows, black-and-white-checkered corridor floors, high ceilings and working fireplaces, whereas New State is severely functional and has been called the "the world's best-appointed penitentiary."

The handful of assistants who helped early Secretaries of State to perform their duties has grown to about 27,000 employees—not including workers in autonomous and semiautonomous agencies—about 6,700 of them in the United States and most of these in Washington. The diplomatic pouch that once moved by windjammer and saddlebag has given way to long banks of Teletype machines, handling as many as half a million words in a day; to thousands of pieces of mail a day; to some 80 couriers who log as many as 12.5 million miles of travel a year. All of this is to keep contact with nearly 300 embassies, consulates, missions and other offices. Their personnel may include experts in budget planning, tropical medicine and other recondite fields, and their daily routines may vary from issuing visas to barricading windows against mob attacks. And each morning Washington wants to know exactly what took place yesterday.

Not only has the scope of U.S. foreign policy changed in recent decades, but so has the content, and this is reflected in the department's structure. State still divides the world into segments, each of which is expected to generate, in the nicely ambiguous old word, "affairs" that are an assistant secretary's responsibility. But in addition to the sections that handle African, European, Near Eastern and South Asian, East Asian and Pacific, and Inter-American "Affairs," there are now others dealing with Economic Affairs, Educational and Cultural Affairs, and International Organization Affairs. There are assistant secretaries and directors for, among others, Congressional Relations (to keep Capitol Hill happy), Public Affairs (to get the good word to the voters) and Intelligence and Research (to spot trouble before it happens). All of these jobs could once be adequately handled by a Secretary of State who had friends in Congress, a generous manner with the press, and a sharp set of eyes and ears.

Besides the traditional Foreign Service, the department administers such relatively recent operations as the U.S. Mission to the United Nations, the Peace Corps and the Agency for International Development. Among them, these various cells in the honeycomb of State Department offices supervise the execution of more than 40 collective-security pacts and some 4,500 treaties and other agreements with foreign powers on subjects as varied as disarmament, control of outer space, scientific cooperation in the Antarctic and the control of traffic in narcotics. They also prepare for American participation in as many as 600 international conferences a year, most of them rising out of our membership in permanent, specialized international bodies such as the General Agreement on Tariffs and Trade (GATT), the International Labor Organization (ILO), the Food and Agriculture Organization (FAO), and a great variety of others.

Sometimes it is difficult for even veteran State Department employees to remember that only a few decades have passed since the work consisted primarily of supervising ambassadors and consuls and presenting the American viewpoint, via formal notes and calls, on a limited range of such standard subjects of international discussion as wars, boundaries, alliances and trading rights. Today, as one former department official notes, "the officer who works in the traditional political diplomacy is now in the minority."

The average American is only vaguely aware of

The epithet "Foggy Bottom," often employed derisively to describe the methods or viewpoint of the Department of State, actually refers to a section of Washington. The name was first applied to a little-used tract of often misty bogland southeast of Georgetown, shown in the center of the upper picture in the 1890s. The State Department acquired the name in its new connotation when it moved to its present quarters (upper left, bottom picture).

this expanded State Department structure, of its labyrinthine complexity, or of the occasional struggles of its chieftains to retain foreign policy control against the encroachments of Congress, other Cabinet departments, White House experts and independent agencies with overseas functions. As a tourist in Washington he may attend one of the twice-weekly public briefings offered by the department—a gallant effort to convince the visitor from Mattoon, Illinois, or Kelso, Oregon, that the bromides about dilettante "striped-pants" diplomats are untrue. But otherwise, his only physical contact with the department is likely to come if affluence leads him to a passport-issuing office as a prelude to foreign travel. That becomes a more likely event each year. In 1950 the government issued or renewed about 300,000 passports. In the late 1960s the number was nearly 1.7 million a year. A crowded schedule in the Passport Office is a simple, easily recognizable sign of a shrinking world.

In Washington itself the human facets of global involvement generally elude statistical definition. But the by-products of the capital's evolution into an international center are evident in such places as the departure lounges for the international flights leaving Dulles Airport, where a goodly proportion of the passengers will be departing on government business. They can be felt in classrooms where children of civil servants chirp at "show and tell" time about the fun of riding in a bicycle-ricksha or proudly show the slides they took of the bay at Rio de Janeiro. Some of the children's classmates may themselves be foreign, sons and daughters of embassy staff members. The relatively new internationalism of Washington creates a daily routine for the State Department Foreign Service Institute, whose staff arranges courses in foreign languages and foreign customs for new and reassigned personnel, and for the government accountants who must audit the department-paid moving bills of thousands of families annually, to and from ports all over the globe.

To be sure, not all of this ebb and flow is under State Department auspices. The Pentagon is filled with career officers who expect, as part of their regular progression toward the shining stars of general or flag rank, to be sent overseas often. Their mission may be not only to fight battles or to administer combat-ready forces but to participate in the staff and planning work of such international commands as NATO. The number of Central Intelligence Agency employees who move in and out of the country, with cloaks and daggers presum-

ably secreted in their two-suiters, is not a published figure, but it is probably sizable.

Some government employees, by the very nature of their jobs, "internationalize" Washington without leaving their desks. The Agriculture, Commerce and Treasury Departments, for instance, employ specialists whose chief function is to study possible foreign markets for American growers, manufacturers, investors and shippers. The city is full of men and women to whom a fall in the price of cocoa in Brazil or a flooded tin mine in Indonesia are pieces of news with an immediate impact on their workaday lives. Washington is the home of the International Monetary Fund, the International Bank for Reconstruction and Development (World Bank), the Inter-American Development Bank, and several other agencies concerned with worldwide investment, development and solvency. For numerous young men and women who only recently were economics majors on Midwestern campuses, the rise and fall of the rupee and the yen have come to acquire enormous significance.

Not only the affairs but even the thoughts of people around the globe are crucial to modern Washington. Little more than a block from the White House are the offices of the United States Information Agency, where a large staff lives and labors for no other purpose than to give an accurate and, if possible, pleasing configuration to the world's opinion of the United States. Once upon a time Americans believed that propaganda was something sinister, used only by totalitarian governments. But the requirements of the Cold War forced a change of heart. "Even God," the saying goes, "needs church bells." America's "church bells" ring out from the USIA offices to reach millions of foreigners, some of them in countries that did not exist a few decades ago.

In the late 1960s the government spent nearly $170 million annually on USIA, whose main mission is to counteract not only the coarse, "proletarians-versus-plutocrats" distortions of American life printed in the press of Communist and other unfriendly countries but the misapprehensions held in neutral nations. USIA sends some 10,000 words of speeches, news releases and reports about current government programs—especially those in the areas of antipoverty, race relations and peace-keeping—to U.S. embassies daily, where press information officers put the material in form for friendly foreign news media to use. USIA prints pamphlets and magazines in 26 tongues, conducts English-language classes, schedules lectures on the American problems of past and present by visiting scholars from the United States, and arranges for the distribution of works, often in translation, of American history, biography and social criticism—not all of it gentle by any means. These are distributed to more than 200 libraries and reading rooms run by the organization around the world.

For nonreaders there are films, filmstrips and the well-known Voice of America. It broadcasts about 840 hours weekly in 36 tongues, some as exotic as Tamil and Swahili, from transmitters positioned as far apart as North Carolina and Thailand. The program content is not merely "rah-rah-for-our-side" newscasts, but samples of what Americans themselves hear—music (jazz, symphony, chamber, pop and rock), interviews, panel shows, and social reportage of the kind heard on NBC's "Monitor" and CBS's "Dimension."

So it is that in the "new" Washington, long ruled by a Congress suspicious of government-financed art and propaganda, there are thousands of civil servants (USIA has almost 12,000 employees worldwide) using the kinds of skills found in New York's publishing and broadcasting offices. They are trying to tell the world: "This is how it really is with us. This is what we are made of." The existence of a center in Washington dedicated to that responsibility is yet another example of America's coming of international age.

Yet if the entire corps of federal employees working in Washington could be assembled in one parking lot, it would be impossible by simple observation to distinguish them from any other body of white-collar workers. The more exotic manifestation of the new internationalism is the large colony of foreigners now found in the capital city. Not only has it grown considerably from the handful of ambassadors who braved the bilious fevers of early Washington history, but the functions of many of the present aliens are wholly different. Among the more interesting non-American residents are the specialists from other nations working in such recondite agencies as the International Monetary Fund and the nearly 200 correspondents for the foreign press. The newspapermen come primarily from Western Europe, though there is a large Japanese contingent. Most of them learn to operate like their American counterparts in cultivating official sources, and usually they adopt a similar style of dress and family life as well. Some have openly expressed their pleasure in being able to live in Washington's suburbs, which are still relatively close to their work. Occasionally they voice laments about the cultural thinness of the Amer-

ican capital, but on the other hand the frequency of in-the-home entertainment (especially of visiting Europeans or Asians) among hospitable Americans is a pleasing bonus of a Washington assignment. To some it perhaps is perilously pleasing: "I have fast learned to watch my stomach and liver here," one correspondent has said.

The internationalism of Washington may also be gauged by the number of embassies that now grace the city. There are more than 110 countries, beginning with Afghanistan and concluding with Zambia, that have diplomatic relations with the United States. The offices and living quarters that they maintain for their representatives vary from the splendid and imposing quarters of the British Embassy (which employs more than 500 people) to the small hotel suites maintained by some of the newer nations. It is, in fact, striking testimony to the changed world in which we live that of the 50 diplomatic delegations added to the 61 in the Washington of 1937, almost all are from countries nonexistent 30 years ago. A middle-aged American who grew up with impressions of Asia and Africa cinematically formed by *Tarzan*, *Beau Geste* and *The Lives of a Bengal Lancer* can probably gain much from a walk past buildings whose name plates announce that they are quarters for Their Excellencies the Ambassadors of Burundi, Chad, Gabon, the Ivory Coast, Kuwait, the Maldive Islands, Tanzania and Uganda.

The embassy people are not all diplomats, attachés, economic experts and specialists in the subject matter of treaties. An estimated 6,000 of some 7,600 diplomatic employees are supporting-cast members—clerks, secretaries, chauffeurs, messengers, janitors and guards. (Whether an embassy is staffed from top to bottom by its own nationals, or hires some Americans, usually depends on the country's sensitivity, suspiciousness and operating budget.) Washington's diplomatic community now numbers about 10,000 persons, including wives and children, and its effect is subtle and expressed in a variety of ways, from the demand for particular delicacies in Washington stores to the increased revenues of the commercial cable companies that handle some of the missions' dispatches. (However, about 20 per cent of the embassies have their own radio setups for communication with home.)

The Protocol Office of the State Department, numbering about 40 persons, is very much aware of even the humblest diplomatic presence in the capital. Part of the division's work is traditional, and on lofty levels. It is responsible, for example,

Embassy Row

The aerial photograph at right locates many of the foreign embassies *(black dots)* grouped around a section of Massachusetts Avenue, a street that has become known as Embassy Row. They are largely centered on the converted mansions of turn-of-century millionaires. Many embassies have been split among two or more buildings, with the living quarters of the ambassador and his family separated from the chanceries, or business offices. Some of the embassies still double as the ambassadorial residences. Separate residences of ambassadors are shown by black triangles. Because of the rapid increase in the number of embassies in recent years, chanceries and residences of ambassadors are now also locating outside the center of the city.

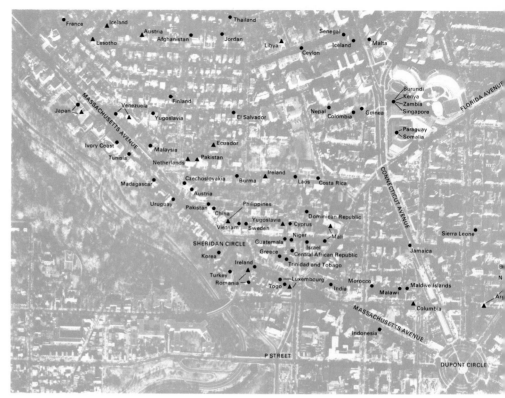

for presenting new ambassadors to the President and for worrying about the order of precedence in seating diplomats at state dinners. It must make sure that when foreign dignitaries visit, bands are properly coached in the appropriate national anthem and chefs do not inadvertently commit some fearful blunder in their choice of the *pièce de résistance*, such as offering pork to the Prime Minister of Israel or wine to a Muslim statesman. Insofar as possible Protocol attempts to see that ambassadors representing unfriendly neighbors like Pakistan and India are not invited to see the Secretary of State at the same day and hour.

But it must also keep a monitorial eye on the encounters that diplomatic personnel may have with Washington's laws and customs. Until the relatively recent unraveling of the fabric of segregation in Washington's residential areas, hotels and restaurants, the consumption of aspirin rose sharply in Protocol corridors whenever dark-skinned diplomats sallied out to seek sustenance not furnished by their own kitchens. Diplomatic license plates are supposed to buy a certain immunity from traffic tickets (though it is not unlimited), but this fact must often be explained to suburban policemen and others unfamiliar with the courtesies that prevail among nations. And members of the diplomat-

ic community who, like common clay, get publicly drunk, seduce secretaries or are caught at other malfeasances can create anxiety both for their own embassies and for the State Department.

It is an entirely reasonable assumption that Washington's foreigners also attract the attentions of the Federal Bureau of Investigation and other security agencies, though this is not often publicly admitted. There was a time when embassy staffs were small, and only the military and naval attachés were presumed to be possibly interested in some polite spying. The post-World War II era has not only raised the stakes, the scope and the cost of intelligence collection but has filled major diplomatic headquarters with strange, professorial figures. Ostensibly promoting exchanges of artists and lecturers or other projects, they may also be bent on some kind of clandestine information gathering. The surveillance of these visitors by the host government's security police is one of the accepted aspects of life in all civilized capitals, and Washington is surely no exception.

Between 1957 and 1967 twenty-eight Russians were arrested or expelled for suspected espionage. In two of several 1967 cases in which U.S. military personnel were charged with planning to reveal or with revealing military secrets, Air Force Sergeant

Herbert W. Boeckenhaupt was found guilty of conspiring to transmit classified information to a onetime assistant commercial counselor in the Soviet embassy, and retired Army Lieutenant Colonel William H. Whalen was convicted of giving data to a former Soviet military attaché and a former first secretary of the Russian embassy.

But the knife cuts both ways, as a 1967 incident reveals. Newspaper reporters discovered, via a leak from the FBI, that two visiting Soviet officials on temporary diplomatic visas were members of the KGB, the Russian spy agency. The printing of the story took care of any threat to national security, since the KGB people, with their cover blown, were harmless. Yet when reporters asked what the State Department's reaction was to this heinous breach of international etiquette the response was a more or less polite yawn. The reason for the indifference was probably, as a *New York Times* reporter wrote, that not all American "diplomats" entering Russia are necessarily what they seem either. "Because it is to their mutual advantage," he said, "both sides wink at the practice and have developed a tacit understanding about granting temporary diplomatic visas."

One consequence of the diplomatic population explosion has been the scattering of embassies out from the original nucleus on Massachusetts Avenue above Dupont Circle. This has come about as old missions outgrew their quarters and new ones were created. The delegations of Ecuador and Spain, for instance, are on 15th Street north of Florida Avenue, the old northern boundary of L'Enfant's original plan. Switzerland's diplomacy in Washington is conducted from a location on Cathedral Avenue, near the National Zoological Park. Representatives of other nations are even farther out from the center of the city. Efforts to find more suitable locations are thwarted not only by a scarcity of space but by a zoning law of 1964, which bears Congressional approval. This law forbids the construction of embassy office buildings except in high-density, high-cost commercial zones. The zones suggested by Congress are inconveniently far from downtown Washington's official centers. Though the Department of State is anxious to help with the problem—and has even suggested the establishment of a 42-acre diplomatic enclave in the central district—Congress has not budged. The embassies and their workers are not a voting constituency. They are not even American!

Embassy personnel and foreign reporters do not make up the entire alien population of Washington. Of the more than 60,000 foreign students in the United States, many are in Washington on government-sponsored exchange programs set up to train future administrators for emergent nations. Many others are in uniform, attending armed services schools in preparation for the day when they will direct the use of American military equipment furnished to their countries under various aid programs.

And there are also the short-term visitors from abroad, divided, like the American visitors to Washington, among tourists seeking pleasure and those with business in hand. Of some 2.6 million foreign travelers to the United States in 1967, many came to Washington merely to see what some of them, rightly or wrongly, regard as the new Rome. Others had more utilitarian goals in mind. A partial list would have included doctors coming for assignment to programs of study in American hospitals, foreign exporters seeking appointments with Commerce Department officials on matters of licenses, and advance men for ballet and theater companies, discussing itineraries with their country's cultural affairs officer in Washington. They touched down at Baltimore's Friendship or Washington's Dulles Airports from Cairo and Singapore, Leningrad and Istanbul, Nairobi and Osaka. Behind them, perhaps, were business stops in other European and Asian and American cities, but eventually necessity led them to the low-lying parcel of land chosen by George Washington and surveyed by Andrew Ellicott less than two centuries ago. History has moved quickly.

Today, the Potomac flows past the panorama of Washington much as it did when the first planters crowded the Indians from its banks. But Washingtonians will never again be able to regard the river and the District lines as boundaries between themselves and the rest of the world. The world, too, is now a kind of Washington constituency. Capital, nation and globe are bound together in the grip of space-age and nuclear technology. Political and military commitments abroad may change in nature; the international duties laid on the United States by the collapse of world order after World War II may be shared with other powers or they may alter in relative importance to one another. But the responsibilities will not grow lighter. They will continue to press on the consciousness of official Washington, influencing the inmost substance and quality of life in the capital city—and sooner or later reaching out to affect the rest of the country. No American can spend time in Washington as it draws near its 200th birthday and be unaware of that truth.

The department's diplomatic entrance on C Street.

Keeping watch on the worl a day at Stat

Of all the power centers that make Washington the focus of global affairs, the most influen (outside of the White House itself) is a concrete-and-glass building *(above)* in an area cal Foggy Bottom, home to the Department of State. Serving overseas as the nation's eyes and e and voice, serving at home as command center for delicate actions that strongly influence unstable world, State has over the years seen its functions expanded hugely. In 1790 t department had only nine employees in the U.S. and 13 small overseas offices; today its to staff numbers about 27,500, of whom some 20,000 maintain nearly 300 foreign missions. M of the remaining 7,500 employees work in the department's huge eight-story headquarters building that not only bulges with expertise on everything from Kurdish culture to the stability the Polish zloty but pulses with communications to and from all corners of the globe. T Secretary of State directs his own department and also coordinates the work of tw semiautonomous agencies, the Agency for International Development (AID) and the Pea Corps, as well as two independent agencies, the Arms Control and Disarmament Agen (ACDA) and the United States Information Agency (USIA). The myriad activities of t department can be seen in a record of a single day at Foggy Bottom, May 8, 1968. Like all oth days, it was jammed with problems, some solved and some not, and all really without beginni or end, because for State the watching, the listening and the decision making never cea

8:00 a.m.

Round-the-clock duty is routine in some offices at State, such as the Operations Center, which maintains 24-hour communications with posts throughout the world and keeps track of the various times in key world cities by means of clocks on its wall *(above)*. But the bulk of State's workers begin arriving about 8 a.m. Many of them enter at the D Street entrance *(right)*, where a guard checks their identification cards. No one is allowed in the building without a card, a pass or special permission.

8:30

One of the first meetings of the day is a question-and-answer session held by Thomas L. Hughes *(at coffee table)*, Director of INR (Bureau of Intelligence and Research), with aides who have been on duty since 5:30 a.m. analyzing overnight world developments. One question concerns enemy infiltration in Vietnam.

8:40

The Assistant Secretary of State for Congressional Relations, William B. Macomber *(left, and far left holding papers)*, leaves his office with two colleagues for a weekly briefing of Congressional leaders. His job is not only to inform Congress on a day-to-day basis about what State is doing but to convey the legislators' reactions back to the department. After meeting with the Congressmen, Macomber will spend a second hour on Capitol Hill speaking on "America and Disarmament" to legislators' wives.

8:50

In the Communications Center, where all telegraph messages in and out of the department are processed, Technical Controller Charles Devoe *(far left, seated)* plans a new line to Paris with the help of a master circuit list and advice from Ernest Field, an International Telephone and Telegraph engineer on permanent duty in the Center. Here incoming messages are decoded if necessary, sent to the proper department and also fed into a computer filing system. Urgent messages go directly to the Operations Center, which notifies the officers concerned. At left, the Center's chief, Willis Naeher, looks over a machine that prints out "spilled" messages—cables that were imperfectly prepared for electronic processing.

8:55

Elizabeth Ann Brown, Director of the United Nations Political Affairs Office, checks over a statement on the Pacific Trust Territory which the United States administers for the U.N. The statement will be read on Capitol Hill later that morning by the Under Secretary of State, Nicholas Katzenbach, when he testifies before a Senate committee; a plebiscite on independence will be held by July 1972. Miss Brown's main responsibility is to handle all business between the State Department and the U.S. Mission to the U.N.

9:00

Congressional Correspondence Officer George Winnett consults a file for a letter he will need to follow up on a job application referred by a Senator. Representatives and Senators are continually asking the department for information or assistance in replying to their constituents on such matters as visas and summer jobs at State, and it is Winnett's job to act on the requests. Some requests involve other countries, in which case Winnett will refer the matter to the U.S. Embassy concerned. He answers about 125 letters a day.

9:00

Accompanied by a security guard, Secretary of State Dean Rusk *(far left)* arrives at a special basement entrance leading to a private elevator that will whisk him to his seventh-floor office. The route his car follows to the department is classified information and it varies daily; the car stays by the entrance all day for his immediate use. Once in his office, Rusk is briefed by Thomas Hughes *(top of page)* on the latest intelligence information. Now and then Rusk interrupts to ask specific questions or pauses to read parts of a "Top Secret Daily Staff Summary" of global developments.

9:10

One of Rusk's principal advisers, veteran diplomat Charles E. Bohlen, Deputy Under Secretary for Political Affairs, is briefed on last-minute events in Eastern Europe by an officer of the Bureau of Intelligence and Research. Bohlen in a long career has been Ambassador to the Soviet Union, France and the Philippines. Like all such briefings this one is over quickly, for at 9:15 Bohlen must report to a daily staff meeting to be held in Rusk's office.

Preparing for a new assignment as Country Director for the United Kingdom, Ireland and Malta—i.e., the officer in charge of matters affecting those countries—Mortimer D. Goldstein reads files of background material. In his new post he must be familiar with a broad range of subjects, from military agreements and balance-of-payment statistics to London's racial problems.

9:15

In Secretary Rusk's office, staff members discuss a U.N. treaty to halt the proliferation of nuclear weapons and the Congressional attitude toward a foreign-aid bill. Among those present are such top advisers as Under Secretary Eugene Rostow *(left)* and Leonard H. Marks, Director of the USIA *(next to Rostow)*. Later, in picture at right, Rusk chats with Winthrop Brown, his assistant for liaison with U.S. state governors.

9:20

A trade agreement on Japanese wall tiles is the problem confronting Peter W. Lande, Chief of the Trade Agreements Division of the department's Bureau of Economics. Tariff rates and other import regulations are usually handled jointly by Lande's office and a similar unit in the Commerce Department. In this case Lande is asking a departmental economist about the need for such tiles in the U.S. and the effect of importing them on rival U.S. manufacturers.

9:30

A weekly meeting of the Bureau of African Affairs is addressed by a Labor Department expert, George Weaver, Assistant Secretary of Labor for International Affairs *(center, back to camera)*. Weaver reports on work in Africa by the International Labor Organization (ILO), a United Nations affiliate. Present are Country Directors for the African continent, their advisers and representatives of other government agencies. Weaver points out that ILO can advise U.S. firms operating in Africa on collective bargaining there and mentions the effective work being done by labor ministers of certain African nations.

9:30

"Let's hurry, gang, I've got a plane to catch," says Joseph Sisco, head of the Bureau of International Organization Affairs, in summoning staff members to his office for a weekly meeting. He asks his assistants to be prepared to brief George Ball, the newly appointed U.S. Ambassador to the U.N.; he hears a report on the activities of the World Health Organization and another on a human rights conference being held in Teheran; he instructs his staff to be prepared to answer questions from the press about a new U.S. policy toward the Pacific Trust Territory, soon to be announced to Congress by Under Secretary Katzenbach *(page 167)*.

9:50

Having ended a talk with a Foreign Service Officer just back from Vietnam, John M. Steeves, Director of the Foreign Service, prepares to call the department's Bureau of Public Affairs. Because of a projected meeting of the Board of Foreign Service, which sets personnel policy for State employees abroad, Steeves wants to cancel one of the two speaking engagements he has in Minneapolis and Chicago.

9:55

John Walck, a department courier *(far left)*, inspects some pouches he will take to 12 U.S. posts in Africa. Pouch Control Officer John C. Grover then confirms Walck's route with him. All classified department mail to overseas posts goes by courier-accompanied pouch. When traveling by plane, a courier must be last on and first off to ensure that pouches are handled safely.

10:00

The Country Director for the Soviet Union, Malcolm Toon, presides at an informal meeting. Discussion ranges over the implications of the new Consular Treaty with Russia; a planned visit to the U.S. by the Mayor of Moscow (Toon has talked with Mayor John Lindsay about arrangements in New York City); Congress' failure to pass an East-West trade bill and the effects of this on Czechoslovakia; and a letter from New York Senator Jacob Javits about a new automobile plant in Russia with which a New York construction firm is involved as an exporter.

10:00

Peace negotiations with the North Vietnamese are about to get underway in Paris, and Dixon Donnelley, Assistant Secretary of State for Public Affairs, talks to his staff about dealing with the crucial news that the meetings will generate. As many as 2,000 reporters are expected to cover the conference, and already the U.S. Embassy in Paris has sent an urgent request for background material to be made available to the press.

10:05

William S. Gaud *(foreground)*, administrator of one of the department's semiautonomous organizations, the Agency for International Development, addresses a committee that is considering the agency's relations with universities. Much of AID's work consists of getting U.S. universities to advise and assist their counterparts in underdeveloped countries. The committee must advise on a form for contracts with universities, on the kind of research needed to improve education in poor nations, and on a delicate matter of policy: what to do about American teachers abroad whose political activities may have diplomatic repercussions.

10:20

Two English journalists sit outside the Secretary's office, waiting for a 10:30 interview. One is William Rees-Mogg, editor of *The Times* of London *(far left)*, who says, "I have come here to form a general view on American policy." With him in near-left picture is the Washington correspondent for *The Times,* Louis Heren. Rees-Mogg is interested in the U.S. attitude toward Vietnam, but he will also ask the Secretary about the State Department's current views on Europe and the Common Market.

10:30

Eugene V. Rostow, Under Secretary for Political Affairs *(center)*, meets with Lucius D. Battle, Assistant Secretary for the Bureau of Near Eastern and South Asian Affairs *(on couch)*, and Robert Grey, a staff assistant, to discuss U.N. peace efforts in the Middle East. Dr. Gunnar Jarring, the U.N. peace envoy, has been visiting Israel and its various Arab opponents in the six-day war of 1967, and the State Department is deeply concerned with his attempts to arrange an agreement between the antagonists.

10:30

The department's Equal Employment Opportunity Program Director, Eddie N. Williams, and an assistant, Eleanor Farrar, confer about ways to recruit Negroes for the Foreign Service—an effort somewhat hampered by the Vietnam War. Because of antiwar sentiment among black students, some who qualify will not apply for jobs at State.

10:30

William C. Foster, Director of the Arms Control and Disarmament Agency *(foreground)*, who has completed talks with Soviet representatives on the Nuclear Non-Proliferation Treaty, meets with his staff to discuss U.N. ratification of the pact. He is optimistic. As he said later, "We have the Russians enthusiastically supporting it." He did not anticipate unanimous ratification: France would be among those opposed, and U.S. diplomats would have to do "a lot of arguing and arm-twisting and explaining," but eventually the treaty would be approved. (The U.N. did approve it on June 12, 1968, by a vote of 95 to 4; 21 nations, including France, abstained.)

10:35

Affairs in Poland, often an arena for East-West confrontations, occupy Doyle Martin as he meets with associates in the Eastern Europe section to line up appointments for the U.S. Ambassador to Poland, due to return to Washington the next day for a short visit. But the meeting also covers a wide range of events affecting Poland: student unrest, political changes in neighboring Czechoslovakia and the possibilities of getting Congress to appropriate funds for an addition to an American-financed children's hospital in Cracow.

10:40

Defectors from the U.S. Armed Forces who have sought asylum in Sweden occupy the attention of David H. McKillop, Country Director for Scandinavia *(right, and behind desk far right picture)*. Parents have been writing Congressmen about the difficulty of learning exactly where the exiles are, and the letters have come to McKillop. Until now the U.S. has had no contact with the men. McKillop asks how many there are. Richard Dwyer *(with pipe)* says no accurate figure is available, but it is known that Sweden granted residence permits to 50 defectors.

10:45

Arranging for a board to review procedures for ranking and promoting Foreign Service Officers, Idar Rimestad, Deputy Under Secretary for Administration, asks an assistant for suggestions. Foreign Service Officers are considered for promotion each year, and those who do not earn promotion periodically are retired. Because Rimestad is the review board's adviser and is in charge of allocating the department's funds, he has been called the most powerful man in the department after the Secretary himself.

11:00

A smallpox inoculation is given young Sandra Whittaker by nurse Alice Davies in the department's medical section. Shots and inoculations are provided for official travel only; Sandra qualifies because she and her brother will be making a summer visit to their father, a Foreign Service Officer in Nigeria. At far right, Mrs. Maud Ulla Sabbagh, who will leave with her husband shortly for Kuwait, notes her shots in her own medical record.

11:00

Roy Melbourne, Country Director for Ghana, Liberia, Nigeria and Sierra Leone, confers with his assistant, Robert Sherwood, on a political upheaval in Sierra Leone. A coup, one of the many that have kept some recently established African nations in almost continuous turmoil, has brought a new administration into office. The U.S. has recognized the new government, and Melbourne will later send a cable to the U.S. Ambassador there commending him for his handling of the affair.

11:25

Having attended the earlier staff meeting of the Bureau of African Affairs *(page 168)*, Alvin M. Rucker, the bureau's Labor Adviser, meets with two specialists. They discuss, among other matters, the serious interruption of U.S.-Nigeria training programs for labor leaders brought about by the Nigerian civil war.

11:25

The launching of an internationally sponsored satellite, to record solar radiation and cosmic rays for several nations, is discussed at a staff meeting by Herman Pollock, Director of International Scientific and Technological Affairs. His section helps promote scientific cooperation between countries and briefs U.S. diplomats on scientific trends in their assigned areas.

11:30

In the Foreign Service Lounge, which provides facilities and services for Foreign Service personnel visiting Washington, Phil Battaglia *(far left)*, who has recently returned to the U.S. from his post as vice consul in Barcelona, Spain, prepares travel vouchers for his trip. At left, Marcella Wheeler signs the Foreign Service Register, a book that lists the arrivals and departures of persons who are serving overseas. The private secretary to the U.S. Ambassador to Togo, Miss Wheeler is about to return to that African country from home leave.

11:30

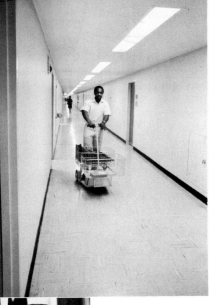

Gary Washington, one of two messengers serving the Bureau of European Affairs, rides a total of about five miles a day on his power-driven cart, delivering memos, cables, letters and documents to the bureau's offices, which are spread over three floors. He has a security clearance for handling all classified messages. Washington makes six runs a day and has 40 stops on each; this is the second time he has made the rounds this morning. His home base is the bureau's own mail room, which has a pneumatic tube that brings in cables from the Communications Center. The tube is one of 65 that handle messages to and from specific departments and bureaus in the building. More than 40 messengers like Washington are needed to cover the building's six and a half miles of corridors.

11:30

A key assistant to William Foster *(opposite page, top)* in the Arms Control and Disarmament Agency is Lieutenant General John J. Davis, Assistant Director for Weapons Evaluation and Control. He pursues his current assignment: helping to organize an extensive test of disarmament inspection techniques to be held later in the year in England. In the test, two-man teams will roam the British countryside during "war games," attempting to discover violations of previously agreed-upon troop levels.

11:45

Preparing for a dinner at the Belgian Embassy, Robert Anderson, Country Director for France and Benelux (Belgium, the Netherlands and Luxembourg), reviews the political situation in Belgium so that he can converse informatively and effectively with other guests. Later Anderson makes a phone call about hiring someone who is needed in the U.S. Embassy in Paris to do special work for the newly appointed Ambassador and his wife.

12:00 p.m.

Clydia Mae Richardson affixes the Great Seal of the United States to the official commission for Henry Cabot Lodge, who will be sworn in as Ambassador to West Germany later in the day *(page 175)*. The seal, which is applied to documents appointing all diplomatic and major executive officials, dates from the early years of the republic, when the department handled not only foreign relations but also copyrights, patents and other domestic matters, and functioned as the government's official certifying agency. The seal is kept in the department's Exhibit Hall near the diplomatic entrance and is a popular attraction for visitors.

12:00 p.m.

In the Passport Office, Reed Paige Clark III, in charge of passport matters involving the Mediterranean area and Africa, considers a request of an American in Israel for citizenship recognition of his foreign-born daughter. (He could not grant it.) Meanwhile the office's director, Frances Knight, makes notes for an upcoming conference on future travel problems.

12:00

The Country Directors for the Soviet Union and other Eastern European nations gather with staff members to discuss cultural exchange agreements with Russia. Such agreements must be renewed regularly, and because the latest ones have expired, dislocations may occur if they are not renewed soon. For example, U.S. universities with summer programs involving student exchanges must be kept informed so that they may allocate funds in time. Some universities will not allocate funds until the agreements are negotiated.

12:15

Developments in certain Arab nations are among the items being examined by Herbert J. Liebesny, who is in charge of affairs in the Near East and South Asia for the Bureau of Intelligence and Research. The bureau gathers political, economic and military data from many sources, including the Central Intelligence Agency, and passes the information along to Country Directors and other officials. Liebesny also teaches Near Eastern law at the George Washington University Law School and speaks German, French, Italian, modern Greek and Arabic.

12:25

The State Department's daily briefing for the press (far right) is conducted by Robert J. McCloskey, Deputy Assistant Secretary for Public Affairs (standing at left in first picture). At this session he describes an inconclusive meeting at Panmunjom, Korea, concerning the U.S.S. Pueblo, the Navy intelligence ship captured by the North Koreans. He also announces the departure time of the American delegation to the upcoming Vietnam peace negotiations in Paris.

12:30

Plans for a conference of educators are discussed at a small working lunch held in the Van Buren Suite on the eighth floor of State. The hostess is Mrs. Charlotte Hubbard (far right), who is Deputy Assistant Secretary for Public Services. The main topic of the conference will be improved teaching of international affairs, and the luncheon group talks about the possibility of inviting as a speaker the head of the Bureau of Educational and Cultural Affairs, Edward D. Re.

1:00

On the phone with the Defense Department, Richard A. Frank, Assistant Legal Adviser for Inter-American Affairs, assesses upcoming elections in Panama and their potential influence on negotiations for a new Panama Canal treaty. The call over, Frank talks with a visitor about mediating a dispute between the United Kingdom and Guatemala over the status of British Honduras. Later he will do some work on a policy paper on Cuba that has been sent to him for suggestions. Relaxed and jovial, Frank enjoys joking with visitors to his office.

1:00

"We have this awesome increase in population to confront," says George Coleman, Deputy Director of the Population Service for the War on Hunger (a branch of AID), "but we don't have any answers yet." Some steps to curb population are being taken, however. A major part of Coleman's job is the supervision of birth control assistance AID gives to the 26 nations that have requested it.

1:00

The chart behind John N. Street, Assistant Disaster Relief Coordinator for AID, shows emergency supplies shipped to such distant places as Okinawa and Iran. Through the use of scientific means to predict certain natural disasters, AID also saves lives by warning people in the areas. In 1967, for example, infrared pictures taken at night with aerial cameras enabled scientists to forecast accurately the time a Philippine volcano would erupt.

1:25

A distinguished state visitor, the Prime Minister of Thailand, is greeted at the department by Secretary Rusk. At top left, the Secretary and Mrs. Rusk await their guest outside the department's diplomatic entrance. Then Rusk walks into the building and through the lobby with the Prime Minister, Thanom Kittikachorn, who had arrived in Washington that morning and had already been welcomed at the White House. At lower left, Rusk and the Thai Ambassador to the U.S., Bunchana Atthakor, sign protocols certifying that the ratifications of the 1966 U.S.-Thai Treaty on Amity and Economic Relations have been exchanged. At the luncheon that follows in the department's formal dining room *(lower right)*, the Secretary converses with Mrs. Kittikachorn through an interpreter *(center)*. The lunch lasts until well past 3 p.m.

2:00

The reassignment of Foreign Service Officers is considered by a panel under the chairmanship of Adrian T. Middleton, Chief of the Officer Assignment and Career Management Division. One staff member described the way the panel operates: "Officers are not footballs or darts being flicked around. . . . We try to make a selection based on the individual, his personality and qualifications as well as the needs and personalities involved in the job openings."

2:00

The Country Director for Caribbean Countries, Edward T. Long, sets up financing for a dam to be built in the Dominican Republic. The dam project, the largest in Dominican history, is to be funded jointly by the International Development Bank, AID and the Dominican Republic, and Long's office is coordinating the combined effort. Although most Country Directors' offices do not have personnel from semiautonomous AID on their staffs, Long's does, in order to unite in one group the political and economic operations of the U.S. in the Caribbean area.

2:30

Lucius Battle, Assistant Secretary for Near Eastern and South Asian Affairs *(left, on couch at window),* who had earlier talked to Eugene Rostow about Middle Eastern conflicts *(page 169),* welcomes officials of the American University in Cairo and a group of AID officers. They have come to discuss assistance to the university, which the U.S. helps support. The educators describe the difficulties they encountered during the 1967 Arab-Israeli war. Also on Battle's schedule for the day is a visit to the Ambassador of India, who is ill. Battle's involvement in the East is reflected by the painting above his desk *(far left):* a view of the Sultan's troops in Constantinople in the 18th Century.

Mr. BATTLE
ASSISTANT SECRETARY

2:30

Two officers in the African regional office of the Peace Corps, Andrew Oerke *(at right)* and Calvin H. Raullerson, use a blackboard as they work out the number of volunteers needed in their area and the types of training to be provided for them. Programs may be reviewed several times each year.

2:30

Debating the future course of world affairs, the Policy Planning Council meets under the chairmanship of Henry D. Owen *(at far end of table)*. Council members, named for two-year terms by the President and the Secretary of State, are mainly State Department officers, though there is usually at least one person from the Pentagon and some from outside the government. Their job is to ponder the long-range implications of current foreign policy and to question all assumptions about potential developments. Their work is inevitably secret; they could not, for example, divulge what they were discussing on this day. One participant did, however, hint at the tone of such sessions: "It's not a satisfactory meeting unless there is an inch of blood on the floor."

2:30

A course in economics under the auspices of the Foreign Service Institute is attended by some 20 men *(two shown at immediate right)*, selected from various branches of the government, who want to gain special knowledge in such matters as statistics, international trade and economic growth patterns. One of the men, Harry Coburn, 33 *(far right)*, was a political science major in college and has been in the department for seven years; he expects to use his new knowledge to good advantage in his next assignment—a post in the Bureau of International Organization Affairs.

2:45

Jack Frankel, training specialist for the Peace Corps, has just written a memo concerning the recruitment of more veterinarians into the corps. Frankel's particular responsibility is agricultural programs, and heretofore there has been a shortage of veterinarians, partly because their assignments have not been made attractive enough. He is attempting to realign their responsibilities so that more will apply. Frankel has just returned from a two-week trip to Ecuador, visiting corps workers and government officials and checking on the progress of agricultural activities.

2:45

A request from the Somali government occupies Frank Scordato, who is Somali desk officer in AID. The Somalis have asked to upgrade a teacher-training college that was built and staffed with AID funds, making it into a full-scale college (and eventually transforming it into a university). Scordato will have to decide what effect this may have on AID's original plan, which was to phase out the program in another two years and turn the college over completely to the Somalis.

3:00

A conference of U.S. and Spanish officials convenes with the U.S. participants sitting on one side of a long table *(far right)*. Two American delegates *(center picture)* hold a private talk before the meeting begins. The two countries had agreed in 1963 to hold periodic consultations on political and economic matters, and the afternoon session starts with an address by Under Secretary of the Treasury Frederick L. Deming *(immediate right)*, who describes the U.S. balance of payments situation.

3:00

Rudi Klaus, Peace Corps Operations Officer for Iran and Afghanistan, addresses a meeting of regional corps officers. Klaus describes a test of the "total immersion" method of language training being tried out on volunteers learning Parsi before departing for Iran. He points out, however, that other needed courses must be postponed during the test.

3:15

A class in Urdu—a major language of Pakistan and India—is conducted by Mrs. Lubna Iqbal, a Pakistani *(at left in picture)*, under the auspices of the Foreign Service Institute. James Holmes *(center, with glasses)* is a Foreign Service Officer; the others are from the USIA. Nearby, classes in Turkish and Swahili are being held.

3:25

Lieutenant Colonel Rolf Kahrs Baardvik, who is in charge of defense planning for the Norwegian Shipowners Association, checks out of the State Department after attending a meeting of the North Atlantic Treaty Organization's Planning Board for Ocean Shipping. The board meets each year to discuss the disposition of merchant vessels among the NATO countries in the event of war. Baardvik is secretary of the six-man Norwegian delegation to the meeting.

3:30

In the Vietnam Training Center, operated by the Foreign Service Institute, officers from the department and related agencies are given speeded-up courses for work in that country. Dang Phuong Lan *(far left)* is one of 37 instructors teaching Vietnamese. At right, Dr. Jerry Winfield, the deputy director of the center, describes the Vietnamese coastal fishing industry. Using a projection machine, he shows how fishermen cover their craft with tough basketry to protect them from barnacles and how the U.S. is helping motorize the boats.

3:35

Under Secretary of State Nicholas deB. Katzenbach, who earlier in the day testified on the Pacific Trust Territory before a Senate committee *(page 167)*, holds a staff meeting in his office to prepare for still another appearance on the Hill. He is to appear before the House Banking and Currency Committee to request more funds for the International Development Association, a World Bank affiliate.

4:00

Returning from a meeting of the Council for Latin America (an organization of U.S. businessmen who have interests in Latin America), Jack B. Kubisch, Country Director for Brazil, reads a letter from the President of Brazil. The letter, which is intended for transmission to the U.S. President, proposes an extension of the existing International Coffee Agreement that controls production and pricing of coffee. Because Brazil is the world's largest exporter of coffee and the U.S. the largest consumer, this is of great importance to Brazil. A number of U.S. Senators, however, have said that they are opposed to continuing the agreement because it artificially raises the price of coffee for the consumer. (The Senate did approve the extension, however.)

4:05

Henry Cabot Lodge *(at right in picture)*, former U.S. Ambassador to the United Nations and former Ambassador to South Vietnam, is sworn in as the new Ambassador to West Germany. The oath is administered by Angier Biddle Duke, the department's Chief of Protocol, as Secretary Rusk looks on. After the ceremony both Rusk and Lodge make a few remarks: Lodge's comments draw chuckles from the assembled onlookers because he proceeds to name all of the numerous departments, branches and posts of the State Department in which he has served, rattling them off quickly by their initials.

4:15

The legal adviser to Nigeria's Minister of Defense, S. S. Arthur-Worrie, a guest of the U.S. government for a two-month study of the American military legal system, is greeted in the Bureau of Educational and Cultural Affairs by two bureau officers, William G. Allen *(center)* and J. Roland Jacobs. Arthur-Worrie hopes to set up a uniform code of military law for the Nigerian Army. 175

4:30

The problem of sending enough fertilizer to Vietnam to last through the summer engrosses Milton Mapes, who is Deputy Director of Commodity Import Programs for AID's Bureau for Vietnam. Fertilizer purchasing in Vietnam was once controlled by the government but is now handled by private enterprise, and Mapes will cable the AID mission in Saigon to ask them to urge commercial buyers to file their orders early.

4:30

Cloistered with a colleague in a secluded anteroom, Guy A. Wiggins *(hand to head)*, desk officer for Guatemala, ponders the Guatemalan situation. He must draw up a briefing paper for an Assistant Secretary that will sum up Guatemala's political, military and economic situation. Once Wiggins has finished his draft, he will show it to other experts on the area. Back in his main office, Wiggins prepares to act on a request from Guatemala for information about a compressed-air device for administering mass inoculations—Guatemala's Minister of Health has learned of the instrument's successful use in Costa Rica and hopes it can be put into use in his own country.

4:35

William O. Boswell, Director of the Office of International Conferences, discusses with assistants a forthcoming NATO Council of Ministers conference in Reykjavik, Iceland. His office handles all arrangements for such multilateral conferences, working out transportation, local accommodations, supplies and the like, and even coordinating lists of participants at specific sessions. Boswell will accompany the American delegation to the meeting to take care of details and to insure the security of the delegates.

4:55

Whether to tighten up on contracts made between AID and "host" countries (i.e., those accepting AID help) is the subject of a discussion between R. Peter Straus *(right, and far right at desk)*, AID's Assistant Administrator for African Affairs, and two associates. Some countries are lax in administering the contracts, and with Congress showing increased resistance to foreign aid, Straus thinks the terms of the contracts may have to be stiffer.

5:00

The two negotiators representing the U.S. in the Vietnam peace talks in Paris, Cyrus Vance and W. Averell Harriman, stop by the Secretary's office to say goodbye before departing for Paris. Vance arrives first and waits in Rusk's outer office. Then Ambassador-at-Large Harriman joins him *(center picture)* and they go in for a chat with the Secretary. Rusk makes a point of talking with every important U.S. diplomat or negotiator who is leaving or arriving in town.

5:00

A provocative piece of news has just come to John C. Hill, Country Director for a number of Latin American countries, including Venezuela, via a daily summary of local press stories that is prepared by the U.S. Embassy in Caracas. The newly elected Governor of Caracas has said he wants to reorganize the city's police force; this is crucial to the State Department because the present police organization was set up with AID assistance. Fully a fifth of Venezuela's population lives in Caracas, and the police are a key element in preserving a stable government. Hill must find out what the Governor intends and consult with other officials so that the department can decide whether or not the current technical assistance program there is affected.

5:10

Worried about the Prime Minister of Thailand's schedule, which is running late, Moncrieff Spear, Country Director for Thailand and Burma, phones the Pentagon, where the Thais went after leaving State *(page 173)*. They must still attend a briefing at the CIA, yet have time to change for an 8 p.m. black-tie dinner at the White House.

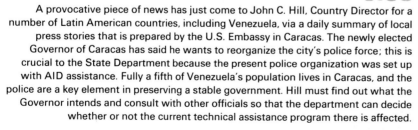

5:25

Alfred L. Atherton Jr., Country Director for Israel and Arab-Israeli Affairs *(right)*, talks with J. Owen Zurhellen Jr., the new Deputy Chief of Mission in Tel Aviv, about such matters as the diplomatic problems that have arisen since the 1967 Arab-Israeli war.

5:25

Following security regulations, Leona Marti, scretary to Moncrieff Spear *(opposite page, bottom)*, cuts off the used portion of her typewriter ribbon at the end of the day's work and puts it with classified waste material to be burned. The ribbon, which goes through the machine only once, clearly shows each letter she strikes; anyone who had it could read everything she has typed.

5:30

The day is over for most of the department's employees; some have left as early as 5 p.m., but the main rush occurs now as they stream out the building's various entrances. At the D Street entrance a man stops to buy some flowers. On the seventh floor, Security Guard Al Boyd holds open the door of Secretary Rusk's private elevator for Vance, Harriman and Rusk, who are leaving together. Rusk will be driven home so that he may change for dinner, reporting to the White House in time for the formal reception honoring the Prime Minister of Thailand.

5:50

A rush order for multiple copies of background information on the U.S. role in Vietnam has come from the U.S. Embassy in Paris in anticipation of the arrival of some 2,000 newspapermen for the peace talks. The request is handled by William Blair Jr., Director of the Office of Media Services for the Bureau of Public Affairs. Blair later cables Paris that the material will be on its way tomorrow on the plane with Vance and Harriman. He also makes alternate plans for air-freighting the releases in case they miss the Vance-Harriman flight.

10:10

Working late to finish a report on the economy of the Philippines, AID's Dr. Richard M. Kirby in effect steps out of his area. He is desk officer for Malaysia, Singapore and the Pacific Islands, a responsibility that does not include the Philippines, but he is helping his colleagues as an expert in economics. The report is needed for talks to be held with the Governor of one of the Philippine provinces, who has come to Washington to discuss a loan. No loan request may be granted without an economic report.

10:55

Special Police Officer C. E. McDaniel checks a vault door on the fifth floor as part of his regular security patrol. Then with another officer he thoroughly inspects an office area nearby. Each evening the security force picks a different area to comb in detail, checking carbon paper, wastebaskets and files and making sure no telltale typewriter ribbons remain in their machines. The cart contains forms that McDaniel must fill out if he finds a violation. At right he checks the contents of a partially filled "Burn Bag," which, if it contains classified material, should already have gone to the incinerator. He goes through the entire bag item by item and is relieved to learn that there is nothing classified in the waste.

12:45 a.m.

In the Operations Center, which handles all urgent overseas messages and never closes down, a new watch is about to take over from Senior Watch Officer James D. Relph, seated at the desk in the background. During the nighttime hours—often crucial because of worldwide time differentials—the Watch Officer and his crew *are* the State Department. If there is a crisis, he will hear of it first; he must decide whom to call (possibly the Secretary) and coordinate any actions taken. If the crisis is serious, the Center itself becomes a command post as officials concerned with the area involved arrive to take over. During the night the Center also prepares the "Top Secret Daily Staff Summary" that will go early in the morning to the President and the Secretary of State *(page 167)*, thus helping to start a brand-new State Department day.

Suggested areas to tour

The maps that follow show six sections of the District of Columbia and its environs, emphasizing features of particular interest to tourists. The first map suggests an overall automobile tour; the numbered rectangles surprinted on it indicate smaller areas covered by the subsequent maps, in which points of interest can be visited at will.

1. Outskirts of Washington

Before the idea of building the nation's capital on t banks of the Potomac was ever conceived, the region su rounding what is now the District of Columbia h already left its mark on history. The map below provic a suggested route for touring the environs of Washir ton. Also shown—and keyed by outline and number are the areas covered in the following five tour maps.

Six miles south of Washington, via the George Was ington Memorial Parkway, is Alexandria, Virginia, city that retains much of its 18th Century flavor al boasts of numerous landmarks of American histor Christ Church, a fine example of Georgian church a chitecture of the pre-Revolutionary period, is one of t foremost attractions. Completed in 1773, the church w attended by George Washington and, later, by Robe E. Lee. Both men owned pews in the church; these a now designated with silver plaques. Also of interest Alexandria are Gadsby's Tavern, which served as Was ington's military headquarters in 1754; the Carly House, where General Braddock planned the campaig

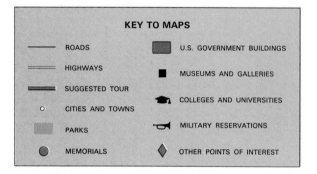

KEY TO MAPS

— ROADS

═ HIGHWAYS

━ SUGGESTED TOUR

○ CITIES AND TOWNS

░ PARKS

● MEMORIALS

▮ U.S. GOVERNMENT BUILDINGS

■ MUSEUMS AND GALLERIES

🎓 COLLEGES AND UNIVERSITIES

🎺 MILITARY RESERVATIONS

◆ OTHER POINTS OF INTEREST

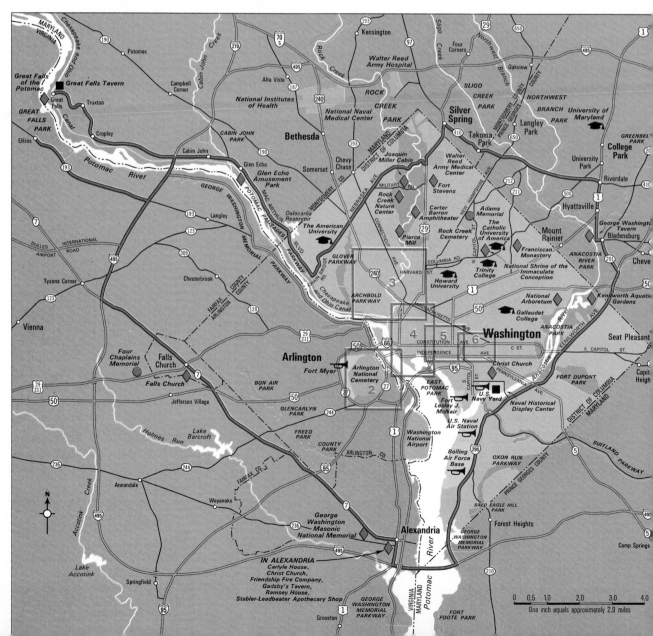

against the French and Indians in 1755; Stabler-Lead-eater Apothecary Shop, which was founded in 1792 and operated continuously as a pharmacy until 1933 when it was converted into a museum; and the George Washington Masonic National Memorial, an enormous structure built as a tribute to Washington the Mason, which contains such Washington memorabilia as the trowel he used in laying the cornerstone of the Capitol and the clock that was stopped at the moment of his death.

Moving northeast via Interstate 295 into the District, one passes the U.S. Navy Yard and the Naval Historical Display Center. In the Center is an extensive exhibit of naval trophies and mementos, including President Kennedy's private ship-model collection. Farther north are two sites of great natural beauty, the National Arboretum and the Kenilworth Aquatic Gardens. The arboretum, an experimental forest maintained by the Department of Agriculture, contains 32 distinct types of soil that permit the growth of a great variety of trees not indigenous to the region, while the Kenilworth gardens present an immense display of water plants, both exotic and native. To the north is historic Bladensburg, a commercial center for half a century before Washington was founded. In Bladensburg is the George Washington Tavern, at which the first President stopped on his way to the First Continental Congress.

To the west, in rustic Rock Creek Park (which extends into the District), the visitor can tour the nature center; it offers exhibits of wildlife of the area and has a small planetarium. Farther to the west are the Great Falls of the Potomac, where the river cascades off the Piedmont plateau. The only major waterfall in this part of the U.S., the Great Falls offer a spectacular view and are usually pleasantly cool, even during Washington's hot summers.

To the south of the falls, just outside Falls Church, is the Four Chaplains Memorial. The monument, a notable piece of modern sculpture, is dedicated to the four chaplains—two Protestant, one Catholic, one Jewish—who gave their life jackets to four soldiers when their troopship was sunk off Greenland during World War II.

2. Arlington and the Pentagon

Across the Potomac from Washington via the Arlington Memorial Bridge lies Arlington National Cemetery, the nation's largest and most revered military shrine, and the Pentagon, headquarters of the Department of Defense. The world's largest office building, the Pentagon is a miniature city in itself, bulging with 30,000 employes of the Department of Defense. Despite its imposing air of secrecy, visitors are welcome on weekdays and can freely roam most of the building's 17.5 miles of corridors. Parking is a problem, and so visitors are advised to travel to the Pentagon in buses and taxis.

Northwest of the Pentagon, in the Arlington cemetery, is the Tomb of the Unknown Soldier, continuously guarded by volunteers from the First Battle Group of the Third Infantry Regiment (pages 24-25). The impressive guard-changing ceremony occurs every hour on the hour during the day. North of the tomb lies the Custis-Lee Mansion National Memorial, which commands a panoramic view of Washington and which was once the home of Robert E. Lee. On the front lawn of the mansion is the grave of Pierre Charles L'Enfant, who designed the plans for the city of Washington in 1791. And just down the hill from the mansion is the grave of President John F. Kennedy. Marked by a flame that burns continuously, the grave is surprisingly simple—no statue, memorial building or vertical tombstone.

Just north of the Arlington National Cemetery is the Netherlands Carillon, a gift to the United States from the people of the Netherlands. At 3:45 each afternoon except Sunday, its 39 bells can be heard throughout the surrounding area. North of the carillon is the U.S. Marine Corps War Memorial, dedicated in 1954 by President Eisenhower. The memorial, which portrays the raising of the flag on Mount Suribachi on Iwo Jima in 1945, is cast in bronze and stands more than 70 feet tall.

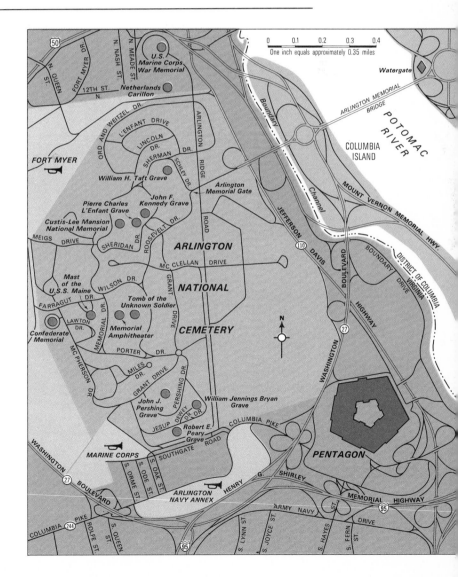

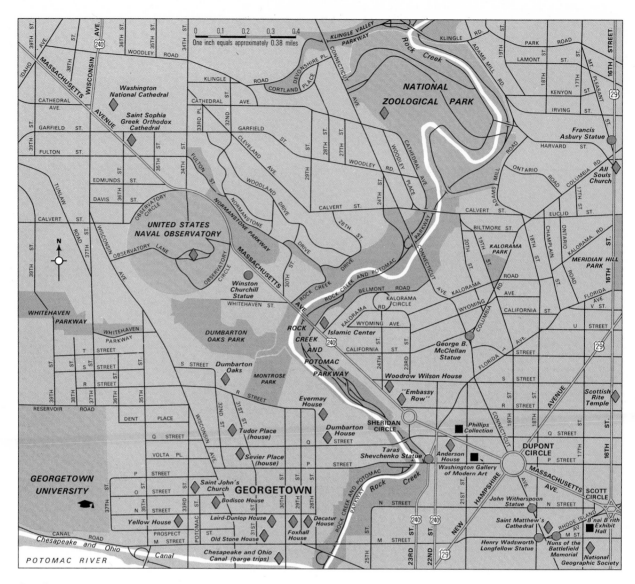

3. Georgetown and Embassy Row

These adjoining sections of residential Washington are noted both for their architecture and for being the homes for many of the city's most distinguished citizens. Georgetown, a former Potomac port that in time was engulfed by the capital city, retains much of its late-18th and early-19th Century charm in its cobblestone streets and colonial and Federal period houses. Today it is Washington's most fashionable address. Its southern boundary is the old Chesapeake and Ohio Canal, refurbished by the National Park Service, which offers mule-drawn barge trips from the foot of 30th Street. Among its oldest houses are the Laird-Dunlop House, owned for a time by Robert Todd Lincoln (eldest son of the President), and Tudor Place, designed by William Thornton (who also planned the Capitol).

Dumbarton Oaks Park, bordering Georgetown on the north, was once the estate of Robert Woods Bliss, a wealthy drug manufacturer; its mansion was the site of

the 1944 conference which drew up proposals for the United Nations charter. In the mansion is Bliss's collection of Byzantine art, one of the world's finest.

To the east, on 21st Street just off Massachusetts Avenue, the famous Phillips Collection of Impressionist and modern paintings is admired partly for its tasteful display, arranged just as collector Duncan Phillips enjoyed it before converting his home into a museum in 1918. The Massachusetts Avenue area known as Embassy Row, stretching along the avenue and on side streets northwest from Dupont Circle, contains the embassies of more than 60 countries. (Individual embassies are located in the photograph on page 164.)

At Observatory Circle, the U.S. Naval Observatory provides daily tours. Farther to the northwest is the Washington National Cathedral, a mammoth, partially completed Gothic church that is one of the principal U.S. sanctuaries of the Protestant Episcopal Church.

White House and major monuments

many Americans a visit to Washington means a visit the White House, the handsome residence at 1600 nnsylvania Avenue that has housed every American esident since John Adams. Although the White House echnically a private residence, loaned to the President the government, it is open to the public each Tuesday rough Saturday from 10 a.m. until noon. Visitors come through a special entrance on East Executive Avenue d can examine many of the historic building's elegant-furnished rooms. On rare occasions they may even be eted by the President himself.

Across Pennsylvania Avenue from the White House is fayette Square, a landscaped rectangle offering an ex-lent view of the White House. In the center of the uare stands a statue of Andrew Jackson on horseback, d in the corners are statues of four Europeans—the arquis de Lafayette, Jean Baptiste Rochambeau, naddeus Kosciuszko and Friedrich von Steuben—who led the American cause in the Revolutionary War. ar the square are many restored historic buildings, tably Blair House, the President's official guesthouse.

South of the White House lies The Ellipse, a park med for its circular roadway; in it or nearby are such ms as the Zero Milestone (the point from which dis-nces from Washington are supposedly measured); the rst Division Memorial (built in 1924 to honor a famous it); and a statue of General William T. Sherman. est of The Ellipse is the Corcoran Gallery of Art, nich houses an excellent collection of American paint-g and sculpture. Also in this area are the American ed Cross headquarters, which has a museum contain-g Red Cross relics (including a battered ambulance ed in World War I), and the national headquarters of e Daughters of the American Revolution. The D.A.R. aintains one of the nation's largest genealogical librar-s, where for a small fee a visitor can research his family ee. Near the D.A.R. building stands the Department the Interior, which has a museum where the work of e department's branches, such as the National Park rvice, are explained and a shop that sells arts and afts made by American Indians.

South of The Ellipse rises the Washington Monument, e of the tallest masonry structures in the world. To joy a breathtaking view of Washington most visitors de to the top of this 555-foot-tall structure in an electric evator, but the more energetic can walk up the mon-nent's 898 steps. Farther south, across the Tidal Basin, the Jefferson Memorial with its bronze statue of the ird President; the statue can be glimpsed by today's esident all the way from the second-floor Oval Room the White House. Washington's famed Japanese cher-trees, which bloom profusely every spring, are nearby. orthwest of the Jefferson Memorial, on the banks of e Potomac, is the Lincoln Memorial, an edifice that aws more visitors than any other building in Wash-gton. In its central chamber is the famous seated atue of Lincoln by the sculptor Daniel Chester French.

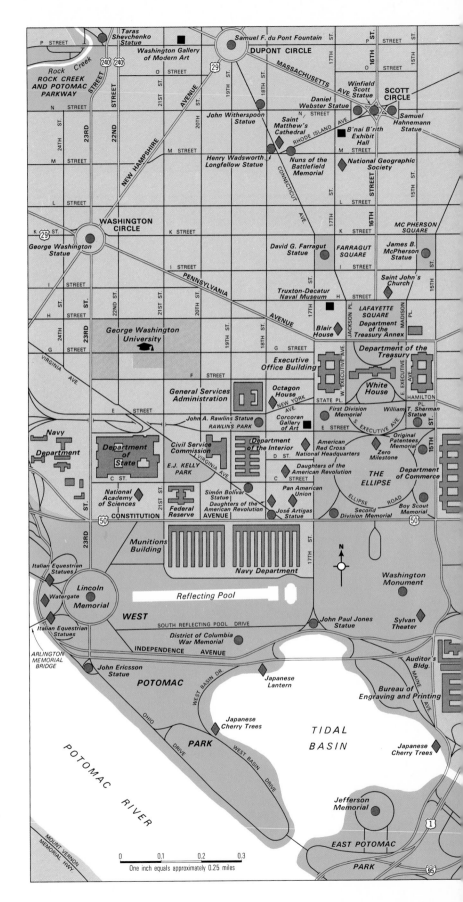

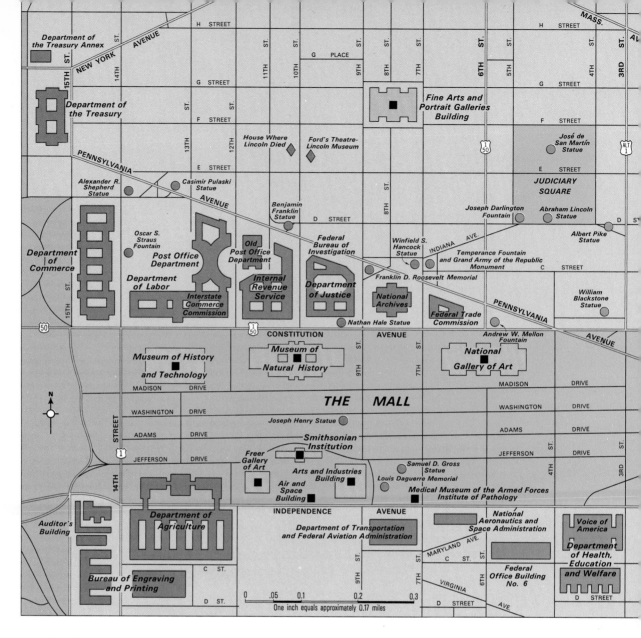

5. The Mall area

The long greensward called the Mall, which stretches from the Capitol to the Washington Monument, is lined with government museums. Five of them contain the collections of the Smithsonian Institution, an organization so vast and varied that Mark Twain dubbed it "the nation's attic." The Museum of Natural History's hundreds of exhibits include the Hope Diamond. The Museum of History and Technology's displays range from a real Telstar satellite to the giant 30-by-34-foot flag that flew over Fort McHenry in 1814, inspiring Francis Scott Key's "Star-Spangled Banner." The Air and Space Building and the Arts and Industries Building are primarily devoted to astronautical and aeronautical exhibits, including the Gemini IV space capsule in the former and Charles A. Lindbergh's *Spirit of St. Louis* in the latter. The building actually named the Smithsonian Institution is now used largely for administration.

Two art museums on the Mall, the Freer Gallery (which is known for its Oriental art) and the National Gallery of Art (described on page 156) are both associated with the Smithsonian. Another nearby institution, the Medical Museum of the Armed Forces Institute of Pathology, interests medical students and, perhaps predictably, children through such exhibits as specimens of war wounds and embryos at various stages of growth.

Flanking the Mall are many government office buildings, and several of these offer tours. At the Bureau of Engraving and Printing, south of the Mall, the printing of money and stamps can be observed. At the headquarters of the Federal Bureau of Investigation, north of the Mall, a popular tour includes a target-shooting demonstration. Next door, at the National Archives, the original manuscripts of the Declaration of Independence and the Constitution are displayed.

A few blocks farther north, Ford's Theatre, where Lincoln was shot, and the house in which he died are now museums. In the same area the new Fine Arts and Portrait Galleries occupy the old Patent Office Building.

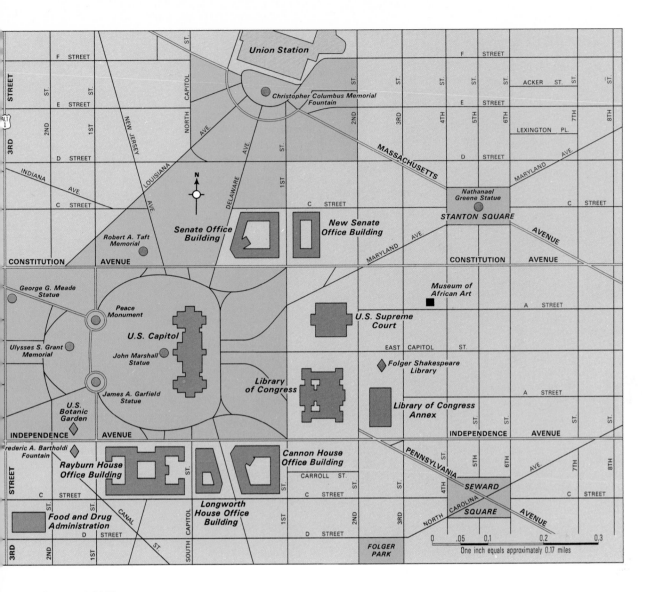

6. Capitol Hill area

The Capitol Hill area is a square mile of majestic landscape dotted with some of the nation's stateliest buildings. Dominated by Capitol Hill, which rises to 88 feet above the tidewater of the Potomac, this area is the seat of two of the nation's three governmental branches. A good way to see "the Hill" and its environs is to start from the cavernous Union Station. In front of the station sprawls the ornate Christopher Columbus Memorial Fountain, where a marble figure of the great explorer scans modern traffic from a ship's prow, flanked by figures representing the Old and New Worlds.

A walk down Louisiana Avenue brings the visitor to the strikingly modern Robert A. Taft Memorial, a 100-foot Tennessee marble bell tower below which a bronze statue of the late Senator stands in wistful solitude. Moving southward along 1st Street, one passes the Peace Monument, the Ulysses S. Grant Memorial with the world's second-largest equestrian statue (the first is that of Victor Emmanuel II in Rome) and the James A. Gar-

field Statue before arriving at the U.S. Botanic Garden. Among the garden's collections are its 55 species of orchids, 150 varieties of chrysanthemums and 25 kinds of azaleas. Farther south is a splashing fountain with three female figures by the Frenchman Frédéric Auguste Bartholdi, designer of the Statue of Liberty.

To the east rises the Capitol, a major symbol of American democracy executed in neoclassic style (pages 58-67). In its majestic Rotunda under the great dome one may join a tour to view the enormous four-acre building that seats the nation's legislators. From the Capitol itself mini-subways and underground walkways connect the five vast Senate and House Office Buildings.

East of the Capitol is the U.S. Supreme Court, a classical temple of justice, and the ornate Library of Congress with its modern annex. Visitors can attend certain Court sessions. At the library some 58 million books, pamphlets and other items are catalogued and kept on 270 miles of bookshelves and in other facilities.

Museums and galleries

District of Columbia

American Friends of the Middle East, 1607 New Hampshire Ave., N.W. Paintings and handicrafts of Middle Eastern artists. Mon-Fri 9-5; Sat 11-5.

The American University, Watkins Gallery, Massachusetts and Nebraska Aves., N.W. Exhibits of contemporary American art. Summer: Sun-Fri 2-5; winter: Mon-Fri 2-5.

The Association for the Study of Negro Life and History, 1538 9th St., N.W. Historic letters, papers, family histories, research relating to Negro history. Mon-Fri 8:30-5.

B'nai B'rith Exhibit Hall, 1640 Rhode Island Ave., N.W. American Jewish history and art. Mon, Tues, Thurs, Fri 1:30-5; Sun 10-5.

Bureau of Engraving and Printing, 14th and C Sts., S.W. Electronically guided tour showing high-speed printing presses from behind glass-enclosed galleries. Mon-Fri 8-2:30.

Columbia Historical Society, 1307 New Hampshire Ave., N.W. Books, prints, maps and diaries on the history of the District of Columbia. Mon, Wed, Sat 2-4.

The Corcoran Gallery of Art, New York Ave. and 17th St., N.W. American, Dutch, Flemish, French and English paintings; sculpture; decorative arts. Tues-Fri 10-4:30; Sat 9-4:30; Sun 2-5.

Daughters of the American Revolution Museum, 1776 D St., N.W. Eighteenth Century furniture; silver; costumes; paintings; 28 period rooms; D.A.R. memorabilia. Mon-Fri 9-4.

Decatur House, 748 Jackson Pl., N.W. House designed by Benjamin Latrobe and built in 1818. Mon-Sat 10-4.

The Dumbarton Oaks Research Library and Collection, 1703 32nd St., N.W. Art museum; house built in 1801 that was the site of a 1944 conference that led to the founding of the United Nations; collections of pre-Columbian and Byzantine art; estate with formal gardens. Labor Day—July 4. Collections: Tues-Sun 2-5; gardens: Mon-Fri 10-4, Sun 1-4.

Federal Bureau of Investigation, 9th St. and Pennsylvania Ave., N.W. Pictures of famous criminals; displays showing how the FBI solves crimes; laboratories; weapons displays. Mon-Fri 9:15-4:15.

Folger Shakespeare Library, 201 E. Capitol St., S.E. Sixteenth and 17th Century British history and culture; theatrical history from 16th to 19th Century; replica of Elizabethan theater. Mon-Sat 10-4:30.

Food and Drug Administration, 200 C St., S.W. Laboratories where scientists test drugs, foods, etc. Mon-Fri 10-12, 1:30-4:30.

Ford's Theatre-Lincoln Museum, 511 10th St., N.W. Restored theater where President Lincoln was shot; period furnishings. Daily 9-9.

Franciscan Monastery, 14th and Quincy Sts., N.E. Landscaped grounds and gardens; reproduction of chapel where St. Francis established the order in 1209. Daily 8-5.

House Where Lincoln Died, 516 10th St., N.W. Petersen House built in 1849; period furniture. Daily 9-9.

Howard University Gallery of Art, 2455 6th St., N.W. American and Italian paintings and sculpture; Alain LeRoy Locke African collection. Mon-Fri 9-5; during academic year: Sat 8:30-12:30.

Kenilworth Aquatic Gardens, 42nd and Douglas Sts., N.E. Native and exotic water plants. Daily 7:30-sundown.

Library of Congress, 1st St. between E. Capitol St. and Independence Ave., S.E. More than 14 million books and pamphlets; Thomas Jefferson's private library; papers of Presidents and other eminent Americans; motion-picture reels; prints; photographs; microfilm. Sat 9 a.m.-10 p.m.; Sun, hols 11:30-10.

Museum of African Art, 316 A St., N.E. House of ex-slave Frederick Douglass, who rose to high rank in the federal government, contains African sculpture and contemporary paintings. Mon-Thurs 11-5:30; Sat, Sun 2-5:30.

Museum of the Society of the

Cincinnati, 2118 Massachusetts Ave., N.W. Anderson House built in 1905; American Revolution relics; European and Oriental art objects. Mon-Sat 2-4.

National Aquarium, 14th St. and Constitution Ave., N.W. Fresh-water fish and turtles common to the U.S.; tropical fish. Daily 9-5.

The National Archives, 8th St. and Pennsylvania Ave., N.W. Records of the federal government, including the Declaration of Independence, the Constitution and the Bill of Rights. Mon-Sat 9 a.m.-10 p.m.; Sun, hols 1-10.

National Gallery of Art, Constitution Ave. and 6th St., N.W. European and American painting, sculpture, graphic and decorative arts; Renaissance bronzes; Chinese porcelains; 18th Century period rooms; prints; drawings; American primitive painting. Labor Day—Mar: Mon-Sat 10-5; Sun 2-10; Apr—Labor Day: Mon-Sat 10-10; Sun 2-10.

National Geographic Society Explorer's Hall, 17th and M Sts., N.W. Items of the past and present relating to land, sea and space explorations. Mon-Fri 9-6; Sat 9-5; Sun 12-5.

The Octagon House, 1799 Massachusetts Ave., N.W. Handsome small house built in 1798-1800; museum of architecture and allied arts. Tues-Sat 9-5; Sun 2-5.

Old Stone House, 3051 M St., N.W. House built in 1764-1765 as home and shop for cabinetmaker; period furniture. Wed-Sun, hols 11-5.

Pan American Union, Constitution Ave. and 17th St., N.W. Exhibits present the development of contemporary Latin American art; patio and Aztec garden. Mon-Fri 8:45-5:30; Sat 8:45-4.

The Phillips Collection, 1600-1612 21st St., N.W. Contemporary and early American paintings; European works of various periods. Mon 11-10; Tues-Sat 11-6; Sun 2-7.

Post Office Department Exhibition Hall, 12th St. and Pennsylvania Ave. N.W. The government's stamp collection, worth millions of dollars; sales desk where all current stamps can be bought. Mon-Sat 9-5.

Red Cross National Headquarters Museum, 17th St. between D and

E Sts., N.W. Civil War items; Red Cross items pertaining to World Wars I and II. Mon-Fri 8:30-4

Scottish Rite Temple, 1733 16th St., N.W. Masonic history items. Mon-Fri 9-4:30; Sat 9-12.

Smithsonian Institution, 10th and Jefferson Dr., S.W. Original Smithsonian building begun in 1847; tomb of James Smithson, British scientist, who gave $500,000 to "diffuse knowledge." Apr—Aug: daily 9 a.m.-10 p.m.; Sept—Mar: daily 9-4:30.

Smithsonian Institution, Air and Space Building, Independence Ave. between 9th and 12th Sts., S.W. Aircraft engines and equipment; scale models of aircraft; actual guided missiles and space vehicles. Apr—Aug: daily 9 a.m.-10 p.m.; Sept—Mar: daily 9-4:30.

Smithsonian Institution, Arts and Industries Building, 9th St. and Jefferson Dr., S.W. Lindbergh's Spirit of St. Louis, the plane that flew the Atlantic in 1927; art exhibits pertaining to astronautics; photographs. Apr—Aug: daily 9 a.m.-10 p.m.; Sept—Mar: daily 9-4:30.

Smithsonian Institution, Fine Arts and Portrait Galleries (formerly Patent Office building, built in 1867), 9th and F Sts., N.W. American and European painting, decorative arts, sculpture; portraits of men and women who made significant contributions to the U.S. Apr—Aug: daily 9 a.m.-10 p.m.; Sept—Mar: daily 9-4:30.

Smithsonian Institution, Freer Gallery of Art, Jefferson Dr. at 12th St., N.W. Near and Far Eastern art; paintings, sculpture, ceramics, jades, glass, bronzes; 19th Century American painting; Peacock Room by Whistler. Apr—Aug: daily 9 a.m.-10 p.m.; Sept—Mar: daily 9-4:30.

Smithsonian Institution, Museum of History and Technology, Constitution Ave. at 14th St., N.W. Items pertaining to U.S. social, cultural, political and military history; engineering; electricity; medical sciences; industrial arts and manufacturing. Apr—Aug: daily 9 a.m.-10 p.m.; Sept—Mar: daily 9-4:30.

Smithsonian Institution, Museum of Natural History, Constitution Ave. at 10th St., N.W. Anthropological, zoological,

mological, botanical and
eralogical exhibits. Apr—Aug:
9 a.m.-10 p.m.; Sept—Mar:
9-4:30.

thsonian Institution, National
ogical Park, 3000
hecticut Ave. N.W. One of the
zoos in the U.S. Sept—Mar:
9-4:30; Apr—Aug: daily
-6.

Textile Museum, 2320 S St.,
. Rugs from Asia and Spain;
ics from Egypt and Peru;
ples of hand weaving;
ics from B.C. to the present.
—Sept: Mon-Fri 1-5; Oct—
: Tues-Sat 1-5.

tun-Decatur Naval Museum,
O H St., N.W. Carriage house
gned by Benjamin Latrobe
built in 1819; items relating
aval and maritime history.
-Sun 10:30-4.

ed States Botanic Garden,
yland Ave. between 1st and
Sts., S.W. Tropical and
ropical plants; native plants
flowers in season. Sun-Fri 9-
at 9-12.

United States Capitol, Capitol
Sculpture, painting and
ture of historic interest;
oes by Brumidi on dome of
Rotunda. Passes to visitors'
ries in both House and
ate chamber are available
offices of specific
gressmen. June—Oct: daily 9
-10 p.m.; Nov—May: daily 9-
.

ed States Department of
rior Museum, C St. between
and 19th Sts., N.W.
dicrafts and artifacts of
an, Eskimo and South Sea
d natives; exhibits of the
ory and activities of the
artment of Interior. Mon-Fri
.

ted States Information
ncy, Voice of America, 330
ependence Ave., S.W. Visitors
observe broadcasting and

publishing operations aimed at
both sides of the Iron Curtain.
Mon-Fri 9:30-4:30.

United States National
Arboretum, 28th and M Sts., N.E.
Azaleas, camellias, hollies,
cultivated plants and willow
collection. Mid-Apr—mid-May:
Mon-Fri 8-7; Sat, Sun 10-7; mid-
May—mid-Apr: Mon-Fri 8-4; first
two weeks in Nov: Sat, Sun 10-
5.

United States Naval Historical
Display Center, 8th and M Sts.,
S.E. Exhibits depicting wars and
events in which the Navy has
participated from 1775 to the
present. Mon-Sat 9-4.

United States Naval Observatory,
Massachusetts Ave. at 34th St.,
N.W. Research institution;
displays of historical timepieces.
Tours: Mon-Fri 2 p.m.

United States Treasury
Department Exhibit Room, 15th
and Pennsylvania Ave., N.W.
Exhibits depicting the history of
the Treasury Department; items
from each bureau; coins and
currency. Mon-Fri 9-5.

Washington Gallery of Modern
Art, 1503 21st St., N.W.
Contemporary painting, sculpture,
drawings and prints. Tues-Sat
10-5; Sun 2-6.

The White House, 1600
Pennsylvania Ave., N.W. Among
rooms open to the public are the
Main Lobby, State Dining Room
and Green Room. Tues-Sat 10-
12.

Woodrow Wilson House, 2340 S
St., N.W. Home of the 27th
President; World War I
memorabilia; original furnishings.
Daily 10-4.

District environs

Maryland

Great Falls
Chesapeake and Ohio Canal

Museum, end of MacArthur Blvd.
on C & O Canal. Great Falls
Tavern built in 1828; Indian
artifacts; displays relating to the
canal's history. June—Labor Day:
daily 10-6; Labor Day—May:
weekends.

Oxon Hill
John Hanson Memorial Museum
and Library, 6295 Oxon Hill Rd.
Art relating to American history;
portraits; busts; Oriental art
collection. Daily.

Silesia
Fort Washington, Old Fort Dr., off
Rte. 210. An unusually fine
example of early 19th Century
coastal defense installation; dry
moat; drawbridge; guardroom.
Fort: daily, daylight hours;
museum: June—Labor Day: daily
10-6.

Virginia

Alexandria
Carlyle House, 121 N. Fairfax St.
House built in 1752; served as
headquarters for British General
Edward Braddock in 1775; period
furniture. Daily 10-6.

Fort Ward Museum, 4301 W.
Braddock Rd. Civil War fort that
has been reconstructed; Civil War
items. Mon-Sat, hols 9-5; Sun
12-5.

Gadsby's Tavern, Cameron and
N. Royal Sts. House built in
1752; George Washington's
headquarters during French and
Indian War in 1754. Daily 10-5.

George Washington National
Masonic Memorial. Large
structure designed to resemble
the Pharos lighthouse in
Alexandria, Egypt; items of
Masonic history; portrait of Lord
Fairfax by Reynolds; chapel. Daily
9-5.

Stabler-Leadbeater Apothecary
Shop, 107 S. Fairfax St. Built in
1792; collection of apothecary
bottles, jars and equipment. Mon-
Sat 10-5.

Arlington
Custis-Lee Mansion, Arlington
National Cemetery. Home of
Robert E. Lee; 18th and 19th
Century furnishings; Lee
memorabilia. Apr—Oct: daily 8-
7; Nov—Mar: daily 8-5.

Fort Belvoir
U.S. Army Corps of Engineers
Museum, 21st and Flagler Rd.
Displays of military engineering
accomplishments; photographs;
paintings; flags; uniforms; rare
books; Presidential letters; rare
maps. Mon-Fri 8-5; Wed eve. 5-
9; Sat 8-12.

Lorton
Gunston Hall, Rte. 242. House
built in 1755-1758; home of
George Mason, signer of the
Declaration of Independence;
family portraits; furniture of the
18th Century. Daily 9:30-5.

Manassas
Manassas National Battlefield
Park. Preserved battlefields of
two Civil War engagements, First
and Second Battles of Bull Run.
Daily 8:30-5.

Mount Vernon
Mount Vernon. Home of George
Washington, built between 1735
and 1787; furniture; prints;
paintings; personal memorabilia;
gardens; stables; tombs of
George and Martha Washington.
Mar—Sept: daily 9-5; Oct—Feb:
daily 9-4.

Quantico
The U.S. Marine Corps Museum,
Marine Corps School. Displays
revealing history and traditions
of the Marine Corps; history of
automatic weapons. Mon-Fri 9-6;
Sat 9-6; Sun 12-4.

Woodlawn
Woodlawn Plantation, Rte. 1.
Two historic houses on the
grounds: Martha Washington's
granddaughter's house, built in
1799-1805; and Pope-Leighey
House designed by Frank Lloyd
Wright and built in 1940. Daily
9:30-4:30.

Statistical information

Population

District of Columbia: 811,000.
Metropolitan Area: 2,632,000.
The Standard Metropolitan
Statistical Area includes (in
addition to the District) Arlington,
Fairfax, Loudoun and Prince
William Counties and the
communities of Alexandria,
Fairfax and Falls Church in
Virginia, and Montgomery and
Prince Georges Counties in
Maryland.

Land area

District of Columbia: 69 square
miles.
Metropolitan Area: 2,368 square
miles.

Federal civilian employees

Metropolitan Area: 312,000.
Other places: 2,688,000.
Total: 3,000,000.

Presidential succession

Vice President
Speaker of the House
President pro tempore of the
  Senate
Secretary of State
Secretary of the Treasury
Secretary of Defense
Attorney General
Postmaster General
Secretary of the Interior
Secretary of Agriculture
Secretary of Commerce
Secretary of Labor
Secretary of Health, Education,
  and Welfare
Secretary of Housing and Urban
  Development
Secretary of Transportation

Executive departments

	Date established	Total employees	Metropolitan Area employ...
State	1789	27,000	6,750
Treasury	1789	91,000	12,000
Defense*	1789	1,250,000	93,500
Justice	1870	34,000	10,000
Post Office	1872	710,500	19,000
Interior	1849	72,000	9,000
Agriculture	1862	114,000	13,000
Commerce†	1913	39,000	16,000
Labor†	1913	10,000	5,000
Health, Education, and Welfare	1953	110,000	29,500
Housing and Urban Development	1965	14,500	4,000
Transportation	1966	59,000	8,500

* Originally Department of War; in 1949 became Department of Defe...
† Prior to 1913 these departments were combined in the Departmer...
Commerce and Labor.

The Congress

	Number	Term	Salary
Senate	100	6 years	$30,000
House of Representatives	435	2 years	$30,000

Credits and acknowledgments

The sources for the illustrations
that appear in this book are
shown below. Credits for the
pictures from left to right are
separated by commas or
semicolons and from top to
bottom by dashes.
Cover—Henri Dauman.
Chapter 1: 8—Frank Scherschel.
10—Map, no credit. 12—Library
of Congress, Carl Fischer, Inc. 15
—United Press International. 17
through 19—Bud Lee. 20, 21—
Bud Lee, courtesy The White
House; White House Collection,
courtesy White House Historical
Association (10); Bud Lee,
courtesy the Smithsonian
Institution. 22, 23—Bud Lee, Bill
Binzen. 24—Bill Binzen, 25—
Bud Lee. 26, 27—Evelyn Hofer,
Henri Dauman. 28—Henri
Dauman, Bill Binzen. 29—Bud
Lee, Dennis Brack from Black
Star. 30, 31—Henri Dauman—
Bud Lee.

Chapter 2: 32—Fred J. Maroon
from Louis Mercier. 37—United
Press International, courtesy New
York State Historical Association,
Cooperstown, New York. 38—
National Capital Planning
Commission. 40—Library of
Congress from American Scenery
by N. P. Willis. 42—Brady-Handy
Collection, Library of Congress.
43—The Kean Archives,
Philadelphia, Pennsylvania. 44—
Evelyn Hofer in The Evidence of
Washington by William Walton,
Harper & Row, 1966. 47—
Library of Congress. 48—Library
of Congress, Culver Pictures, Inc.
—Fred Ward from Black Star. 49
—Library of Congress—National
Capital Planning Commission.
50, 51—The Smithsonian
Institution; Charles Phillips
courtesy Commission of Fine
Arts; Henry Beville, courtesy
National Archives—Charles
Phillips, courtesy Commission of
Fine Arts; Fred Ward from Black
Star; Culver Pictures, Inc. 52, 53
—Culver Pictures, Inc., Brown
Brothers (2), Culver Pictures, Inc.,
Brown Brothers—National
Archives—Charles Phillips,
courtesy Commission of Fine Arts
(2). 54, 55—Fred Ward from
Black Star, Henri Dauman, Fred
J. Maroon from Louis Mercier,
Henri Dauman, Fred J. Maroon

from Louis Mercier (2)—Howard
Sochurek. 56, 57—National
Archives; Howard Sochurek;
Skidmore, Owings, and Merrill—
Robert Rising. 58, 59—Lee
Boltin, courtesy Maryland
Historical Society (2); Lee Boltin,
courtesy Library of Congress; Lee
Boltin, courtesy Maryland
Historical Society—Dr. William
Thornton, painting by C. B. J.
Fevret de St. Memin, courtesy
The Corcoran Gallery of Art;
Library of Congress. 60—Henry
Groskinsky, courtesy Office of the
Architect of the Capitol; Gift of
Francis V. Bulfinch, Fogg Art
Museum, Harvard University,
Cambridge, Massachusetts;
Library of Congress (3). 61—
Courtesy Princeton University
Library (2), Lee Boltin, Library of
Congress (3)—U.S. Capitol
Historical Society, The Old House
of Representatives, painting by
Samuel F. B. Morse, courtesy The
Corcoran Gallery of Art. 62—
Henri Dauman, Library of
Congress. 63—Library of
Congress (2). 64, 65—Library of
Congress (4)—Evelyn Hofer in
The Evidence of Washington by
William Walton, Harper & Row,
1966; Fred Ward from Black
Star. 66, 67—Office of the
Architect of the Capitol—drawing
by Don Spaulding adapted from
Theodore Kautzky.
Chapter 3: 68—Bill Binzen. 71—
Maryland Historical Society (2)—

Library of Congress (2). 72—
Culver Pictures, Inc. (2)—map,
no credit. 73—Library of
Congress (2). 74—Culver
Pictures, Inc., except
center Brown Brothers. 75—
Currier—Brown Brothers; Ale...
Millar, courtesy Columbia
Historical Society. 76—Culver
Pictures, Inc. 77—Map, no cr...
—National Archives. 78, 79—
Abbie Rowe for National Park
Service, Department of the
Interior; Noel Clark; Abbie Ro...
for National Park Service,
Department of the Interior;
Noel Clark; Brown Brothers;
courtesy National Park Servic...
Department of the Interior;
Walker Evans for FORTUNE. 8...
—© by Harris & Ewing from
Gilloon Agency—Brown Broth...
—© H. H. Rideout—Culver
Pictures, Inc. 81—Courtesy
Department of Housing and
Urban Development—courtes...
NASA—Jerry Spearman. 82
through 85—Gary Renaud.
Chapter 4: 86, 87—Henri
Dauman. 89—Keystone View
Co. 95 through 107—
Steinbicker/Houghton. 108
through 119—Sketches by
Alan Cober.
Chapter 5: 120, 121—Francis
Miller. 124—Drawing by Mat...
Greene.
Chapter 6: 130—Fritz Goro. 1...
—Library of Congress, Robert
Cottrol. 135—Arthur Shay;

rtesy Office of Economic
oortunity; Ted Polumbaum—
ed Press International. 137
ough 149—Evelyn Hofer.
pter 7: 150—Dennis Brack
n Black Star. 152, 153—Wide
rld Photos, Arthur Rickerby.
—Wide World Photos;
rtesy Mellon Collection,
ional Gallery of Art,
shington, D.C.—Underwood
Underwood; courtesy
ener Collection, National
ery of Art—Pach Brothers;
rtesy Samuel H. Kress
lection, National Gallery of Art
arris & Ewing from Gilloon
ency; courtesy Rosenwald
lection, National Gallery of Art
o credit; courtesy Chester
e Collection, National Gallery
Art.
pter 8: 158—George Haling.
—National Archives. 164—
Photographics, Inc. 166—
Steffen—courtesy U.S.
artment of State—Don
ffen. 167—Charles Phillips—
ce Roberts from Rapho
llumette—Fred Ward from
ck Star—Charles Phillips—
ce Roberts from Rapho
llumette—Francis Miller—
n Steffen. 168—Fred Ward
m Black Star—Francis Miller
Don Steffen—Bruce Roberts
m Rapho Guillumette—Charles
lips—Francis Miller. 169—
n Steffen—Bruce Roberts
m Rapho Guillumette—Charles
lips—Fred Ward from Black
r—Francis Miller (3)—Bruce
erts from Rapho Guillumette.
)—Charles Phillips—Fred
rd from Black Star (3)—
ncis Miller—Don Steffen—
ce Roberts from Rapho
llumette—Fred Ward from
ck Star. 171—Francis Miller
Don Steffen—Bruce Roberts
m Rapho Guillumette—Charles

Phillips—Fred Ward from Black
Star—Don Steffen. 172—Bruce
Roberts from Rapho Guillumette
—Charles Phillips—Fred Ward
from Black Star—Don Steffen—
Francis Miller—Bruce Roberts
from Rapho Guillumette—Charles
Phillips. 173—Charles Phillips—
Francis Miller (5)—Don Steffen—
Bruce Roberts from Rapho
Guillumette (5). 174—Fred Ward
from Black Star—Don Steffen—
Charles Phillips—Fred Ward from
Black Star—Don Steffen—Bruce
Roberts from Rapho Guillumette
—Fred Ward from Black Star.
175—Charles Phillips—Francis
Miller—Charles Phillips—Francis
Miller—Bruce Roberts from
Rapho Guillumette—Francis
Miller—Don Steffen. 176—
Charles Phillips—Bruce Roberts
from Rapho Guillumette—Don
Steffen—Fred Ward from Black
Star—Francis Miller—Bruce
Roberts from Rapho Guillumette
—Francis Miller. 177—Fred
Ward from Black Star—Francis
Miller (3)—Don Steffen—Fred
Ward from Black Star (5).

The author would like to express
his particular thanks to John
Steele, Bonnie Angelo, Donn
Downing, Edwin Goodpaster and
Wallace Terry of the TIME-LIFE
News Bureau in Washington; to
Mrs. Bess Abell, the White
House; Mark Ferber, the
University of California; Daniel
Greenberg, American Association
for the Advancement of Science;
Louis Heren, the London *Times*;
Philip Ritterbush, The
Smithsonian Institution; Richard
Simons, The Brookings
Institution; Atlee E. Shidler,
Washington Center for
Metropolitan Studies,
Washington; Mrs. John Steele,
former member, Board of

Education, Washington; Eugene
Thoré, Life Insurance Association
of America; and to Clark Clifford,
Edwin C. Fishel, Mrs. Constance
M. Green, Frederick Gutheim and
Joseph L. Rauh.

The editors of this book wish
to thank the following persons
and institutions for their help:
In Washington: Lamar
Alexander, Legislative Assistant
to Senator Howard Baker;
Lieutenant David D. Allen, First
Battalion, Third Infantry,
Headquarters, Military District,
U.S. Army; Warrant Officer Joan
Ambrose, U.S. Marine Corps;
Charles H. Atherton, Secretary
and Administrative Officer,
Commission of Fine Arts; William
D. Blair Jr., Director, Office of
Media Services, Department of
State; Marvin Caplan, Director of
Washington Office, Leadership
Conference on Civil Rights;
Charles H. Conrad, Executive
Director, National Capital
Planning Commission; Virginia
Daiker, Picture Librarian, Library
of Congress, Prints and
Photographs Division; Peggy
DeMichele, Administrative
Assistant to Senator Michael J.
Mansfield; Joseph J. Diamond,
Manager, U.S. Senate
Restaurants; Robert G. Dunphy,
Sergeant at Arms, U.S. Senate;
William F. Dwyer, former
Administrative Assistant to
Representative Frank Horton;
Clyde Flynn, Legislative Assistant
to Senator Everett Dirksen; C.
Alton Frye, Legislative Assistant
to Senator Edward Brooke;
Captain Dale L. Harpham, U.S.
Marine Corps; Milton Kaplan,
Curator of Historical Prints,
Library of Congress; Mary T.
Kennedy, Office of Media
Services, Department of State;

James Ketchum, Curator, the
White House; Margaret Brown
Klapthor, Associate Curator,
Division of Political History, The
Smithsonian Institution; Joseph
Laitin, Assistant to the Director,
Bureau of the Budget; Eleanor M.
McPeck, The President's
Temporary Commission on
Pennsylvania Avenue; Donald R.
McPherron, Assistant Chief,
Standards Division, Bureau of
Policies and Standards, U.S. Civil
Service Commission; John L.
Monahan, Clerk, Office of the
Speaker, House of
Representatives; Cotys M.
Mouser, Chief Clerk, Agriculture
and Forestry Committee, U.S.
Senate; Simone Poulaine,
Assistant to Mrs. Johnson, the
White House; Herbert J. Sanborn,
Exhibits Officer, Library of
Congress; Carolyn Hagner Shaw,
Editor, *The Social List of
Washington, D.C.* Colonel
Leonard H. Sims, First Battalion,
Third Infantry, Headquarters,
Military District, U.S. Army; and
J. George Stewart, Architect of
the Capitol.
Outside of Washington: Robert
W. Bell, Antietam-Chesapeake
and Ohio National Park Service
Group, Sharpsburg, Maryland;
Philip Cocco, Coordinator,
Community Relations, Perkin-
Elmer Corporation, Norwalk,
Connecticut; Eugene DuBois,
Regional Manager of Public
Relations, Eastern Airlines, New
York City; James Marston Fitch,
Professor of Architecture, School
of Architecture, Columbia
University, New York City;
Nathaniel A. Owings, Skidmore
Owings and Merrill, San
Francisco, California; and Robert
Rising, Engineer, Perkin-Elmer
Corporation, Norwalk,
Connecticut.

Bibliography

* Available also in paperback.
† Available only in paperback.

General and historical reading

Anthony, Katharine, *Dolly Madison: Her Life and Times.* Doubleday, 1949.

Baker, Russell, *An American in Washington.* Knopf, 1961.

Caemmerer, H. Paul, *Historic Washington: Capital of the Nation.*† Columbia Historical Society, 1948.

Carpenter, Frank G., *Carp's Washington.* McGraw-Hill, 1960.

Green, Constance McLaughlin: *Washington: Capital City 1879-1950.* Princeton University Press, 1963. *Washington: Village and Capital, 1800-1878.* Princeton University Press, 1962.

Gutheim, Frederick, *The Potomac.* Rinehart, 1949.

Leech, Margaret, *Reveille in Washington: 1860-1865.** Harper, 1941.

Nicolay, Helen, *Our Capital on the Potomac.* Century, 1924.

Schlesinger, Arthur M., Jr., *The Age of Jackson.* Little, Brown, 1950.

Smith, A. Robert, and Eric Sevareid, *Washington: Magnificent Capital.* Doubleday, 1965.

Smith, Merriman, *The Good New Days.* Bobbs-Merrill, 1962.

Stevens, William Oliver, *Washington: The Cinderella City.* Dodd, Mead, 1943.

Tindall, William, *Standard History of the City of Washington.* H. W. Crew, 1914.

Walton, William, *The Evidence of Washington.* Harper & Row, 1966.

West, Dick, *The Backside of Washington.* Doubleday, 1961.

Whitney, Janet, *Abigail Adams.* Little, Brown, 1947.

Whyte, James H., *The Uncivil War: Washington During the Reconstruction—1865-1878.* Twayne, 1958.

Government and politics

Alsop, Stewart, *The Center: People and Power in Political Washington.* Harper & Row, 1968.

American Assembly, The: Don K. Price, ed., *The Secretary of State.*† Prentice-Hall, 1960. David B. Truman, ed., *The Congress and America's Future.** Prentice-Hall, 1965.

Berding, Andrew, *Foreign Affairs and You!* Doubleday, 1962.

Cater, Douglass, *Power in Washington.** Random House, 1964.

Cleveland, Harlan, *The Obligations of Power: American Diplomacy in the Search for Peace.* Harper & Row, 1966.

Crown, James Tracy, *Introduction to American Government.*† Doubleday, 1963.

Deakin, James, *The Lobbyists.* Public Affairs Press, 1966.

Ferguson, John H., and Dean E. McHenry, *The American System of Government,* 9th ed. McGraw-Hill, 1967.

Galloway, George B., *The Legislative Process in Congress.* Crowell, 1953.

Harris, Joseph P., *Congress and the Legislative Process.*† McGraw-Hill, 1967.

Hobbs, Edward H., *Behind the President: A Study of Executive Office Agencies.* Public Affairs Press, 1954.

Keefe, William J., and Morris S. Ogul, *The American Legislative Process: Congress and the States.* Prentice-Hall, 1964.

Koenig, Louis W., *The Chief Executive.* Harcourt, Brace & World, 1964.

Mollenhoff, Clark R., *The Pentagon: Politics, Profits and Plunder.* Putnam, 1967.

Neustadt, Richard E., *Presidential Power: the politics of leadership.** Wiley, 1960.

Salinger, Pierre, *With Kennedy.** Doubleday, 1966.

Schriftgiesser, Karl, *The Lobbyists.* Little, Brown, 1951.

Seabury, Paul, *Power, Freedom, and Diplomacy: The Foreign Policy of the United States of America.** Random House, 1963.

Simpson, Smith, *Anatomy of the State Department.** Houghton Mifflin, 1967.

Thayer, Charles W., *Diplomat.* Harper, 1959.

Walker, Harvey, *The Legislative Process: Lawmaking in the United States.* Ronald Press, 1948.

Wanamaker, Temple, *American Foreign Policy Today.*† Bantam, 1964.

Special topics

Adams, Henry, *The Education of Henry Adams.** Random House, 1931.

Aikman, Lonnelle, *We, the People: The Story of the United States Capitol.** The United States Capitol Historical Society, 1967.

Buchanan, Wiley T., Jr., and Arthur Gordon, *Red Carpet at the White House: Four Years as Chief of Protocol in the Eisenhower Administration.* Dutton, 1964.

Burchard, John, and Albert Bush-Brown, *The Architecture of America.** Little, Brown, 1961.

Caemmerer, H. Paul, *A Manual on the Origin and Development of Washington.* U.S. Government Printing Office, 1939.

Carmichael, Leonard, and J. C. Long, *James Smithson and the Smithsonian Story.* Putnam, 1965.

Cater, Douglass, *The Fourth Branch of Government.** Houghton Mifflin, 1959.

Derthick, Martha, *City Politics in Washington, D.C.*† Harvard University Press, 1962.

Dunbar, Seymour, *A History of Travel in America.*† Tudor, 1937.

Fitch, James Marston, *American Building,* Vol. I, *1: The Historical Forces That Shaped It,* rev. ed. Houghton Mifflin, 1966.

Frary, I. T., *They Built the Capitol.* Garrett and Massie, 1940.

Freidel, Frank, and Lonnelle Aikman, *George Washington: Man and Monument.** Washington National Monument Association, 1965.

Green, Constance McLaughlin, *The Secret City: A History of Race Relations in the Nation's Capital.* Princeton University Press, 1967.

Gurney, Gene, *The Library of Congress.* Crown, 1966.

Hamlin, Talbot, *Benjamin Henry Latrobe.* Oxford University Press, 1955.

Helm, Edith Benham, *The Captains and the Kings.* Putnam, 1954.

Hitchcock, Henry-Russell, *Architecture: Nineteenth and Twentieth Centuries,* 2nd ed. Penguin, 1963.

Hundley, Mary Gibson, *The Dunbar Story (1870-1955).* Vantage, 1965.

Hurd, Charles: *The White House: A Biography.* Harper, 1940. *The White House Story.* Hawthorn, 1966.

Jacobsen, Hugh Newell, ed., *A Guide to the Architecture of Washington, D.C.** Praeger, 1965.

Kite, Elizabeth S., *L'Enfant and Washington: 1791-1792.* Johns Hopkins Press, 1929.

LaFollette, Suzanne, *Art in America.* Norton, 1929.

Larkin, Oliver W., *Art and Life in America,* rev. ed. Holt, Rinehart and Winston, 1960.

Means, Marianne, *The Woman in the White House: The Lives, Times and Influence of Twelve Notable First Ladies.** Random House, 1963.

Moore, Charles, *Daniel H. Burnham: Architect—Planner of Cities.* 2 vols. Houghton Mifflin, 1921.

Murdock, Myrtle M., *Constantino Brumidi: Michelangelo of the United States Capitol.* Monumental Press, 1950.

Newell, Frederick Haynes, ed., *Planning and Building the City of Washington.* Ransdell, 1932.

President's Council on Pennsylvania Avenue, *Pennsylvania Avenue: Report of the President's Council on Pennsylvania Avenue.* U.S. Government Printing Office, 1964.

Reps, John W., *Monumental Washington: The Planning and Development of the Capital Center.* Princeton University Press, 1967.

Sanderlin, Walter S., *The Great National Project: A History of the Chesapeake and Ohio Canal.* Johns Hopkins Press, 1946.

Walker, John: *National Gallery of Art: Washington, D.C.** Harry N. Abrams, 1963. *The White House: An Historic Guide.** White House Historical Association, 1966.

Wolff, Perry, *A Tour of the White House with Mrs. John F. Kennedy.* Doubleday, 1962.

Guidebooks

Allison, Charles G. and Ellen W., *Heritage Cavaliers Guide to the Nation's Capital.*† Heritage Cavaliers, 1967.

Hepburn, Andrew, *Complete Guide to Washington, D.C.*† Doubleday, 1964.

Shuster, Alvin, ed., *Washington: The New York Times Guide to the Nation's Capital.* Robert B. Luce, 1967.

Truett, Randall Bond, ed., *Washington, D.C.: A Guide to the Nation's Capital,* rev. ed. Hastings House, 1968.

PRODUCTION STAFF FOR TIME INCORPORATED

John L. Hallenbeck (Vice President and Director of Production),
Robert E. Foy and Caroline Ferri

Text photocomposed under the direction of Albert J. Dunn and Arthur J. Dunn

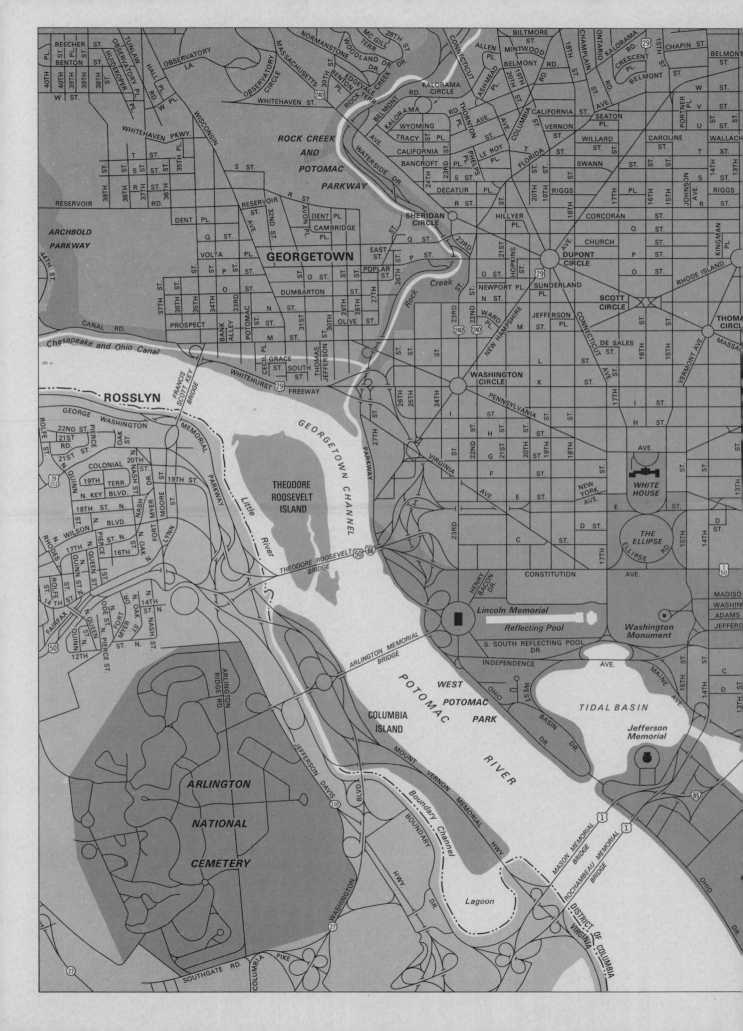